THE RITES

OF THE

CATHOLIC CHURCH

as Revised by Decree of the
Second Vatican Ecumenical Council
and Published
by Authority of Pope Paul VI

English translation
prepared by
The International Commission
on English in the Liturgy

VOLUME TWO

PUEBLO PUBLISHING CO

New York

Nihil Obstat:
Daniel V. Flynn, J.C.D.
Censor Librorum

Imprimatur:
Joseph T. O'Keefe
Vicar General, Archdiocese of New York
September 18, 1979

All the liturgical texts in this volume have been approved by the
National Council of Catholic Bishops and confirmed by the
Apostolic See.

Design: Frank Kacmarcik

English translation of *The Ordination of Deacons, Priests, and Bishops* ©
1969, International Committee on English in the Liturgy, Inc. (ICEL);
excerpts from the English translation of the *Rite of Confirmation, Rite
of the Blessing of Oils, Rite of Consecrating the Chrism* © 1972, ICEL;
English translation of the *Rite of Blessing of an Abbot or Abbess and
the Rite of Consecration to a Life of Virginity* © 1975, ICEL; English
translation of *The Institution of Readers and Acolytes, The Admission to
Candidacy for Ordination as Deacons and Priests* © 1976, ICEL; English
translation of *The Dedication of a Church and Altar* © 1978, ICEL;
English translation of the *Rite of Commissioning Special Ministers of
Holy Communion* © 1978, ICEL; English translation of *The Reception
of the Bishop in the Cathedral Church and the Blessing of the Pontifical
Insignia* © 1979, ICEL. All rights reserved.

CONTENTS

PREFACE

This volume is a collection of the liturgical rites and texts which constitute a part of the Roman Pontifical as revised by mandate of the Second Vatican Council.[1]

The content of this book corresponds to the *Pontificale Romanum* of 1596, issued by Clement VIII[2] in accord with the decree of the Council of Trent.[3] The individual rites were revised and published in Latin by authority of Pope Paul VI during the period from 1968 to 1972.

The English version of the Latin texts has been prepared by the International Commission on English in the Liturgy, a Joint Commission of Catholic Bishops' Conferences, established in 1964 for this purpose. This version has been approved by the various conferences of bishops and is published by authority of those conferences and is thus the official and authentic text for the dioceses of the respective territories.[4]

On October 25, 1973, Pope Paul VI reserved to himself the power to approve directly all the translations into the vernacular of the sacramental forms.[5] In the case of English and other major languages the approbation is given by the Congregation for Divine Worship (now the Congregation for the Sacraments and Divine Worship) after consultation with the conferences of bishops. Thus, in this volume those parts of the sacramental form of orders (for the ordination of deacons, priests, and bishops) "which belong to the nature of the rite and are consequently required for validity"[6] have been directly approved by the Apostolic See (rather than being approved by the respective conferences of bishops and confirmed by the Apostolic See).[7]

---

[1]Const. on the liturgy nos. 25, 71, 76, 80.
[2]Constitution *Ex quo in Ecclesia*, February 10, 1596: *Bullarium Romanum* 10: 246-248.
[3]Session XXV, December 4, 1563, decree on the index etc.: *Conciliorum Oecumenicorum Decreta*, 3 ed., p. 797.
[4]See Const. on the liturgy, no. 36, 3-4.
[5]Congregation for Divine Worship, circular letter of the Secretary of State: *AAS* 66 (1974): 98-99.
[6]Paul VI, apostolic constitution *Pontificalis Romani*, June 18, 1968: *AAS* 60 (1968): 372-373.
[7]See Const. on the liturgy, no. 36, 3.

INSTITUTION OF LAY MINISTRIES

These ministries were established by Paul VI by the apostolic letter *Ministeria quaedam*.[8] The new ministries, which are now carried out by lay persons, replace the corresponding minor orders, which were suppressed along with tonsure and subdiaconate; the two ministries are also to be exercised by candidates for ordination, either before or after they are admitted to candidacy for holy orders. (In the apostolic letter provision was also made for the restoration or establishment of other lay ministries, in addition to the two ministries common to the Latin Church).

The Latin text of the rites of institution or blessing of readers and acolytes was issued by decree of the Congregation for Divine Worship dated December 3, 1972.[9]

ORDINATIONS

With the suppression of the canonical institute of tonsure,[10] a new rite was created for admission to candidacy for ordination as deacons and priests, in accord with the apostolic letter of Paul VI, *Ad pascendum*.[11] This letter, which also provides for a rite of commitment to celibacy on the part of unmarried men who are candidates for the order of deacons, is printed in this volume before the rite of admission to candidacy.

The rite of admission was issued by decree of the Congregation for Divine Worship, dated December 3, 1972.[12] (The commitment to celibacy for unmarried candidates for the diaconate, referred to in the decree has been incorporated into the rite of ordination of deacons.)

Next, an English translation is given of the apostolic constitution of Paul VI, *Pontificalis Romani*,[13] in which the new rites are approved and the essential forms and matter for the sacrament of orders are determined for the Latin Church.

The Latin text of the several rites of ordination, prepared by the Consilium for the Implementation of the Constitution on

[8]Motu proprio, August 15, 1972: *AAS* 64 (1972): 529-534.
[9]*AAS* 65 (1973): 274-275.
[10]Paul VI, motu proprio *Ministeria quaedam*, August 15, 1972: *AAS* 64 (1972): 529-534.
[11]Motu proprio, August 15, 1972: *AAS* 64 (1972): 534-540.
[12]*AAS* 65 (1973): 274-275.
[13]June 18, 1968: *AAS* 60 (1968): 369-373.

the Liturgy, was issued by decree of the Congregation of Rites, August 15, 1968.[14]

BLESSING OF PERSONS

The third part of this book contains rites for the blessing of persons who are publicly consecrated to God.

Among these rites is the traditional consecration of unmarried women to the life of religious virginity. The revision, which has been formally decreed by the Second Vatican Council,[15] was published by the decree of the Congregation for Divine Worship, May 31, 1970,[16] not only for nuns but also for individual consecrated women who do not live in religious communities.[17]

The decree of promulgation explains the development of the venerable rite in this way: "The rite for the consecration of virgins is one of the most treasured in the Roman liturgy. Consecrated virginity is among the most excellent gifts bequeathed by our Lord to his Bride, the Church. From apostolic times women have dedicated their virginity to God, so adding to the beauty of the mystical body of Christ and making it fruitful in grace. Even from the earliest times, as the Fathers of the Church bear witness, mother Church in her wisdom set her seal on this high vocation by her practice of consecrating those who followed it by means of a solemn prayer. This prayer, enriched in the course of time by other ritual elements to bring out more clearly the symbolism of virginity in relation to the Church, the Bride of Christ, was incorporated into the Roman Pontifical."

Two other rites in this part of the volume are for the blessing of an abbot of a monastery of men and the blessing of an abbess of a monastery of women. In the decree of the Congregation of Divine Worship, dated November 9, 1970,[18] by which the Latin text was published, the following explanation of the rites is given: "The blessing, after canonical election, of an abbot or an abbess of a monastery is a traditional rite in the Church's liturgy. The whole religious community is then seen

---

[14]The text of the decree, which was not published in *AAS*, is found in the Latin edition of the rites, *De Ordinatione Diaconi, Presbyteri, et Episcopi*.
[15]Const. on the liturgy, no. 80.
[16]*AAS* 62 (1970): 650.
[17]See introduction, no. 5.
[18]*AAS* 63 (1971): 710-711.

praying for God's grace to come upon the person they have chosen to lead them along the way to perfection. In the course of the centuries this rite took on different forms for different times and places. In our own day, therefore, it seems fitting that these traditional rites should be revised by removing from them what no longer suits our modern mentality so that they may express more clearly the spiritual responsibilities of the head of a religious family."

The Rite of Commissioning Special Ministers of Holy Communion is authorized by the instruction *Immensae Caritatis* which granted bishops the opportunity to approve, when there is true pastoral need, upon request from the local pastor, lay persons to assist ordained ministers and instituted acolytes in the administration of the holy eucharist.

DEDICATION OF A CHURCH AND AN ALTAR

On May 29, 1977, the Congregation for the Sacraments and Divine Worship published the revised rite of Dedication of a Church and an Altar. The decree notes that this "is properly considered among the most solemn liturgical services." The building where the community gathers to worship is an image of the Church itself, which is God's temple built from living stones. The first six chapters provide the community with rites to be celebrated at the time of the laying of a foundation stone or commencement of work on the building, the dedication of a church and altar, or the blessing of a church and altar. The seventh chapter presents the revised rite for the blessing of a chalice and paten. The rite clearly states that these vessels, intended solely and permanently for the celebration of the eucharist, are blessed and become sacred by their use.

In the several decrees referred to above, the day on which the respective rite was to have been put into effect (in the Latin version) is determined, either as a specified day or simply upon publication of the rite. The English and other vernacular versions are to be put into effect on the day determined by the respective conferences of bishops, after they have approved translations and received confirmation from the Apostolic See.

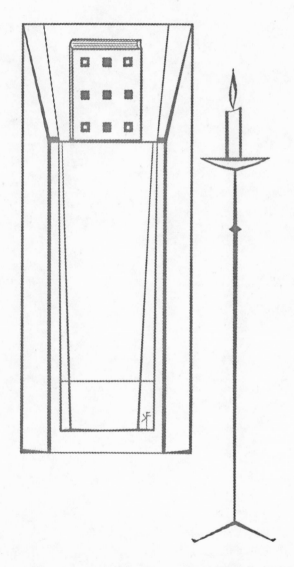

INSTITUTION OF READERS AND ACOLYTES

INSTITUTION OF READERS AND ACOLYTES

Decree
Apostolic Letter

CHAPTER I
INSTITUTION OF READERS

Introduction (1)

Liturgy of the Word (2)

Institution of Readers (3-7)

Calling of the Candidates (3)

Homily (4)

Invitation to Prayer (5)

Prayer (6)

Institution (7)

Liturgy of the Eucharist (8)

CHAPTER II
INSTITUTION OF ACOLYTES

Introduction (1)

Liturgy of the Word (2)

Institution of Acolytes (3-7)

Calling of the Candidates (3)

Homily (4)

Invitation to Prayer (5)

Prayer (6)

Institution (7)

Liturgy of the Eucharist (8-10)

CHAPTER III
BIBLICAL READINGS

SACRED CONGREGATION FOR DIVINE WORSHIP

Prot. n. 1500/72

DECREE

By the apostolic letter *Ministeria quaedam*, issued *motu proprio* on August 15, 1972, Pope Paul VI reformed the discipline of ministries; in the apostolic letter *Ad pascendum*, issued on the same day, he set norms for the holy order of diaconate, both for the diaconate leading to the presbyterate and for the permanent diaconate. The Congregation for Divine Worship has therefore prepared rites for the institution of readers and acolytes, for the admission to candidacy for ordination as deacons and priests, and for the commitment to celibacy.

By his own authority Pope Paul VI has approved these rites and ordered that they be published, so that they may be used in Latin beginning on January 1, 1973, and in the vernacular on the day determined by the episcopal conferences for their respective countries, after they have approved translations and received the confirmation from the Apostolic See.

Anything to the contrary notwithstanding.

From the office of the Congregation for Divine Worship, December 3, 1972, the memorial of Saint Francis Xavier.

Arturo Cardinal Tabera
Prefect

✠ Annibale Bugnini
Titular Archbishop of Diocletiana
Secretary

APOSTOLIC LETTER

ISSUED *MOTU PROPRIO*
BY WHICH THE DISCIPLINE
OF FIRST TONSURE, MINOR ORDERS,
AND SUBDIACONATE
IN THE LATIN CHURCH IS REFORMED

POPE PAUL VI

Even in the most ancient times certain ministries were established by the Church for the purpose of suitably giving worship to God and for offering service to the people of God according to their needs. By these ministries, duties of a liturgical and charitable nature, deemed suitable to varying circumstances, were entrusted to the performance of the faithful. The conferring of these functions often took place by a special rite, in which, after God's blessing had been implored, a Christian was established in a special class or rank for the fulfillment of some ecclesiastical function.

Some of these functions, which were more closely connected with the liturgical celebration, slowly came to be considered as preparatory institutions for the reception of sacred orders, so that the offices of porter, reader, exorcist, and acolyte were called minor orders in the Latin Church in relation to the subdiaconate, diaconate, and presbyterate, which were called major orders. Generally, though not everywhere, these minor orders were reserved to those who received them on their way to the priesthood.

Nevertheless, since the minor orders have not always been the same and many tasks connected with them, as at present, have also been exercised by the laity, it seems fitting to reexamine this practice and to adapt it to contemporary needs, so that what is obsolete in these offices may be removed, what is useful retained, what is necessary defined, and at the same time what is required of candidates for holy orders may be determined.

While the Second Vatican Council was in preparation, many pastors of the Church requested that the minor orders and subdiaconate should be reexamined. Although the Council did not decree anything concerning this for the Latin Church, it enunciated certain principles for solving the question. There is no doubt that the norms laid down by the Council regarding the general and orderly renewal of the liturgy[1] also include those areas which concern ministries in the liturgical assembly, so that from the very arrangement of the celebration the Church clearly appears structured in different orders and ministries.[2] Thus the Second Vatican Council decreed that "in liturgical celebrations each individual, minister or lay person, who has an office to perform, should do all, and only, those parts which pertain to his office by the nature of the rite and the principles of liturgy."[3]

With this assertion is closely connected what was written a little before in the same constitution: "Mother Church earnestly desires that all the faithful be led to that full, conscious, and active participation in liturgical celebrations which is demanded by the nature of the liturgy. Such participation by the Christian people as 'a chosen race, a royal priesthood, a holy nation, a purchased people' (1 Peter 2:9; see 2:4-5) is their right and duty by reason of their baptism. In the restoration and promotion of the sacred liturgy, this full and active participation by all the people is the aim to be considered before all else; for it is the primary and indispensable source from which the faithful are to derive the true Christian spirit. Therefore, through the needed program of instruction, pastors of souls must zealously strive to achieve it in all their pastoral work."[4]

Among the particular offices to be preserved and adapted to contemporary needs are those which are in a special way more closely connected with the ministries of the word and of the altar and in the Latin Church are called the offices of reader and acolyte and the subdiaconate. It is fitting to preserve and adapt these in such a way, that from this time on there will be two offices: that of reader and that of acolyte, which will include the functions of the subdiaconate.

Besides the offices common to the Latin Church, there is nothing to prevent conferences of bishops from requesting

[1]See const. on the liturgy, no. 62.
[2]See General Instruction of the Roman Missal, no. 58.
[3]Const. on the liturgy, no. 28.
[4]*Ibid.*, no. 14.

others of the Apostolic See, if they judge the establishment of such offices in their region to be necessary or very useful because of special reasons. To these belong, for example, the offices of porter, exorcist, and catechist,[5] as well as other offices to be conferred upon those who are dedicated to works of charity, where this service has not been given to deacons.

It is in accordance with the reality itself and with the contemporary outlook that the above-mentioned ministries should no longer be called minor orders; their conferring will not be called "ordination," but "institution." Only those, however, who have received the diaconate will be properly known as clerics. Thus there will better appear the distinction between clergy and laity, between what is proper and reserved to the clergy and what can be entrusted to the laity; thus there will appear more clearly their mutual relationship, insofar as "the common priesthood of the faithful and the ministerial or hierarchical priesthood, while they differ in essence and not only in degree, are nevertheless interrelated. Each of them shares in its own special way in the one priesthood of Christ."[6]

Having weighed every aspect of the question well, having sought the opinion of experts, having consulted with the conferences of bishops and taken their views into account, and having taken counsel with our venerable brothers who are members of the Sacred Congregations competent in this matter, by our apostolic authority we enact the following norms, derogating—if and insofar as necessary—from provisions of the Code of Canon Law now in force, and we promulgate them with this letter.

1. First tonsure is no longer conferred; entrance into the clerical state is joined to the diaconate.

2. What up to now were called minor orders are henceforth called "ministries."

---

[5] See decree on missionary activity, nos. 15 and 17.
[6] Const. on the Church, no. 10.

3. Ministries may be committed to lay Christians; hence they are no longer to be considered as reserved to candidates for the sacrament of orders.

4. Two ministries, adapted to present-day needs, are to be preserved in the whole of the Latin Church, namely those of reader and acolyte. The functions heretofore committed to the subdeacon are entrusted to the reader and the acolyte; consequently, the major order of subdiaconate no longer exists in the Latin Church. There is nothing, however, to prevent the acolyte being also called a subdeacon in some places, if the conference of bishops judges it opportune.

5. The reader is appointed for a function proper to him, that of reading the word of God in the liturgical assembly. Accordingly, he is to read the lessons from sacred Scripture, except for the gospel, in the Mass and other sacred celebrations; he is to recite the psalm between the readings when there is no psalmist; he is to present the intentions for the general intercessions in the absence of a deacon or cantor; he is to direct the singing and the participation by the faithful; he is to instruct the faithful for the worthy reception of the sacraments. He may also, insofar as necessary, take care of preparing other faithful who by a temporary appointment are to read the Scriptures in liturgical celebrations. That he may more fittingly and perfectly fulfill these functions, let him meditate assiduously on sacred Scripture.

Let the reader be aware of the office he has undertaken and make every effort and employ suitable means to acquire that increasingly warm and living love[7] and knowledge of Scripture that will make him a more perfect disciple of the Lord.

6. The acolyte is appointed in order to aid the deacon and to minister to the priest. It is therefore his duty to attend to the service of the altar and to assist the deacon and the priest in liturgical celebrations, especially in the celebration of Mass; he is also to distribute holy communion as an auxiliary minister when the ministers spoken of in canon 845 of the Code of

[7]See const. on the liturgy, no. 24; const. on revelation, no. 25.

Canon Law are not available or are prevented by ill health, age, or another pastoral ministry from performing this function, or when the number of those approaching the sacred table is so great that the celebration of Mass would be unduly prolonged.

In the same extraordinary circumstances he may be entrusted with publicly exposing the blessed sacrament for adoration by the faithful and afterward replacing it, but not with blessing the people. He may also, to the extent needed, take care of instructing other people who by temporary appointment assist the priest or deacon in liturgical celebrations by carrying the missal, cross, candles, etc., or by performing other such duties. He will perform these functions more worthily if he participates in the holy eucharist with increasingly fervent piety, receives nourishment from it, and deepens his knowledge of it.

Destined as he is in a special way for the service of the altar, the acolyte should learn all matters concerning public divine worship and strive to grasp their inner spiritual meaning: in that way he will be able each day to offer himself entirely to God, be an example to all by his seriousness and reverence in the sacred building, and have a sincere love for the Mystical Body of Christ, the people of God, especially the weak and the sick.

7. In accordance with the venerable tradition of the Church, institution in the ministries of reader and acolyte is reserved to men.

8. The following are requirements for admission to the ministries:
a) the presentation of a petition freely made out and signed by the aspirant to the Ordinary (the bishop or, in clerical institutes, the major superior) who has the right to accept the petition;
b) a suitable age and special qualities to be determined by the conference of bishops;
c) a firm will to give faithful service to God and the Christian people.

9. The ministries are conferred by the Ordinary (the bishop or, in clerical institutes, the major superior) according to the

liturgical rite *De institutione lectoris* and *De institutione acolythi* revised by the Apostolic See.

10. Intervals, determined by the Holy See or the conferences of bishops, shall be observed between the conferring of the ministries of reader and acolyte whenever more than one ministry is conferred on the same person.

11. Candidates for ordination as deacons and priests are to receive the ministries of reader and acolyte, unless they have already done so, and are to exercise them for a suitable time, in order to be better disposed for the future service of the word and of the altar. Dispensation from receiving these ministries on the part of such candidates is reserved to the Holy See.

12. The conferring of ministries does not confer the right to sustenance or remuneration from the Church.

13. The rite of institution of readers and acolytes is to be published by the competent department of the Roman Curia.

All that has been decreed by us in this letter, issued *motu proprio*, we order to be confirmed and ratified, anything to the contrary notwithstanding. We also determine that it shall come into force on January 1, 1973.

Given in Rome, at Saint Peter's, on August 15, 1972, the Solemnity of the Assumption, the tenth year of our pontificate.

Paul VI

CHAPTER I

INSTITUTION OF READERS

INTRODUCTION

1. Readers are instituted by the bishop or major superior of a clerical religious institute. The rite takes place during Mass or during a celebration of the word of God.

LITURGY OF THE WORD

2. The readings are taken in whole or in part from the liturgy of the day or from the texts listed in Chapter III.

INSTITUTION OF READERS

CALLING OF THE CANDIDATES

3. After the gospel, the bishop, wearing his miter, sits, and the appointed deacon or priest calls the candidates:

Those to be instituted in the ministry of reader please come forward.

The candidates are called by name, and each one answers: **Present**, and goes to the bishop, before whom he makes a sign of reverence.

HOMILY

4. Then all sit, and the bishop gives the homily, which he concludes by speaking to the candidates in these or similar words:

Dear sons in Christ, through his Son, who became man for us, God the Father has revealed the mystery of salvation and brought it to fulfillment. Jesus Christ made all things known to us and then entrusted his Church with the mission of preaching the Gospel to the whole world.

As readers and bearers of God's word, you will assist in this mission, and so take on a special office within the Christian community; you will be given a respon-

sibility in the service of the faith, which is rooted in the word of God. You will proclaim that word in the liturgical assembly, instruct children and adults in the faith, and prepare them to receive the sacraments worthily. You will bring the message of salvation to those who have not yet received it. Thus with your help men and women will come to know God our Father and his Son Jesus Christ, whom he sent, and so be able to reach eternal life.

In proclaiming God's word to others, accept it yourselves in obedience to the Holy Spirit. Meditate on it constantly, so that each day you will have a deeper love of the Scriptures, and in all you say and do show forth to the world our Savior, Jesus Christ.

INVITATION TO PRAYER

5. Then all stand, and the bishop, without his miter, invites the people to pray:

Brothers and sisters, let us ask God our Father to bless these servants who have been chosen for the ministry of reader. Let us pray that they may be faithful to the work entrusted to them, proclaim Christ to the world, and so give glory to our Father in heaven.

All pray in silence for a brief period.

PRAYER

6. Then the bishop, with hands joined, continues:

Lord God,
source of all goodness and light,
you sent your only Son, the Word of life,
to reveal to mankind the mystery of your love.

Bless ✠ our brothers
who have been chosen for the ministry of reader.
Grant that as they meditate constantly on your word
they may grow in its wisdom
and faithfully proclaim it to your people.

We ask this through Christ our Lord.
℟. Amen.

INSTITUTION

7. Each candidate goes to the bishop, who gives him the Bible, saying:

**Take this book of holy Scripture
and be faithful in handing on the word of God,
so that it may grow strong in the hearts of his people.**
The reader answers: **Amen.**

Meanwhile, Psalm 19 or another appropriate song may be sung, especially if there are many candidates.

LITURGY OF THE EUCHARIST

8. If the institution of readers takes place during Mass, the Mass continues as usual. If the institution takes place during a celebration of the word, the bishop blesses the assembly and dismisses it in the usual manner.

CHAPTER II

INSTITUTION OF ACOLYTES

INTRODUCTION

1. Acolytes are instituted by the bishop or the major superior of a clerical religious institute. The rite takes place during Mass.

LITURGY OF THE WORD

2. The readings are taken in whole or in part from the liturgy of the day or from the texts listed in Chapter III.

INSTITUTION OF ACOLYTES

CALLING OF THE CANDIDATES

3. After the gospel, the bishop, wearing his miter, sits, and the appointed deacon or priest calls the candidates:

Those to be instituted in the ministry of acolyte please come forward.

The candidates are called by name, and each one answers: **Present**, and goes to the bishop, before whom he makes a sign of reverence.

HOMILY

4. Then all sit, and the bishop gives the homily, which he concludes by speaking to the candidates in these or similar words:

Dear sons in Christ, as people chosen for the ministry of acolyte, you will have a special role in the Church's ministry. The summit and source of the Church's life is the eucharist, which builds up the Christian community and makes it grow. It is your responsibility to assist priests and deacons in carrying out their ministry, and as special ministers to give holy communion to the faithful at the liturgy and to the sick. Because you are specially called to this ministry, you should strive

to live more fully by the Lord's sacrifice and to be molded more perfectly in its likeness. You should seek to understand the deep spiritual meaning of what you do, so that you may offer yourselves daily to God as spiritual sacrifices acceptable to him through Jesus Christ.

In performing your ministry bear in mind that, as you share the one bread with your brothers and sisters, so you form one body with them. Show a sincere love for Christ's Mystical Body, God's holy people, and especially for the weak and the sick. Be obedient to the commandment which the Lord gave to his apostles at the Last Supper: "Love one another as I also have loved you."

INVITATION TO PRAYER

5. Then all stand, and the bishop, without his miter, invites the people to pray:

Brothers and sisters, let us pray to the Lord for those chosen by him to serve in the ministry of acolyte. Let us ask him to fill them with his blessing and strengthen them for faithful service in his Church.

All pray in silence for a brief period.

PRAYER

6. Then the bishop, with hands joined, continues:

God of mercy
through your only Son
you entrusted the bread of life to your Church.
Bless ✠ our brothers
who have been chosen for the ministry of acolyte.
Grant that they may be faithful
in the service of your altar
and in giving to others the bread of life;
may they grow always in faith and love,
and so build up your Church.

We ask this through Christ our Lord.
℟. Amen.

INSTITUTION

7. Each candidate goes to the bishop, who gives him a vessel with the bread or wine to be consecrated, saying:

Take this vessel with bread (wine)
for the celebration of the eucharist.
Make your life worthy of your service
at the table of the Lord and of his Church.
The acolyte answers: **Amen.**

LITURGY OF THE EUCHARIST

8. At the preparation of the gifts, the acolytes (or some of them, if the number is large) present the patens with the bread and the chalice with the wine.

9. The acolytes receive communion immediately after the deacons.

10. In the Mass of institution the bishop may direct the acolyte as a special minister to help in giving communion to the faithful.

CHAPTER III

BIBLICAL READINGS

FOR THE INSTITUTION OF READERS

READING FROM THE OLD TESTAMENT

1. **Deuteronomy 6:3-9** (L 737)
Keep these words in your heart.

2. **Deuteronomy 30:10-14** (L 106)
Let the instruction of the Lord be near you.

3. **Isaiah 55:10-11** (L 104)
The rain makes the earth fruitful.

4. **Nehemiah 8:1-4a, 5-6, 8-10** (L 70)
They read from the book of Law and they understood what was read.

READING FROM THE NEW TESTAMENT

1. **1 Corinthians 2:1-5** (L 74)
I have told you of the mystery of God.

2. **2 Timothy 3:14-17** (L 648)
All Scripture is inspired by God and can profitably be used for teaching.

3. **2 Timothy 4:1-5** (L 722)
Preach the Good News; fulfill your ministry.

4. **Hebrews 4:12-13** (L 144)
The word of God discerns the thoughts and intentions of the heart.

5. **1 John 1:1-4** (L 697)
What we have seen and heard we are making known to you.

RESPONSORIAL PSALM

1. Psalm 19:8, 9, 10, 11 (L 727)
℟. (see John 6:64b) **Your words, Lord, are spirit and life.**

2. Psalm 119:9, 10, 11, 12 (L 727)
℟. (12b) **Lord, teach me your decrees.**

3. Psalm 147:15-16, 17-18, 19-20
℟. (12) **Praise the Lord, Jerusalem.**

ALLELUIA VERSE AND VERSE BEFORE THE GOSPEL

1. John 6:64b and 69b (L 164)
Your words, Lord, are spirit and life:
you have the words of everlasting life.

2. See Acts 16:14b (L 509)
Open our hearts, O Lord,
to listen to the words of your Son.

3. (L 224)
The seed is the word of God, Christ is the sower;
all who come to him will live for ever.

4. See Luke 4:18 (L 7)
The Spirit of the Lord is upon me;
he sent me to bring Good News to the poor.

GOSPEL

1. Matthew 5:14-19
You are the light of the world.

2. Mark 1:35-39
He came preaching in their synagogues.

3. Luke 4:16-21 (L 39)
The Spirit of the Lord is upon me; he sent me to bring Good News to the poor.

4. Luke 24:44-48 (L 756)
Jesus sent the apostles to preach repentance for the forgiveness of sins.

5. John 7:14-18
My teaching is not mine, but of him who sent me.

FOR THE INSTITUTION OF ACOLYTES

READING FROM THE OLD TESTAMENT

1. Genesis 14:18-20 (L 170)
Melchizedek offered bread and wine to God.

2. Exodus 16:2-4, 12-15 (L 114)
I will rain bread from heaven upon you.

3. Exodus 24:3-8 (L 169)
This is the blood of the covenant that the Lord has made with you.

4. Deuteronomy 8:2-3, 14b-16a (L 168)
He gave you food which you and your ancestors did not know.

5. 1 Kings 19:4-8 (L 117)
Strengthened by the food, he walked to the mountain of the Lord.

6. Proverbs 9:1-6 (L 120)
Come and eat my bread, drink the wine I have prepared.

READING FROM THE NEW TESTAMENT

1. Acts 2:42-47 (L 44)
They remained faithful in prayer and the breaking of the bread.

2. Acts 10:34a, 37-43 (L 43)
We have eaten and drunk with him after his resurrection from the dead.

3. 1 Corinthians 10:16-17 (L 168)
Though we are many, we form a single body because we share this one loaf.

4. 1 Corinthians 11:23-26 (L 40)
Until the Lord comes, every time you eat this bread and drink this cup, you proclaim his death.

5. Hebrews 9:11-15 (L 169)
The blood of Christ will purify our inner selves.

RESPONSORIAL PSALM

1. Psalm 23:1-3a, 3b-4, 5, 6 (L 906)
℟. (1) **The Lord is my shepherd; there is nothing I shall want.**

2. Psalm 34:2-3, 4-5, 6-7, 8-9, 10-11 (L 906)
℟. (9a) **Taste and see the goodness of the Lord.**

3. Psalm 78:3 and 4bc, 23-24, 25, 54 (L 906)
℟. (24b) **The Lord gave them bread from heaven.**

4. Psalm 110:1, 2, 3, 4 (L 906)
℟. (4bc) **You are a priest for ever, in the line of Melchizedek.**

5. Psalm 116:12-13, 15 and 16bc, 17-18 (L 906)
℟. (13) **I will take the cup of salvation, and call on the name of the Lord.**

6. Psalm 145:10-11, 15-16, 17-18 (L 906)
℟. (see 16) **The hand of the Lord feeds us; he answers all our needs.**

7. Psalm 148:12-13, 14-15, 19-20 (L 906)
℟. (John 6:59b) **Whoever eats this bread will live for ever.**

ALLELUIA VERSE AND VERSE BEFORE THE GOSPEL

1. John 6:57 (L 908)
All who eat my flesh and drink my blood
will live in me and I in him, says the Lord.

2. John 6:58 (L 908)
As the living Father sent me, and I live because of the Father,
so whoever feeds on me will live because of me.

3. John 6:35
The Lord says: I am the bread of life.
Whoever comes to me will never be hungry,
and whoever believes in me will never thirst.

4. John 6:51-52 (L 908)
I am the living bread from heaven, says the Lord;
whoever eats this bread will live for ever.

GOSPEL

1. **Mark 14:12-16, 22-26** (L 169)
This is my body. This is my blood.

2. **Luke 9:11b-17** (L 170)
They all ate and were filled.

3. **Luke 24:13-35** (L 43)
They had recognized him at the breaking of the bread.

4. **John 6:1-15** (L 111)
He gave the food to those who were sitting around, as much as they wanted.

5. John 6:24-35 (L 114)
Whoever comes to me will never be hungry; whoever believes in me will never thirst.

6. John 6:41-52a (L 909)
I am the living bread that came down from heaven.

7. John 6:51-59 (L 793)
My flesh is real food and my blood is real drink.

8. John 21:1-14 (L 909)
Jesus came and took the bread and gave it to them and the same with the fish.

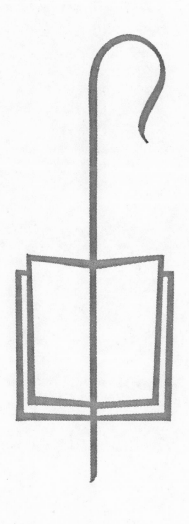

ORDINATION OF DEACONS, PRIESTS
AND BISHOPS

ORDINATION OF DEACONS, PRIESTS, AND BISHOPS

Apostolic Letter

CHAPTER I
ADMISSION TO CANDIDACY FOR ORDINATION AS DEACONS AND PRIESTS

Introduction (1-3)

Liturgy of the Word (4)

Celebration of Admission (5-11)

Homily (5)

Calling of the Candidates (6)

Examination (7)

Acceptance of the Candidates (7)

Invitation to Prayer (8)

Intercessions (9)

Concluding Prayer (10)

Liturgy of the Eucharist (11)

Apostolic Constitution

CHAPTER II
ORDINATION OF A DEACON

Introduction (1-5)

Liturgy of the Word (6-8)

Ordination of a Deacon (9-26)

Calling of the Candidate (10-11)

Presentation of the Candidate (12)

CHAPTER III
ORDINATION OF A PRIEST

Investiture with Stole and Chasuble (23)

Anointing of Hands (24-25)

Presentation of the Gifts (26)

Kiss of Peace (27-28)

Liturgy of the Eucharist (29)

CHAPTER IV
ORDINATION OF DEACONS AND PRIESTS IN THE SAME CELEBRATION

Liturgy of the Word (1-2)

Ordination of Deacons and Priests (3-32)

For Deacons
Calling of the Candidates (3)
Presentation of the Candidates (4)
Election by the Bishop and Consent of the People (5)

For Priests
Calling of the Candidates (6-7)
Presentation of the Candidates (8)
Election by the Bishop and Consent of the People (9)

For Deacons and Priests
Homily (10)
Commitment to Celibacy for Deacons (10)

For Deacons
Examination of the Candidates (11)
Promise of Obedience (12)

For Priests
Examination (12)
Promise of Obedience (13)

For Deacons and Priests
Invitation to Prayer (14)
Litany of the Saints (15-16)

For Deacons
Laying on of Hands (17)
Prayer of Consecration (18)

CHAPTER V
ORDINATION OF A BISHOP

CHAPTER VI
TEXTS FOR USE IN ORDINATION

Readings

Litany of the Saints

APOSTOLIC LETTER

ISSUED *MOTU PROPRIO* LAYING DOWN CERTAIN NORMS REGARDING THE HOLY ORDER OF DEACONS

POPE PAUL VI

For the nurturing and constant growth of the people of God, Christ the Lord instituted in the Church a variety of ministries which work for the good of the whole body.[1]

From the apostolic age the diaconate has had a clearly outstanding position among these ministries, and it has always been held in great honor by the Church. Explicit testimony of this is given by the apostle Saint Paul both in his letter to the Philippians, in which he sends his greetings not only to the bishops but also to the deacons,[2] and in a letter to Timothy, in which he highlights the qualities and virtues that deacons must have in order to be proved worthy of their ministry.[3]

Later, when the early writers of the Church acclaim the dignity of deacons, they do not fail to extol also the spiritual qualities and virtues that are required for the performance of that ministry, namely, fidelity to Christ, moral integrity, and obedience to the bishop.

Saint Ignatius of Antioch declares that the office of the deacon is nothing other than "the ministry of Jesus Christ, who was with the Father before all ages and has been manifested in the final time."[4] He also made the following observation: "The deacons too, who are ministers of the mysteries of Jesus Christ, should please all in every way, for they are not servants of food and drink, but ministers of the Church of God."[5]

Saint Polycarp of Smyrna exhorts deacons to "be moderate in all things, merciful, diligent, living according to the truth of

---

[1]See const. on the Church, no. 18.
[2]See Philippians 1:1.
[3]See 1 Timothy 3:8-13.
[4]*Ad Magnesios*, VI, 1: *Patres Apostolici*, ed. F. X. Funk, I (Tübingen, 1901), p. 235.
[5]*Ad Trallianos*, II, 3: *Patres Apostolici*, ed. F. X. Funk, I (Tübingen, 1901), p. 245.

the Lord, who became the servant of all."[6] The author of the *Didascalia Apostolorum*, recalling the words of Christ: "Anyone who wants to be great among you must be your servant,"[7] addresses the following fraternal exhortation to deacons: "Accordingly you deacons also should behave in such a way that, if your ministry obliges you to lay down your lives for a brother, you should do so. . . . If the Lord of heaven and earth served us and suffered and sustained everything on our behalf, should not this be done for our brothers all the more by us, since we are imitators of him and have been given the place of Christ?"[8]

Furthermore, when the writers of the first centuries insist on the importance of the deacons' ministry, they give many examples of the manifold important tasks entrusted to them and clearly show how much authority they held in the Christian communities and how great was their contribution to the apostolate. The deacon is described as "the bishop's ear, mouth, heart and soul."[9] The deacon is at the disposal of the bishop in order that he may serve the whole people of God and take care of the sick and the poor;[10] he is correctly and rightly called "one who shows love for orphans, for the devout and for the widowed, one who is fervent in spirit, one who shows love for what is good."[11] Furthermore, he is entrusted with the mission of taking the holy eucharist to the sick confined to their homes,[12] of conferring baptism,[13] and of attending to preaching the word of God in accordance with the express will of the bishop.

Accordingly, the diaconate flourished in a wonderful way in the Church and at the same time gave an outstanding witness of love for Christ and the brethren through the performance

---

[6]Epistula *Ad Philippenses*, V, 2: *Patres Apostolici*, ed. F. X. Funk, I (Tübingen, 1901), pp. 301-303.

[7]Matthew 20:26-27.

[8]*Didascalia Apostolorum*, III, 13, 2-4: *Didascalia et Constitutiones Apostolorum*, ed. F. X. Funk, I (Paderborn, 1906), p. 214.

[9]*Didascalia Apostolorum*, II, 44, 4; ed. F. X. Funk, I, p. 138.

[10]See *Traditio Apostolica*, 39 and 34; *La Tradition Apostolique de Saint Hippolyte. Essai de reconstitution* by B. Botte (Münster, 1963), pp. 87 and 81.

[11]*Testamentum D. N. Iesu Christi*, I, 38; ed. and trans. into Latin by I. E. Rahmani (Mainz, 1899), p. 93.

[12]See Saint Justin, *Apologia* I, 65, 5 and 67, 5: Saint Justin, *Apologiae duae*; ed. G. Rauschen (Bonn, 1911), pp. 107 and 111.

[13]See Tertullian, *De Baptismo*, XVII, 1: *Corpus Christianorum*, I, *Tertulliani Opera*, pars I (Turnholt, 1954), p. 291.

of works of charity,[14] the celebration of sacred rites,[15] and the fulfillment of pastoral duties.[16]

The exercise of the office of deacon enabled those who were to become presbyters to give proof of themselves, to display the merit of their work, and to acquire preparation—all of which were requirements for receiving the dignity of the priesthood and the office of pastor.

As time went on, the discipline concerning this holy order was changed. The prohibition against conferring ordination without observing the established sequence of orders was strengthened, and there was a gradual decrease in the number of those who preferred to remain deacons all their lives instead of advancing to a higher order. As a consequence, the permanent diaconate almost entirely disappeared in the Latin Church. It is hardly necessary to mention what was decided by the Council of Trent when it proposed to restore the holy orders in accordance with their own nature as ancient functions within the Church;[17] it was only much later that the idea matured of restoring this important order also as a truly permanent rank. Our predecessor Pius XII briefly alluded to this matter.[18] Finally, the Second Vatican Council supported the wishes and requests that, where such would lead to the good of souls, the permanent diaconate should be restored as an intermediate order between the higher ranks of the Church's hierarchy and the rest of the people of God, as an expression of the needs and desires of the Christian communities, as a driving force for the Church's service or *diaconia* toward the local Christian communities, and as a sign or sacrament of the Lord Christ himself, who "came not to be served but to serve."[19]

---

[14]See *Didascalia Apostolorum*, II, 31, 2: ed. F. X. Funk, I, p. 112; see *Testamentum D. N. Iesu Christi*, I, 31: ed. and trans. into Latin by I. E. Rahmani (Mainz, 1899), p. 75.

[15]See *Didascalia Apostolorum* II, 57, 6; 58, 1: ed. F. X. Funk, 1, pp. 162 and 166.

[16]See Saint Cyprian, Epistolae XV and XVI: ed. G. Hartel (Vienna, 1971), pp. 513-520; see Saint Augustine, *De catechizandis rudibus*, I, cap. I, 1: PL 40, 309-310.

[17]Session XXIII, capp. I-IV: *Mansi* XXXIII, 138-140.

[18]Address to the Participants in the Second International Congress of the Lay Apostolate, October 5, 1957; *AAS* 49 (1957) 925.

[19]Matthew 20:28.

For this reason, at the third session of the Council, in October 1964, the Fathers ratified the principle of the renewal of the diaconate and in the following November the dogmatic constitution *Lumen gentium* was promulgated. In article 29 of this document a description is given of the principal characteristics proper to that state: "At a lower level of the hierarchy are deacons, upon whom hands are imposed 'not for priesthood, but for ministry.' For, strengthened by sacramental grace, in communion with the bishop and his presbyterium, they serve the people of God in the *diaconia* of the liturgy, of the word, and of charity."[20]

The same constitution made the following declaration about permanency in the rank of deacon: "These duties [of deacons], so very necessary for the life of the Church, can in many areas be fulfilled only with difficulty according to the prevailing discipline of the Latin Church. For this reason, the diaconate can in the future be restored as a proper and permanent rank of the hierarchy."[21]

However, this restoration of the permanent diaconate required that the instructions of the Council be more profoundly examined and that there be mature deliberation concerning the juridical status of both the celibate and married deacon. Similarly, it was necessary that matters connected with the diaconate of those who are to become priests should be adapted to contemporary conditions, so that the time of diaconate would furnish that proof of way of life, of maturity, and of aptitude for the priestly ministry which ancient discipline demanded from candidates for the presbyterate.

Thus on June 18, 1967, we issued *motu proprio* the apostolic letter *Sacrum Diaconatus Ordinem*, by which suitable canonical norms for the permanent diaconate were established.[22] On June 17 of the following year, through the apostolic constitution *Pontificalis Romani Recognitio*,[23] we authorized the new rite for conferring of the sacred orders of deacons, presbyters, and bishops, and at the same time defined the matter and the form of the ordination itself.

Now that we are proceeding further and are today promulgating the apostolic letter *Ministeria Quaedam*, we consider it fit-

[20]*AAS* 57 (1965) 36.
[21]*Ibid.*
[22]*AAS* 59 (1967) 697-704.
[23]*AAS* 60 (1968) 369-373.

ting to issue certain norms concerning the diaconate. We also desire that candidates for the diaconate should know what ministries they are to exercise before sacred ordination and what and how they are to take upon themselves the responsibilities of celibacy and liturgical prayer.

Since entrance into the clerical state is deferred until diaconate, there no longer exists the rite of first tonsure, by which a layman used to become a cleric. But a new rite is introduced, by which one who aspires to ordination as deacon or presbyter publicly manifests his will to offer himself to God and the Church, so that he may exercise a sacred order. The Church, accepting this offering, selects and calls him to prepare himself to receive a sacred order, and in this way he is properly numbered among candidates for the diaconate or presbyterate.

It is especially fitting that the ministries of reader and acolyte should be entrusted to those who, as candidates for sacred orders, desire to devote themselves to God and to the Church in a special way. For the Church, which "does not cease to receive the bread of life from the table of the word of God and the body of Christ and offer it to the faithful,"[24] considers it to be very opportune that, both by study and by gradual exercise of the ministry of the word and of the altar, candidates for sacred orders should through intimate contact understand and reflect upon the double aspect of the priestly office. Thus it comes about that the authenticity of the ministry shines out with the greatest effectiveness. In this way the candidates are to approach holy orders fully aware of their vocation, fervent in spirit, serving the Lord, constant in prayer, and aware of the needs of the faithful.[25]

Having weighed every aspect of the question well, having sought the opinion of experts, having consulted with the conferences of bishops and taken their views into account, and having taken counsel with our venerable brothers who are members of the Sacred Congregations competent in this matter, by our apostolic authority we enact the following norms, derogating—if and insofar as necessary—from provisions of the Code of Canon Law now in force, and we promulgate them with this letter.

[24]See const. on revelation, no. 21.
[25]See Romans 12:11-13.

1. a) A rite of admission for candidates for ordination as deacons and presbyters is now introduced. In order that this admission be properly made, the free petition of the aspirant, made out and signed in his own hand, is required, as well as the written acceptance of the competent ecclesiastical superior, by which the selection by the Church is brought about.

Professed members of clerical congregations who seek the presbyterate are not bound to this rite.

b) The competent superior for this acceptance is the ordinary (bishop and, in clerical institutes, the major superior). Those can be accepted who give signs of an authentic vocation and, endowed with good moral qualities and free from mental and physical defects, wish to dedicate their lives to the service of the Church for the glory of God and the good of souls. It is necessary that those who aspire to the diaconate leading to the presbyterate will have completed at least their twentieth year and have begun their course of theological studies.

c) In virtue of the acceptance the candidate must care for his vocation in a special way and foster it. He also acquires the right to the necessary spiritual assistance by which he can develop his vocation and submit unconditionally to the will of God.

2. Candidates for the permanent diaconate and for the diaconate leading to the presbyterate, as well as candidates for the presbyterate itself, are to receive the ministries of reader and acolyte, unless they have already done so, and are to exercise them for a fitting time, in order to be better disposed for the future service of the word and of the altar.

Dispensation from receiving these ministries on the part of such candidates is reserved to the Holy See.

3. The liturgical rites by which admission of candidates for ordination as deacons and presbyters takes place and by which the above-mentioned ministries are conferred should be performed by the ordinary of the aspirant (the bishop and, in clerical institutes, the major superior).

4. The intervals established by the Holy See or by the conferences of bishops between the conferring—during the course

of theological studies—of the ministry of readers and that of acolytes, and between the ministry of acolytes and the order of deacons, must be observed.

5. Before ordination candidates for the diaconate shall give to the ordinary (the bishop and, in clerical institutes, the major superior) a declaration made out and signed in their own hand, by which they testify that they are about to receive the order freely and of their own accord.

6. The special consecration of celibacy observed for the sake of the kingdom of heaven and its obligation for candidates to the priesthood and for unmarried candidates to the diaconate are linked with the diaconate. The public commitment to celibacy before God and the Church is to be celebrated in a particular rite, even by religious, and it is to precede ordination to the diaconate. Celibacy taken on in this way is a diriment impediment to entering marriage.

In accordance with the traditional discipline of the Church, a married deacon who has lost his wife cannot enter a new marriage.[26]

7. a) Deacons called to the presbyterate are not to be ordained until they have completed the course of studies prescribed by the norms of the Apostolic See.

b) In regard to the course of theological studies to precede the ordination of permanent deacons, the conferences of bishops, with attention to the local situation, will issue the proper norms and submit them for the approval of the Sacred Congregation for Catholic Education.

8. In accordance with norms 29-30 of the General Instruction for the Liturgy of the Hours:

a) Deacons called to the presbyterate are obliged by their sacred ordination to celebrate the liturgy of the hours.

b) It is most fitting that permanent deacons should recite daily at least a part of the liturgy of the hours, to be determined by the conference of bishops.

[26]See Paul VI, apostolic letter *Sacrum Diaconatus Ordinem*, no. 16: *AAS* 59 (1967) 701.

9. Entrance into the clerical state and incardination into a diocese are brought about by ordination to the diaconate.

10. The rite of admission for candidates for ordination as deacons and presbyters and of the special consecration of celibacy is to be published soon by the competent department of the Roman Curia.

Transitional Norms: Candidates for the sacrament of orders who have already received first tonsure before the promulgation of this letter retain all the duties, rights, and privileges of clerics. Those who have been promoted to the order of subdiaconate are held to the obligations taken on in regard to both celibacy and the liturgy of the hours. But they must celebrate once again their public commitment to celibacy before God and the Church by the new special rite preceding ordination to the diaconate.

All that has been decreed by us in this letter, issued *motu proprio*, we order to be confirmed and ratified, anything to the contrary notwithstanding. We also determine that it shall come into force on January 1, 1973.

Given in Rome, at Saint Peter's, August 15, 1972, the Solemnity of the Assumption, the tenth year of our pontificate.

Paul VI

CHAPTER I

ADMISSION TO CANDIDACY FOR ORDINATION AS DEACONS AND PRIESTS

INTRODUCTION

1. The rite of admission to candidacy for ordination as deacons and priests is celebrated when the candidates have reached a maturity of purpose and are shown to have the necessary qualifications.

Those professed in clerical religious institutes are not bound to the celebration of this rite.

2. The intention of receiving orders is to be expressed publicly by the candidates. The bishop or the major superior of a clerical religious institute accepts their intention publicly.

3. The rite of admission may be celebrated on any day, preferably on feast days, in a church or other appropriate place, either during Mass or during a celebration of the word of God. Because of its nature, the rite is never joined to an ordination or the institution of readers or acolytes.

LITURGY OF THE WORD

4. The readings are taken in whole or in part from the liturgy of the day or from the texts suggested below.

CELEBRATION OF ADMISSION

HOMILY

5. After the gospel, the bishop, wearing his miter, sits, and gives the homily, which he concludes with these or similar words:

Dear brethren in Christ, our brothers stand here today in the presence of the Church, recommended to us and to you for admission among the candidates for holy orders.

Christ gave this command: "Ask the Lord of the harvest to send laborers into his harvest." Our brothers know the Lord's concern for his flock, they see the needs of the Church, and they feel ready to respond generously to the Lord in the words of the prophet: "Here I am, send me forth." They put their hope in the Lord, trusting that they may answer his call faithfully.

This call from the Lord should be recognized and understood from the daily signs which reveal God's will to men of discernment. When God chooses men to share in the ordained priesthood of Christ, he moves and helps them by his grace. At the same time, he entrusts us with the task of calling suitable and approved candidates and of consecrating them by a special seal of the Holy Spirit to the ministry of God and of the Church. By the sacrament of holy orders they will be appointed to share in the ministry of salvation that Christ accomplished in the world. When the time comes, they will be given a part in our ministry of service to the Church, and build up by word and sacrament the Christian communities to which they will be sent.

Our brothers here have already begun their preparation so that later they may be called to ordination by the bishop. Day by day they will learn to live the life of the Gospel and deepen their faith, hope, and love. In the practice of these virtues they will gain the spirit of prayer and grow in zeal to win the world to Christ.

Urged on by his love and strengthened by the Holy Spirit, they have come here to declare in public their desire to bind themselves to the service of God and of mankind.

When each one is called by name, he should come forward and declare his intention before the Church assembled here.

CALLING OF THE CANDIDATES

6. The appointed deacon or priest calls the candidates by name. Each one answers: **Present**, and goes to the bishop, before whom he makes a sign of reverence.

EXAMINATION

7. Then the bishop speaks to the candidates in these words or in others which the conference of bishops may determine:

My sons, the pastors and teachers in charge of your formation, and others who know you, have given a favorable account of you, and we have full confidence in their testimony.

In response to the Lord's call are you resolved to complete your preparation so that in due time you will be ready to be ordained for the ministry of the Church?
Together the candidates answer: **I am.**

The bishop:
Are you resolved to prepare yourselves in mind and spirit to give faithful service to Christ the Lord and his body, the Church?
The candidates: **I am.**

ACCEPTANCE OF THE CANDIDATES

If it wishes, the conference of bishops may determine the manner in which the bishop is to accept the candidates.

The bishop adds:
The Church receives your declaration with joy. May God who has begun the good work in you bring it to fulfillment.
All: **Amen.**

INVITATION TO PRAYER

8. Then all stand, and the bishop, without his miter, invites the people to pray:

Brothers and sisters, let us ask our God and Lord to pour out his grace and blessing on these servants of his

who desire to give their lives to the ministry of the Church.

INTERCESSIONS

9. The deacon or another qualified minister proposes the following intentions or others adapted to the circumstances. All respond with an appropriate acclamation.

Deacon or minister:
That our brothers may draw closer to Christ and be his witnesses in the world, let us pray to the Lord:
℟. **Lord, hear our prayer.**

Deacon or minister:
That they may share the burdens of others and always listen to the voice of the Holy Spirit, let us pray to the Lord:
℟. **Lord, hear our prayer.**

Deacon or minister:
That they may become ministers of the Church who will strengthen the faith of their brothers and sisters by word and example, and gather them together to share in the eucharist, let us pray to the Lord:
℟. **Lord, hear our prayer.**

CONCLUDING PRAYER

10. The bishop continues:

Lord,
hear our prayers for your sons
who wish to dedicate themselves
to your service and the service of your people
in the sacred ministry.
Bless them ✠ in your fatherly love,
that they may persevere in their vocation,
and through their loving fidelity to Christ the Priest
be worthy to carry out
the Church's apostolic mission.

We ask this through Christ our Lord.
℟. **Amen.**

Or:
**Lord,
help your servants
to understand and live the mystery of your love
more completely every day.
Deepen their sense of purpose
as they prepare for the sacred ministry of the Church
and fill them with the spirit of your love
so that they may be wholehearted
in bringing salvation to mankind
for the glory of your name.**

**We ask this through Christ our Lord.
℟. Amen.**

LITURGY OF THE EUCHARIST

11. If the rite of admission takes place during Mass, the celebration continues as usual. If it takes place during a celebration of the word, the bishop blesses the assembly and dismisses it in the usual way.

APOSTOLIC CONSTITUTION

APPROVAL OF NEW RITES FOR THE ORDINATION OF DEACONS, PRESBYTERS, AND BISHOPS

PAUL, BISHOP

Servant of the Servants of God For an Everlasting Memorial

The revision of the Roman Pontifical is prescribed in a general way by the Second Vatican Ecumenical Council[1] and is also governed by special norms in which the holy Synod ordered that the rites of ordination be changed "in ceremonies and in texts."[2]

Among the rites of ordination the first to be considered are those which constitute the hierarchy through the sacrament of orders, conferred in several grades: "Thus the divinely instituted ministry of the Church is exercised in various orders by those who already in antiquity are called bishops, presbyters, and deacons."[3]

In the revision of the rites of sacred ordination, besides the general principles which must direct the entire restoration of the liturgy according to the decrees of the Second Vatican Council, the greatest attention should be paid to the Council's important teaching, in the constitution on the Church, on the nature and effects of the sacrament of orders. It is evident that the liturgy itself should express this doctrine in its own way, for "the texts and rites should be drawn up so that they express more clearly the holy things they signify; the Christian people, so far as possible, should be able to understand them with ease and to take part in them fully, actively, and as befits a community."[4]

The holy Synod teaches that "by episcopal consecration the fullness of the sacrament of orders is conferred, that fullness which is truly called—in the Church's liturgical usage and in the language of the Fathers—the high priesthood, the apex of the sacred ministry. But together with the office of sanctify-

---

[1]Const. on the liturgy, no. 25.
[2]*Ibid.*, no. 76.
[3]Const. on the Church, no. 28.
[4]Const. on the liturgy, no. 21.

ing, episcopal consecration also confers the offices of teaching and governing. These, however, of their very nature can be exercised only in hierarchical communion with the head and members of the college [of bishops]. From tradition which is expressed especially through liturgical rites and through the practice of the Church in both East and West, it is clear that by the laying on of hands and the words of consecration the grace of the Holy Spirit is so conferred and the sacred character so impressed that bishops undertake Christ's own role as Teacher, Shepherd, and Bishop in an eminent and visible way and that they act in his person."[5]

To these words should be added a number of important doctrinal statements [of the Council] concerning the apostolic succession of bishops and their duties and functions. Even if these matters are now found in the rite of episcopal consecration, still it seems that they should be better and more precisely expressed. To achieve this, it appeared appropriate to take from ancient sources the consecratory prayer which is found in the document called the *Apostolic Tradition of Hippolytus of Rome*, written at the beginning of the third century. This consecratory prayer is still used, in large part, in the ordination rites of the Coptic and West Syrian liturgies. Thus the very act of ordination is witness to the harmony of tradition in East and West concerning the apostolic office of bishops.

With regard to presbyters, the following should be recalled from acts of the Second Vatican Council: "Although presbyters do not possess the highest degree of pontificate and although they are dependent upon the bishops in the exercise of their power, they are nevertheless united with the bishops in priestly dignity; and in virtue of the sacrament of orders they are consecrated in the image of Christ the eternal high priest (see Hebrews 5:1-10; 7:24; 9:11-28) as true priests of the New Testament to preach the Gospel, shepherd the faithful, and celebrate the worship of God."[6] In another place the Council says: "By sacred ordination and by the mission they receive from the bishops, presbyters are promoted to the service of Christ the Teacher, the Priest, and the King. They share in his ministry of unceasingly building up the Church on earth into the people of God, the body of Christ, and the

[5]Const. on the Church, no. 21.
[6]*Ibid.*, no. 28.

temple of the Holy Spirit."[7] In the ordination of presbyters, as found in the Roman Pontifical, the mission and grace of the presbyter as a helper of the episcopal order have been very clearly described. Yet it seemed necessary to restore the entire rite, which had been divided into several parts, to greater unity and to express in sharper light the central part of the ordination, that is, laying on of hands and the consecratory prayer.

Finally, with regard to deacons, in addition to the content of our apostolic letter *Sacrum Diaconatus Ordinem* issued *motu proprio* on June 18, 1967, the following should be especially recalled: "In the lower grade of the hierarchy are deacons, on whom hands are laid 'not for the priesthood, but for the ministry' (Constitutions of the Church of Egypt, III, 2). Strengthened by sacramental grace, they serve the people of God in the *diaconia* of liturgy, word, and charity, in communion with the bishop and his presbyterium."[8] In the ordination of deacons a few changes had to be made to satisfy the recent prescriptions about the diaconate as a distinct and permanent grade of the hierarchy in the Latin Church or to achieve a greater simplicity and clarity in the rites.

Among the other documents of the supreme magisterium pertaining to sacred orders, we consider one worthy of particular mention, namely, the apostolic constitution *Sacramentum Ordinis* published by our predecessor, Pius XII, on November 30, 1947. In this constitution he declared that "the sole matter of the sacred orders of diaconate and presbyterate is the laying on of hands; likewise the sole form is the words determining the application of this matter, which univocally signify the sacramental effects—namely, the power of orders and the grace of the Holy Spirit—and are accepted and used as such by the Church."[9] After this, the document determines which laying on of hands and which words constitute the matter and form in the conferring of each order.

It was necessary in the revision of the rite to add, delete, or change certain things, either to restore texts to their earlier integrity, to clarify the meaning, or to bring out more clearly the sacramental effects. We therefore think it necessary, in

[7]Decree on priestly ministry and life, no. 1.
[8]Const. on the Church, no. 29.
[9]*AAS* 40 (1948) 6.

order to remove all controversy and to avoid anxiety of conscience, to declare what is to be considered as belonging to
the very nature of the rite in each case. By our supreme apostolic authority we decree and establish the following with
regard to the matter and form in the conferring of each order.

In the ordination of deacons, the matter is the laying of the
bishop's hands upon the individual candidates, which is
done in silence before the consecratory prayer; the form consists of the words of the consecratory prayer, of which the
following belong to the nature of the rite and are consequently required for validity:

Lord,
send forth upon them the Holy Spirit,
that they may be strengthened
by the gift of your sevenfold grace
to carry out faithfully the work of the ministry.

In the ordination of presbyters, the matter is likewise the
laying of the bishop's hands upon the individual candidates,
which is done in silence before the consecratory prayer; the
form consists of the words of the consecratory prayer, of
which the following belong to the nature of the rite and are
consequently required for validity:

Almighty Father,
grant to these servants of yours
the dignity of the priesthood.
Renew within them the Spirit of holiness.
As co-workers with the order of bishops
may they be faithful to the ministry
that they receive from you, Lord God,
and be to others a model of right conduct.

Finally, in the ordination of a bishop, the matter is the laying
of hands upon the head of the bishop-elect by the consecrating bishops, or at least by the principal consecrator, which is
done in silence before the consecratory prayer; the form consists of the words of the consecratory prayer, of which the
following belong to the nature of the rite and are consequently required for validity:

So now pour out upon this chosen one
that power which is from you,

the governing Spirit
whom you gave to your beloved Son, Jesus Christ,
the Spirit given by him to the holy apostles,
who founded the Church in every place to be your
    temple
for the unceasing glory and praise of your name.

This rite for the conferring of the sacred orders of diaconate, presbyterate, and episcopate, has been revised by the Consilium for the Implementation of the Constitution on the Sacred Liturgy "with the assistance of experts, and with the consultation of bishops, from various parts of the world."[10] By our apostolic authority we approve this rite so that it may be used in the future for the conferral of these orders in place of the rite now found in the Roman Pontifical.

It is our will that these our decrees and prescriptions be firm and effective now and in the future, notwithstanding, to the extent necessary, the apostolic constitutions and ordinances issued by our predecessors and other prescriptions, even those requiring particular mention and derogation.

Given at Rome, at Saint Peter's, June 18, 1968, the fifth year of our pontificate.

                                                                    Paul VI

[10]See const. on the liturgy, no. 25.

CHAPTER II

ORDINATION OF A DEACON

INTRODUCTION

1. The ordination of a deacon should take place on a Sunday or holyday, when a large number of the faithful can attend, unless pastoral reasons suggest another day.

The public commitment to celibacy by the candidate for ordination as a priest and by an unmarried candidate for the diaconate, including a religious, must be made before the rite of ordination of a deacon (see no. 14 below).

2. The ordination should take place ordinarily at the *cathedra* or bishop's chair; or, to enable the faithful to participate more fully, a chair for the bishop may be placed before the altar or elsewhere. A seat for the one to be ordained should be placed so that the faithful may have a complete view of the liturgical rites.

3. The one to be ordained wears an alb (with amice and cincture unless other provisions are made).

4. In addition to what is needed for the celebration of Mass, there should be ready: (a) the Roman Pontifical; (b) stole and dalmatic for the candidate.

5. When everything is ready, the procession moves through the church to the altar in the usual way. A deacon carries the Book of the Gospels; he is followed by the candidate and finally by the bishop between two deacons.

LITURGY OF THE WORD

6. The liturgy of the word takes place according to the rubrics.

7. The readings may be taken in whole or in part from the Mass of the day or from the texts listed in Chapter VI.

8. The profession of faith is not said, nor are the general intercessions.

ORDINATION OF A DEACON

9. The ordination of a deacon begins after the gospel. The bishop, wearing his miter, sits at his chair.

CALLING OF THE CANDIDATE

10. The candidate is called by the deacon:
Let N. who is to be ordained deacon please come forward.

11. The candidate answers: **Present**, and goes to the bishop, before whom he makes a sign of reverence.

PRESENTATION OF THE CANDIDATE

12. When the candidate is in his place before the bishop, the priest designated by the bishop says:

Most Reverend Father, holy mother Church asks you to ordain this man, our brother, for service as deacon.

The bishop asks:
Do you judge him to be worthy?

He answers:
After inquiry among the people of Christ and upon recommendation of those concerned with his training, I testify that he has been found worthy.

ELECTION BY THE BISHOP
AND CONSENT OF THE PEOPLE

13. Bishop:
We rely on the help of the Lord God and our Savior Jesus Christ, and we choose this man, our brother, for the order of deacons.

All present say: **Thanks be to God**, or give their assent to the choice in some other way, according to local custom.

HOMILY

14. Then all sit, and the bishop gives the homily. He begins with the text of the readings from Scripture and then speaks to the people and the candidate about the office of deacon and the meaning and importance of celibacy in the Church. He may use these words:

This man, your relative and friend, is now to be raised to the order of deacons. Consider carefully the ministry to which he is to be promoted.

He will draw new strength from the gift of the Holy Spirit. He will help the bishop and his body of priests as a minister of the word, of the altar, and of charity. He will make himself a servant to all. As a minister of the altar he will proclaim the Gospel, prepare the sacrifice, and give the Lord's body and blood to the community of believers.

It will also be his duty, at the bishop's discretion, to bring God's word to believer and unbeliever alike, to preside over public prayer, to baptize, to assist at marriages and bless them, to give viaticum to the dying, and to lead the rites of burial. Once he is consecrated by the laying on of hands that comes to us from the apostles and is bound more closely to the altar, he will perform works of charity in the name of the bishop or the pastor. From the way he goes about these duties, may you recognize him as a disciple of Jesus, who came to serve, not to be served.

He then addresses the candidate:
My son, you are being raised to the order of deacons. The Lord has set an example for you to follow.

As a deacon you will serve Jesus Christ, who was known among his disciples as the one who served others. Do the will of God generously. Serve God and mankind in love and joy. Look upon all unchastity and avarice as worship of false gods; for no man can serve two masters.

Like the men the apostles chose for works of charity, you should be a man of good reputation, filled with wisdom and the Holy Spirit. Show before God and mankind that you are above every suspicion of blame, a true minister of Christ and of God's mysteries, a man firmly rooted in faith. Never turn away from the hope which the Gospel offers; now you must not only listen to God's word but also preach it. Hold the mystery of faith with a clear conscience. Express in action what you proclaim by word of mouth. Then the people of Christ, brought to life by the Spirit, will be an offering God accepts. Finally, on the last day, when you go to meet the Lord, you will hear him say: "Well done, good and faithful servant, enter into the joy of your Lord."

COMMITMENT TO CELIBACY

After the homily the candidate, if he is to manifest his intention of a commitment to celibacy, stands before the bishop. The bishop speaks to him in these or similar words:

By your own free choice you seek to enter the order of deacons. You shall exercise this ministry in the celibate state for celibacy is both a sign and a motive of pastoral charity, and a special source of spiritual fruitfulness in the world. By living in this state with total dedication, moved by a sincere love for Christ the Lord, you are consecrated to him in a new and special way. By this consecration you will adhere more easily to Christ with an undivided heart; you will be more freely at the service of God and mankind, and you will be more untrammeled in the ministry of Christian conversion and rebirth. By your life and character you will give witness to your brothers and sisters in faith that God must be loved above all else, and that it is he whom you serve in others.

Therefore, I ask you:
In the presence of God and the Church, are you resolved, as a sign of your interior dedication to Christ,

to remain celibate for the sake of the kingdom and in lifelong service to God and mankind?

The candidate answers: **I am.**

If it wishes, the conference of bishops may determine some external sign to express the intention of the candidate.

The bishop adds:
May the Lord help you to persevere in this commitment.

The candidate answers: **Amen.**

EXAMINATION OF THE CANDIDATE

15. The candidate then stands before the bishop who questions him:

My son, before you are ordained a deacon, you must declare before the people your intention to undertake this office.

Are you willing to be ordained for the Church's ministry by the laying on of hands and the gift of the Holy Spirit?
The candidate answers: **I am.**

Bishop:
Are you resolved to discharge the office of deacon with humility and love in order to assist the bishop and the priests and to serve the people of Christ?
Candidate: **I am.**

Bishop:
Are you resolved to hold the mystery of the faith with a clear conscience as the Apostle urges, and to proclaim this faith in word and action as it is taught by the Gospel and the Church's tradition?
Candidate: **I am.**

Bishop:
Are you resolved to maintain and deepen a spirit of prayer appropriate to your way of life and, in keeping with what is required of you, to celebrate faithfully the

liturgy of the hours for the Church and for the whole world?
Candidate: **I am.**

Bishop:
Are you resolved to shape your way of life always according to the example of Christ, whose body and blood you will give to the people?
Candidate: **I am, with the help of God.**

PROMISE OF OBEDIENCE

16. Then the candidate goes to the bishop and, kneeling before him, places his joined hands between those of the bishop. If this gesture seems less suitable in some places, the conference of bishops may choose another gesture or sign.

If the bishop is the candidate's own Ordinary, he asks:
Do you promise respect and obedience to me and my successors?
Candidate: **I do.**

If the bishop is not the candidate's own Ordinary, he asks:
Do you promise respect and obedience to your Ordinary?
Candidate: **I do.**

Bishop:
May God who has begun the good work in you bring it to fulfillment.

INVITATION TO PRAYER

17. Then all stand, and the bishop, without his miter, invites the people to pray:

My dear people, let us pray that the all-powerful Father will pour out his blessing on this servant of his, whom he receives into the holy order of deacons.

Deacon (except during the Easter season):
Let us kneel.

LITANY OF THE SAINTS

18. The candidate prostrates himself and, except during the Easter season, the rest kneel at their places.

The cantors begin the litany (see Chapter VI); they may add, at the proper place, names of other saints (for example, the patron saint, the titular of the church, the founder of the church, the patron saint of the one to be ordained) or petitions suitable to the occasion.

19. The bishop alone stands and, with his hands joined, sings or says:

Lord God,
hear our petitions
and give your help to this act of our ministry.
We judge this man worthy to serve as deacon
and we ask you to bless him
and make him holy.

Grant this through Christ our Lord.
℟. **Amen.**

Deacon: **Let us stand.**

LAYING ON OF HANDS

20. Then all stand. The candidate goes to the bishop and kneels before him. The bishop lays his hands on the candidate's head, in silence.

PRAYER OF CONSECRATION

21. The candidate kneels before the bishop. With his hands extended over the candidate, he sings the prayer of consecration or says it aloud:

Almighty God,
be present with us by your power.
You are the source of all honor,
you assign to each his rank,
you give to each his ministry.

You remain unchanged,
but you watch over all creation and make it new
through your Son, Jesus Christ, our Lord:
he is your Word, your power, and your wisdom.
You foresee all things in your eternal providence
and make due provision for every age.
You make the Church, Christ's body,
grow to its full stature as a new and greater temple.
You enrich it with every kind of grace
and perfect it with a diversity of members
to serve the whole body in a wonderful pattern of
    unity.

You established a threefold ministry of worship and
    service
for the glory of your name.
As ministers of your tabernacle you chose the sons
    of Levi
and gave them your blessing as their everlasting
    inheritance.
In the first days of your Church
under the inspiration of the Holy Spirit
the apostles of your Son appointed seven men of
    good repute
to assist them in the daily ministry,
so that they themselves might be more free for
    prayer and preaching.
By prayer and the laying on of the hands
the apostles entrusted to those chosen men the
    ministry of serving at tables.

Lord
look with favor on this servant of yours,
whom we now dedicate to the office of deacon,
to minister at your holy altar.

Lord,
send forth upon him the Holy Spirit,
that he may be strengthened
by the gift of your sevenfold grace
to carry out faithfully the work of the ministry.

May he excel in every virtue:
in love that is sincere,
in concern for the sick and the poor,
in unassuming authority,
in self-discipline,
and in holiness of life.
May his conduct exemplify your commandments
and lead your people to imitate his purity of life.
May he remain strong and steadfast in Christ,
giving to the world the witness of a pure conscience.
May he in this life imitate your Son,
who came, not to be served but to serve,
and one day reign with him in heaven.

We ask this through our Lord Jesus Christ, your Son,
who lives and reigns with you and the Holy Spirit,
one God, for ever and ever.
℟. Amen.

INVESTITURE WITH STOLE AND DALMATIC

22. After the prayer of consecration, the bishop, wearing his miter, sits, and the newly ordained stands. An assisting deacon or priest puts a deacon's stole and then a dalmatic on him.

23. Meanwhile, the following antiphon may be sung with Psalm 84.

Blessed are they who dwell in your house, O Lord.

The antiphon is repeated after every two verses. **Glory to the Father** is not said. The psalm is interrupted and the antiphon repeated when the dalmatic has been put on the deacon.

Any other appropriate song may be sung.

PRESENTATION OF THE BOOK OF THE GOSPELS

24. Vested as a deacon, the newly ordained goes to the bishop and kneels before him. The bishop places the Book of the Gospels in the hands of the newly ordained and says:

Receive the Gospel of Christ,
whose herald you now are.

Believe what you read,
teach what you believe,
and practice what you teach.

KISS OF PEACE

25. Lastly, the bishop stands and gives the kiss of peace to the new deacon, saying:

Peace be with you.

The deacon responds: **And also with you.**

If circumstances permit, the deacons present also give the kiss of peace to the newly ordained.

26. Meanwhile, the following antiphon may be sung with Psalm 146.

If anyone serves me, says the Lord,
my Father in heaven will honor him.

The antiphon is repeated after every two verses. **Glory to the Father** is not said. The psalm is interrupted and the antiphon repeated when all have received the kiss of peace.

Any other appropriate song may be sung.

LITURGY OF THE EUCHARIST

27. The Order of Mass is followed with these changes:
a) The new deacon brings the offerings for the celebration to the bishop and assists him at the altar.
b) In Eucharistic Prayer I, the special form of **Father, accept this offering** is said:

Father, accept this offering
from your whole family
and from the one you have chosen for the order
    of deacons.

Protect the gifts you have given him,
and let him yield a harvest worthy of you.

[Through Christ our Lord. Amen.]

28. The new deacon receives communion under both kinds and if necessary assists the bishop by ministering the cup. In any event he assists the bishop in giving communion to the people.

CHAPTER III

ORDINATION OF A PRIEST

INTRODUCTION

1. The ordination of a priest should take place on a Sunday or holyday, when a large number of the faithful can attend, unless pastoral reasons suggest another day.

2. The ordination should take place ordinarily at the *cathedra* or bishop's chair; or, to enable the faithful to participate more fully, a chair for the bishop may be placed before the altar or elsewhere. A seat for the one to be ordained should be placed so that the faithful may have a complete view of the liturgical rites.

3. The priest concelebrates with the bishop in his ordination Mass. It is most appropriate for the bishop to admit other priests to the concelebration; in this case and on this day the newly ordained priest takes the first place ahead of the others who concelebrate.

4. The one to be ordained wears an alb (with an amice and cincture unless other provisions are made) and a deacon's stole. In addition to what is needed for the concelebration of Mass, there should be ready: (a) the Roman Pontifical; (b) stoles for the priests who lay hands upon the candidate; (c) a chasuble for the candidate; (d) a linen gremial; (e) holy chrism; (f) whatever is needed for the washing of hands.

5. When everything is ready, the procession moves through the church to the altar in the usual way. A deacon carries the Book of the Gospels; he is followed by the candidate then the concelebrating priests, and finally the bishop between two deacons.

LITURGY OF THE WORD

6. The liturgy of the word takes place according to the rubrics.

7. The readings may be taken in whole or in part from the Mass of the day or from the texts listed in Chapter VI.

8. The profession of faith is not said, nor are the general intercesssions.

ORDINATION OF A PRIEST

9. The ordination of a priest begins after the gospel. The bishop, wearing his miter, sits at his chair.

CALLING OF THE CANDIDATE

10. The candidate is called by the deacon:
Let N. who is to be ordained priest please come forward.

11. The candidate answers: **Present**, and goes to the bishop, before whom he makes a sign of reverence.

PRESENTATION OF THE CANDIDATE

12. When the candidate is in his place before the bishop, the priest designated by the bishop says:

Most Reverend Father, holy mother Church asks you to ordain this man, our brother, for service as priest.

The bishop asks:
Do you judge him to be worthy?

He answers:
After inquiry among the people of Christ and upon recommendation of those concerned with his training, I testify that he has been found worthy.

ELECTION BY THE BISHOP
AND CONSENT OF THE PEOPLE

13. Bishop:
We rely on the help of the Lord God and our Savior Jesus Christ, and we choose this man, our brother, for priesthood in the presbyteral order.

All present say: **Thanks be to God**, or give their assent to the choice in some other way, according to local custom.

HOMILY

14. Then all sit, and the bishop addresses the people and the candidate on the duties of a priest. He may use these words:

This man, your relative and friend, is now to be raised to the order of priests. Consider carefully the position to which he is to be promoted in the Church.

It is true that God has made his entire people a royal priesthood in Christ. But our High Priest, Jesus Christ, also chose some of his followers to carry out publicly in the Church a priestly ministry in his name on behalf of mankind. He was sent by the Father, and he in turn sent the apostles into the world; through them and their successors, the bishops, he continues his work as Teacher, Priest, and Shepherd. Priests are co-workers of the order of bishops. They are joined to the bishops in the priestly office and are called to serve God's people.

Our brother has seriously considered this step and is now to be ordained to priesthood in the presbyteral order. He is to serve Christ the Teacher, Priest, and Shepherd in his ministry which is to make his own body, the Church, grow into the people of God, a holy temple.

He is called to share in the priesthood of the bishops and to be molded into the likeness of Christ, the supreme and eternal Priest. By consecration he will be made a true priest of the New Testament, to preach the Gospel, sustain God's people, and celebrate the liturgy, above all, the Lord's sacrifice.

He then addresses the candidate:

My son, you are now to be advanced to the order of the presbyterate. You must apply your energies to the duty of teaching in the name of Christ, the chief Teacher. Share with all mankind the word of God you have received with joy. Meditate on the law of God, believe what you read, teach what you believe, and put into practice what you teach.

Let the doctrine you teach be true nourishment for the people of God. Let the example of your life attract the followers of Christ, so that by word and action you may build up the house which is God's Church.

In the same way you must carry out your mission of sanctifying in the power of Christ. Your ministry will perfect the spiritual sacrifice of the faithful by uniting it to Christ's sacrifice, the sacrifice which is offered sacramentally through your hands. Know what you are doing and imitate the mystery you celebrate. In the memorial of the Lord's death and resurrection, make every effort to die to sin and to walk in the new life of Christ.

When you baptize, you will bring men and women into the people of God. In the sacrament of penance, you will forgive sins in the name of Christ and the Church. With holy oil you will relieve and console the sick. You will celebrate the liturgy and offer thanks and praise to God throughout the day, praying not only for the people of God but for the whole world. Remember that you are chosen from among God's people and appointed to act for them in relation to God. Do your part in the work of Christ the Priest with genuine joy and love, and attend to the concerns of Christ before your own.

Finally, conscious of sharing in the work of Christ, the Head and Shepherd of the Church, and united with the bishop and subject to him, seek to bring the faithful together into a unified family and to lead them effectively, through Christ and in the Holy Spirit, to God the Father. Always remember the example of the Good Shepherd who came not to be served but to serve, and to seek out and rescue those who were lost.

EXAMINATION OF THE CANDIDATE

15. The candidate then stands before the bishop, who questions him:

My son, before you proceed to the order of the presbyterate, declare before the people your intention to undertake this priestly office.

Are you resolved, with the help of the Holy Spirit, to discharge without fail the office of priesthood in the presbyteral order as a conscientious fellow worker with the bishops in caring for the Lord's flock?
The candidate answers: **I am.**

Bishop:
Are you resolved to celebrate the mysteries of Christ faithfully and religiously as the Church has handed them down to us for the glory of God and the sanctification of Christ's people?
Candidate: **I am.**

Bishop:
Are you resolved to exercise the ministry of the word worthily and wisely, preaching the Gospel and explaining the Catholic faith?
Candidate: **I am.**

Bishop:
Are you resolved to consecrate your life to God for the salvation of his people, and to unite yourself more closely every day to Christ the High Priest, who offered himself for us to the Father as a perfect sacrifice?
Candidate: **I am, with the help of God.**

PROMISE OF OBEDIENCE
16. Then the candidate goes to the bishop and, kneeling before him, places his joined hands between those of the bishop. If this gesture seems less suitable in some places, the conference of bishops may choose another gesture or sign.

If the bishop is the candidate's own Ordinary, he asks:
Do you promise respect and obedience to me and my successors?
Candidate: **I do.**

If the bishop is not the candidate's own Ordinary, he asks:
Do you promise respect and obedience to your Ordinary?
Candidate: **I do.**

Bishop:
May God who has begun the good work in you bring it to fulfillment.

INVITATION TO PRAYER

17. Then all stand, and the bishop, without his miter, invites the people to pray:

My dear people, let us pray, that the all-powerful Father may pour out the gifts of heaven on this servant of his, whom he has chosen to be a priest.

Deacon (except during the Easter season):
Let us kneel.

LITANY OF THE SAINTS

18. The candidate prostrates himself and, except during the Easter season, the rest kneel at their places.

The cantors begin the litany (see Chapter VI); they may add, at the proper place, names of other saints (for example, the patron saint, the titular of the church, the founder of the church, the patron saint of the one to be ordained) or petitions suitable to the occasion.

19. The bishop alone stands and, with his hands joined, sings or says:

Hear us, Lord our God,
and pour out upon this servant of yours
the blessing of the Holy Spirit
and the grace and power of the priesthood.
In your sight we offer this man for ordination:
support him with your unfailing love.

We ask this through Christ our Lord.
℟. **Amen.**

Deacon: **Let us stand.**

LAYING ON OF HANDS

20. Then all stand. The candidate goes to the bishop and kneels before him. The bishop lays his hands on the candidate's head, in silence.

21. Next all the priests present, wearing stoles, lay their hands upon the candidate in silence. After the laying on of hands, the priests remain on either side of the bishop until the prayer of consecration is completed.

PRAYER OF CONSECRATION

22. The candidate kneels before the bishop. With his hands extended over the candidate, the bishop sings the prayer of consecration or says it aloud:

Come to our help,
Lord, holy Father, almighty and eternal God;
you are the source of every honor and dignity,
of all progress and stability.
You watch over the growing family of man
by your gift of wisdom and your pattern of order.
When you had appointed high priests to rule
     your people,
you chose other men next to them in rank and dignity
to be with them and to help them in their task;
and so there grew up
the ranks of priests and the offices of levites,
established by sacred rites.

In the desert
you extended the spirit of Moses to seventy wise men
who helped him to rule the great company of his
     people.
You shared among the sons of Aaron
the fullness of their father's power,
to provide worthy priests in sufficient number
for the increasing rites of sacrifice and worship.
With the same loving care
you gave companions to your Son's apostles
to help in teaching the faith:
they preached the Gospel to the whole world.

Lord,
grant also to us such fellow workers,
for we are weak and our need is greater.

Almighty Father,
grant to this servant of yours

the dignity of the priesthood.
Renew within him the Spirit of holiness.
As a co-worker with the order of bishops
may he be faithful to the ministry
that he receives from you, Lord God,
and be to others a model of right conduct.

May he be faithful in working with the order of
    bishops,
so that the words of the Gospel may reach the ends of
    the earth,
and the family of nations,
made one in Christ,
may become God's one, holy people.

We ask this through our Lord Jesus Christ, your Son,
who lives and reigns with you and the Holy Spirit,
one God, for ever and ever.
℟. Amen.

INVESTITURE WITH STOLE AND CHASUBLE

23. After the prayer of consecration, the bishop, wearing his
miter, sits, and the newly ordained stands. The assisting
priests return to their places, but one of them arranges the
stole of the newly ordained as it is worn by priests and vests
him in a chasuble.

ANOINTING OF HANDS

24. Next the bishop receives a linen gremial and anoints with
chrism the palms of the new priest as he kneels before him.
The bishop says:

The Father anointed our Lord Jesus Christ
through the power of the Holy Spirit.
May Jesus preserve you to sanctify the Christian
    people
and to offer sacrifice to God.

25. While the new priest is being vested in stole and chasuble
and the bishop is anointing his hands, the hymn **Veni,
Creator Spiritus** or the following antiphon may be sung with
Psalm 110.

Christ the Lord,
a priest for ever in the line of Melchizedek,
offered bread and wine.

The antiphon is repeated after every two verses. **Glory to the Father** is not said. The psalm is interrupted and the antiphon repeated when the hands of the priest have been anointed.

Any other appropriate song may be sung.

Then the bishop and the new priest wash their hands.

PRESENTATION OF THE GIFTS

26. The deacon assists the bishop in receiving the gifts of the people and he prepares the bread on the paten and the wine and water in the chalice for the celebration of Mass. He brings the paten and chalice to the bishop, who hands them to the new priest as he kneels before him. The bishop says:

Accept from the holy people of God the gifts to be
  offered to him.
Know what you are doing, and imitate the mystery you
  celebrate:
model your life on the mystery of the Lord's cross.

KISS OF PEACE

27. Lastly, the bishop stands and gives the kiss of peace to the new priest, saying:

Peace be with you.

The priest responds: **And also with you.**

If circumstances permit, the priests present also give the kiss of peace to the newly ordained.

28. Meanwhile, the following antiphon may be sung with Psalm 100.

You are my friends, says the Lord, if you do what I
command you.

The antiphon is repeated after every two verses. **Glory to the Father** is not said. The psalm is interrupted and the antiphon repeated when all have received the kiss of peace.

Any other appropriate song may be sung, or:

**No longer do I call you servants, but my friends,
because you know all that I have done among you
(alleluia).
—Receive the Holy Spirit as an Advocate among you:
it is he whom the Father will send you (alleluia).
You are my friends if you do the things I command
you.
—Receive the Holy Spirit as an Advocate among you.
Glory to the Father...
—It is he whom the Father will send you (alleluia).**

LITURGY OF THE EUCHARIST

29. The rite for the concelebration of Mass is followed with
these changes:
a) The preparation of the chalice is omitted.
b) In Eucharistic Prayer I, the special form of **Father, accept
this offering** is said:

**Father, accept this offering
from your whole family
and from the one you have chosen for the order of
 priests.
Protect the gifts you have given him,
and let him yield a harvest worthy of you.**

[Through Christ our Lord. Amen.]

CHAPTER IV

ORDINATION OF DEACONS AND PRIESTS IN THE SAME CELEBRATION

1. The preparations and the order of the liturgy of the word should follow what has been previously indicated for the individual ordinations.

2. After the gospel is read, the bishop, wearing his miter, sits at his chair.

ORDINATION OF DEACONS AND PRIESTS

FOR DEACONS

CALLING OF THE CANDIDATES

3. First the candidates for the order of deacons are called by the deacon:

Those to be ordained deacons please come forward.

Then their names are called by the deacon. Each one answers: **Present**, and goes to the bishop, before whom he makes a sign of reverence.

PRESENTATION OF THE CANDIDATES

4. When all the candidates are in their place before the bishop, the priest designated by the bishop says:

Most Reverend Father, holy mother Church asks you to ordain these men, our brothers, for service as deacons.

The bishop asks:
Do you judge them to be worthy?

He answers:
After inquiry among the people of Christ and upon recommendation of those concerned with their training, I testify that they have been found worthy.

5. Bishop:

We rely on the help of the Lord God and our Savior Jesus Christ, and we choose these men, our brothers, for the order of deacons.

All present say: **Thanks be to God**, or give their assent to the choice in some other way, according to local custom.

FOR PRIESTS

CALLING OF THE CANDIDATES

6. Then the candidates for priesthood in the presbyteral order are called by the deacon:

Those to be ordained priests please come forward.

7. Then their names are called by the deacon. Each one answers: **Present**, and goes to the bishop, before whom he makes a sign of reverence.

PRESENTATION OF THE CANDIDATES

8. When the candidates are in their places before the bishop, the priest designated by the bishop says:

Most Reverend Father, holy mother Church asks you to ordain these men, our brothers for service as priests.

The bishop asks:
Do you judge them to be worthy?

He answers:
After inquiry among the people of Christ and upon recommendation of those concerned with their training, I testify that they have been found worthy.

ELECTION BY THE BISHOP
AND CONSENT OF THE PEOPLE

9. Bishop:

We rely on the help of the Lord God our Savior Jesus Christ, and we choose these men, our brothers, for priesthood in the presbyteral order.

All present say: **Thanks be to God**, or give their assent to the choice in some other way, according to local custom.

FOR DEACONS AND PRIESTS

HOMILY

10. Then all sit, and the bishop addresses the people and the candidates. He may use these words:

These men, our brothers, are now to be raised to the order of deacons and to the order of priests. Consider carefully the ministry to which they are to be promoted in the Church. They are to serve Christ the Teacher, Priest, and Pastor in his ministry which is to make his own body, the Church, grow incessantly into the people of God and the temple of the Holy Spirit. They are called to share in the priesthood of bishops. By consecration priests and deacons will preach the Gospel, sustain God's people, and celebrate the liturgy, above all, the Lord's sacrifice. From the way they go about these duties, may you recognize them as disciples of Jesus, who came to serve, not to be served.

FOR DEACONS

He then addresses the candidates:

My sons, you are being raised to the order of deacons. The Lord has set an example for you to follow.

As deacons you will serve Jesus Christ, who was known among his disciples as the one who served others. Do the will of God generously. Serve God and mankind in love and joy. Look upon all unchastity and avarice as worship of false gods; for no man can serve two masters.

Like the men the apostles chose for works of charity, you should be men of good reputation, filled with wisdom and the Holy Spirit. Show before God and mankind that you are above every suspicion of blame, true ministers of Christ and of God's mysteries, men

firmly rooted in faith. Never turn away from the hope which the Gospel offers; now you must not only listen to God's word but also preach it. Hold the mystery of faith with a clear conscience. Express in action what you proclaim by word of mouth. Then the people of Christ, brought to life by the Spirit, will be an offering God accepts. Finally, on the last day, when you go to meet the Lord, you will hear him say: "Well done, good and faithful servant, enter into the joy of your Lord."

COMMITMENT TO CELIBACY

Now the candidates who are to manifest their intention of a commitment to celibacy stand before the bishop. He speaks to them in these or similar words:

By your own free choice you seek to enter the order of deacons. You shall exercise this ministry in the celibate state: for celibacy is both a sign and a motive of pastoral charity, and a special source of spiritual fruitfulness in the world. By living in this state with total dedication, moved by a sincere love for Christ the Lord, you are consecrated to him in a new and special way. By this consecration you will adhere more easily to Christ with an undivided heart; you will be more freely at the service of God and mankind, and you will be more untrammeled in the ministry of Christian conversion and rebirth. By your life and character you will give witness to your brothers and sisters in faith that God must be loved above all else, and that it is he whom you serve in others.

Therefore, I ask you:
In the presence of God and the Church, are you resolved, as a sign of your interior dedication to Christ, to remain celibate for the sake of the kingdom and in lifelong service to God and mankind?

The candidates answer: **I am.**

If it wishes, the conference of bishops may determine some external sign to express the intention of the candidates.

The bishop adds:
May the Lord help you to persevere in this commitment.

The candidates answer: **Amen.**

FOR PRIESTS

The bishop now addresses the candidates for priesthood in the presbyteral order:

My sons, you are now to be advanced to the order of the presbyterate. You must apply your energies to the duty of teaching in the name of Christ, the chief Teacher. Share with all mankind the word of God you have received with joy. Meditate on the law of God, believe what you read, teach what you believe, and put into practice what you teach.

Let the doctrine you teach be true nourishment for the people of God. Let the example of your lives attract the followers of Christ, so that by word and action you may build up the house which is God's Church.

In the same way you must carry out your mission of sanctifying in the power of Christ. Your ministry will perfect the spiritual sacrifice of the faithful by uniting it to Christ's sacrifice, the sacrifice which is offered sacramentally through your hands. Know what you are doing and imitate the mystery you celebrate. In the memorial of the Lord's death and resurrection, make every effort to die to sin and to walk in the new life of Christ.

When you baptize, you will bring men and women into the people of God. In the sacrament of penance, you will forgive sins in the name of Christ and the Church. With holy oil you will relieve and console the sick. You will celebrate the liturgy and offer thanks and praise to God throughout the day, praying not only for the people of God but for the whole world. Remember that you are chosen from among God's people and appointed to act for them in relation to God. Do

your part in the work of Christ the Priest with genuine joy and love, and attend to the concerns of Christ before your own.

Finally, conscious of sharing in the work of Christ, the Head and Shepherd of the Church, and united with the bishop and subject to him, seek to bring the faithful together into a unified family and to lead them effectively, through Christ and in the Holy Spirit, to God the Father. Always remember the example of the Good Shepherd who came not to be served but to serve, and to seek out and rescue those who were lost.

FOR DEACONS

EXAMINATION OF THE CANDIDATES

11. The candidates for the order of deacons then stand before the bishop who questions all of them together:

My sons, before you are ordained deacons, you must declare before the people your intention to undertake the office.

Are you willing to be ordained for the Church's ministry by the laying on of hands and the gift of the Holy Spirit?
Together, all the candidates answer: **I am.**

Bishop:
Are you resolved to discharge the office of deacon with humility and love in order to assist the bishop and the priests and to serve the people of Christ?
Candidates: **I am.**

Bishop:
Are you resolved to hold the mystery of the faith with a clear conscience, as the Apostle urges, and to proclaim this faith in word and action as it is taught by the Gospel and the Church's tradition?
Candidates: **I am.**

Bishop:
Are you resolved to maintain and deepen a spirit of prayer appropriate to your way of life and, in keeping

with what is required of you, to celebrate faithfully the liturgy of the hours for the Church and for the whole world?

Candidates: **I am.**

Bishop:
Are you resolved to shape your way of life always according to the example of Christ, whose body and blood you will give to the people?

Candidates: **I am, with the help of God.**

PROMISE OF OBEDIENCE

12. Then each one of the candidates goes to the bishop and, kneeling before him, places his joined hands between those of the bishop. If this gesture seems less suitable in some places, the conference of bishops may choose another gesture or sign.

If the bishop is the candidate's own Ordinary, he asks:
Do you promise respect and obedience to me and my successors?

Candidate: **I do.**

If the bishop is not the candidate's own Ordinary, he asks:
Do you promise respect and obedience to your Ordinary?

Candidate: **I do.**

Bishop:
May God who has begun the good work in you bring it to fulfillment.

FOR PRIESTS

EXAMINATION

Then the candidates for priesthood in the presbyteral order stand before the bishop who questions all of them together:

My sons, before you proceed to the order of the presbyterate, declare before the people your intention to undertake this priestly office.

Are you resolved, with the help of the Holy Spirit, to discharge without fail the office of priesthood in the

presbyteral order as conscientious fellow workers with the bishops in caring for the Lord's flock?
Together, all the candidates answer: **I am.**

Bishop:
Are you resolved to celebrate the mysteries of Christ faithfully and religiously as the Church has handed them down to us, for the glory of God and the sanctification of Christ's people?
Candidates: **I am.**

Bishop:
Are you resolved to exercise the ministry of the word worthily and wisely, preaching the Gospel and explaining the Catholic faith?
Candidates: **I am.**

Bishop:
Are you resolved to consecrate your life to God for the salvation of his people, and to unite yourself more closely every day to Christ the High Priest, who offered himself for us to the Father as a perfect sacrifice?
Candidates: **I am, with the help of God.**

PROMISE OF OBEDIENCE
13. Then each of the candidates goes to the bishop and, kneeling before him, places his joined hands between those of the bishop. If this gesture seems less suitable in some places, the conference of bishops may choose another gesture or sign.

If the bishop is the candidate's own Ordinary, he asks:
Do you promise respect and obedience to me and my successors?
Candidate: **I do.**

If the bishop is not the candidate's own Ordinary, he asks:
Do you promise respect and obedience to your Ordinary?
Candidate: **I do.**

Bishop:
May God who has begun the good work in you bring it to fulfillment.

FOR DEACONS AND PRIESTS

INVITATION TO PRAYER

14. Then all stand, and the bishop, without his miter, invites the people to pray:

My dear people, let us pray that the all-powerful Father may pour out the gifts of heaven on these servants of his, whom he has chosen to be deacons and priests.

Deacon (except during the Easter season):
Let us kneel.

LITANY OF THE SAINTS

15. The candidates prostrate themselves and, except during the Easter season, the rest kneel at their places.

The cantors begin the litany (see Chapter VI); they may add, at the proper place, names of other saints (for example, the patron saint, the titular of the church, the founder of the church, the patron saints of those to be ordained) or petitions suitable to the occasions.

16. The bishop alone stands and, with his hands joined, sings or says:

**Lord God,
hear our petitions
and give your help to this act of our ministry.
We judge these men worthy to serve as deacons and
    priests
and we ask you to bless them
and make them holy.**

**Grant this through Christ our Lord.
℟. Amen.**

Deacon: **Let us stand.**

All stand. The candidates for priesthood in the presbyteral order return to their places, and the ordination of the deacons begins.

FOR DEACONS

LAYING ON OF HANDS

17. Then all stand. One by one the candidates go to the
bishop and kneel before him. The bishop lays his hands on
the head of each, in silence.

PRAYER OF CONSECRATION

18. The candidates kneel before the bishop. With his hands
extended over them, he sings the prayer of consecration or
says it aloud:

Almighty God,
be present with us by your power.
You are the source of all honor,
you assign to each his rank,
you give to each his ministry.

You remain unchanged,
but you watch over all creation and make it new
through your Son, Jesus Christ, our Lord:
he is your Word, your power, and your wisdom.
You foresee all things in your eternal providence
and make due provision for every age.
You make the Church, Christ's body,
grow to its full stature as a new and greater temple.
You enrich it with every kind of grace
and perfect it with a diversity of members
to serve the whole body in a wonderful pattern of
    unity.
You established a threefold ministry of worship and
    service
for the glory of your name.
As ministers of your tabernacle you chose the sons of
    Levi
and gave them your blessing as their everlasting in-
    heritance.
In the first days of your Church
under the inspiration of the Holy Spirit
the apostles of your Son appointed seven men of good
    repute

to assist them in the daily ministry,
so that they themselves might be more free for prayer
and preaching.
By prayer and the laying on of hands
the apostles entrusted to those chosen men the ministry
of serving at tables.

Lord,
look with favor on these servants of yours,
whom we now dedicate to the office of deacon,
to minister at your holy altar.

Lord,
send forth upon them the Holy Spirit,
that they may be strengthened
by the gift of your sevenfold grace
to carry out faithfully the work of the ministry.

May they excel in every virtue:
in love that is sincere,
in concern for the sick and the poor,
in unassuming authority,
in self-discipline,
and in holiness of life.
May their conduct exemplify your commandments
and lead your people to imitate their purity of life.
May they remain strong and steadfast in Christ,
giving to the world the witness of a pure conscience.
May they in this life imitate your Son,
who came, not to be served but to serve,
and one day reign with him in heaven.

We ask this through our Lord Jesus Christ, your Son,
who lives and reigns with you and the Holy Spirit,
one God, for ever and ever.
℟. Amen.

INVESTITURE WITH STOLE AND DALMATIC
19. After the prayer of consecration, the bishop, wearing his miter, sits, and the newly ordained stand. Some of the assisting deacons or priests put a deacon's stole and then a dalmatic on each of them.

20. Meanwhile, the following antiphon may be sung with Psalm 84.

Blessed are they who dwell in your house, O Lord.

The antiphon is repeated after every two verses. **Glory to the Father** is not said. The psalm is interrupted and the antiphon repeated when dalmatics have been put on all of the deacons.

Any other appropriate song may be sung.

PRESENTATION OF THE BOOK OF THE GOSPELS

21. Vested as deacons, the newly ordained go to the bishop and kneel before him. He places the Book of the Gospels in the hands of each one and says:

**Receive the Gospel of Christ,
whose herald you now are.
Believe what you read,
teach what you believe,
and practice what you teach.**

22. The newly ordained deacons return to their places, and the candidates for priesthood in the presbyteral order come forward.

FOR PRIESTS

INVITATION TO PRAYER

23. Then all stand, and the bishop, without his miter, invites the people to pray:

My dear people, let us pray that the all-powerful Father may pour out the gifts of heaven on these servants of his, whom he has chosen to be priests.

Deacon: **Let us kneel.**

All kneel and in silence pray for the candidates.

PRAYER

The bishop alone stands and sings or says:

**Hear us, Lord our God,
and pour out upon these servants of yours**

the blessing of the Holy Spirit
and the grace and power of the priesthood.
In your sight we offer these men for ordination:
support them with your unfailing love.

We ask this through Christ our Lord.
℟. **Amen.**

Deacon: **Let us stand.**

LAYING ON OF HANDS

24. Then all stand. One by one the candidates go to the
bishop and kneel before him. The bishop lays his hands on
the head of each, in silence.

25. Next all the priests present, wearing stoles, lay their
hands upon each of the candidates, in silence. After laying on
of hands, the priests remain on either side of the bishop until
the prayer of consecration is completed.

PRAYER OF CONSECRATION

26. The candidates kneel before the bishop. With his hands
extended over them, he sings the prayer of consecration or
says it aloud:

**Come to our help,
Lord, holy Father, almighty and eternal God;
you are the source of every honor and dignity,
of all progress and stability.
You watch over the growing family of man
by your gift of wisdom and your pattern of order.
When you had appointed high priests to rule your
    people,
you chose other men next to them in rank and dignity
to be with them and help them in their task;
and so there grew up
the ranks of priests and the offices of levites,
established by sacred rites.**

**In the desert
you extended the spirit of Moses to seventy wise men
who helped him to rule the great company of his
    people.**

You shared among the sons of Aaron
the fullness of their father's power,
to provide worthy priests in sufficient number
for the increasing rites of sacrifice and worship.
With the same loving care
you gave companions to your Son's apostles
to help in teaching the faith:
they preached the Gospel to the whole world.

Lord,
grant also to us such fellow workers,
for we are weak and our need is greater.

Almighty Father,
grant to these servants of yours
the dignity of the priesthood.
Renew within them the Spirit of holiness.
As co-workers with the order of bishops
may they be faithful to the ministry
that they receive from you, Lord God,
and be to others a model of right conduct.

May they be faithful in working with the order of
    bishops,
so that the words of the Gospel may reach the ends of
    the earth,
and the family of nations,
made one in Christ,
may become God's one, holy people.

We ask this through our Lord Jesus Christ, your Son,
who lives and reigns with you and the Holy Spirit,
one God, for ever and ever.
℟. Amen.

INVESTITURE WITH STOLE AND CHASUBLE

27. After the prayer of consecration, the bishop, wearing his
miter, sits, and the newly ordained stand. The assisting
priests return to their places, but some of them arrange the
stoles of the newly ordained as they are worn by priests and
vest them in chasubles.

ANOINTING OF HANDS

28. Next the bishop receives a linen gremial and anoints with chrism the palms of each new priest as he kneels before him. The bishop says:

**The Father anointed our Lord Jesus Christ
through the power of the Holy Spirit.
May Jesus preserve you to sanctify the Christian
  people
and to offer sacrifice to God.**

29. While the new priests are being vested in stoles and chasubles and the bishop is anointing their hands, the hymn **Veni, Creator Spiritus** or the following antiphon may be sung with Psalm 110.

**Christ the Lord,
a priest for ever in the line of Melchizedek,
offered bread and wine.**

The antiphon is repeated after every two verses. **Glory to the Father** is not said. The psalm is interrupted and the antiphon repeated when the hands of all the priests have been anointed.

Any other appropriate song may be sung.

Then the bishop and the new priests wash their hands.

PRESENTATION OF THE GIFTS

30. The deacon assists the bishop in receiving the gifts of the people and then he prepares the bread on the paten and the wine and water in the chalice for the celebration of Mass. He brings the paten and chalice to the bishop, who hands them to each of the new priests as he kneels before him. The bishop says:

Accept from the holy people of God the gifts to be offered to him. Know what you are doing, and imitate the mystery you celebrate: model your life on the mystery of the Lord's cross.

FOR DEACONS AND PRIESTS

KISS OF PEACE

31. Lastly, the bishop stands and gives the kiss of peace to each of the newly ordained, first the priests, then the deacons, saying:

Peace be with you.

The priest/deacon responds: **And also with you.**

If circumstances permit, the priests and deacons present also give the kiss of peace to the newly ordained.

32. Meanwhile, the following antiphon may be sung with Psalm 100.

You are my friends, says the Lord, if you do what I command you.

The antiphon is repeated after every two verses. **Glory to the Father** is not said. The psalm is interrupted and the antiphon repeated when all have received the kiss of peace.

Any other appropriate song may be sung, or:

No longer do I call you servants, but my friends, because you know all that I have done among you (alleluia).
—Receive the Holy Spirit as an Advocate among you: it is he whom the Father will send you (alleluia).

You are my friends if you do the things I command you.
—Receive the Holy Spirit as an Advocate among you. Glory to the Father...
—It is he whom the Father will send you (alleluia).

LITURGY OF THE EUCHARIST

33. The rite for the concelebration of Mass is followed with these changes:
a) The preparation of the chalice is omitted.

b) In Eucharistic Prayer I, the special form of **Father, accept this offering** is said:

Father, accept this offering
from your whole family
and from those you have chosen for the order of priests
 and deacons.
Protect the gifts you have given them,
and let them yield a harvest worthy of you.

[Through Christ our Lord. Amen.]

34. The new deacons receive communion under both kinds. The deacon who assists the bishop ministers the cup.

35. Some of the new deacons assist the bishop in giving communion to the people.

CHAPTER V

ORDINATION OF A BISHOP

INTRODUCTION

1. The ordination of a bishop should take place on a Sunday or holyday when a large number of the faithful can attend, unless pastoral reasons suggest another day, such as the feast of an apostle.

2. The principal consecrator must be assisted by at least two other consecrating bishops, but it is fitting for all the bishops present together with the principal consecrator to ordain the bishop-elect.

3. Two priests assist the bishop-elect.

4. It is most appropriate for all the consecrating bishops and the priests assisting the bishop-elect to concelebrate the Mass with the principal consecrator and with the bishop-elect. If the ordination takes place in the bishop-elect's own church, some priests of his diocese should also concelebrate.

5. If the ordination takes place in the bishop-elect's own church, the principal consecrator may ask the newly ordained bishop to preside over the concelebration of the eucharistic liturgy. If the ordination does not take place in the bishop-elect's own church, the principal consecrator presides at the concelebration; in this case the new bishop takes the first place among the other celebrants.

6. The principal consecrator and the concelebrating bishops and priests wear the vestments required for Mass. The bishop-elect wears all the priestly vestments, the pectoral cross, and the dalmatic. If the consecrating bishops do not celebrate, they wear the rochet or alb, pectoral cross, stole, cope, and miter. If the priests assisting the bishop-elect do not concelebrate, they wear the cope over an alb or surplice.

7. The blessing of the ring, pastoral staff, and miter ordinarily takes place at a convenient time prior to the ordination service (see Appendix II).

8. In addition to what is needed for the concelebration of a pontifical Mass, there should be ready: a) the Roman Pontifical; b) copies of the consecratory prayer for the consecrating bishops; c) a linen gremial; d) holy chrism; e) a ring, staff, and miter for the bishop-elect.

9. Seats for the principal consecrator, consecrating bishops, the bishop-elect, and concelebrating priests are arranged as follows:

a) For the liturgy of the word, the principal consecrator should sit at the *cathedra* or bishop's chair, with the consecrating bishops near the chair. The bishop-elect sits between the assisting priests in an appropriate place within the sanctuary.

b) The ordination should usually take place at the bishop's chair; or, to enable the faithful to participate more fully, seats for the principal consecrator and consecrating bishops may be placed before the altar or elsewhere. Seats for the bishop-elect and his assisting priests should be placed so that the faithful may have a complete view of the liturgical rites.

10. When everything is ready, the procession moves through the church to the altar in the usual way. A deacon carries the Book of the Gospels; he is followed by the priests who will concelebrate, the bishop-elect between the priests assisting him, the consecrating bishops, and, finally, the principal consecrator between two deacons.

LITURGY OF THE WORD

11. The liturgy of the word takes place according to the rubrics.

12. The readings may be taken in whole or in part from the Mass of the day or from the texts listed in Chapter VI.

The profession of faith is not said, nor are the general intercessions.

ORDINATION OF A BISHOP

HYMN

13. The ordination of a bishop begins after the gospel. While all stand, the hymn **Veni, Creator Spiritus** is sung, or another hymn similar to it, depending on local custom.

14. The principal consecrator and the consecrating bishops, wearing their miters, go to the seats prepared for the ordination and sit.

15. The bishop-elect is led by his assisting priests to the chair of the principal consecrator, before whom he makes a sign of reverence.

PRESENTATION OF THE BISHOP-ELECT

16. One of the priests addresses the principal consecrator:
Most Reverend Father, the church of N. asks you to ordain this priest, N., for service as bishop.

If the bishop-elect is not to be ordained as a residential bishop:
Most Reverend Father, our holy mother the Catholic Church asks you to ordain this priest, N., for service as a bishop.

APOSTOLIC LETTER

The principal consecrator asks him:
Have you a mandate from the Holy See?

He replies: **We have.**

Principal consecrator: **Let it be read.**

Everyone sits while the document is read.

CONSENT OF THE PEOPLE

17. After the reading, all present say: **Thanks be to God**, or give their assent to the choice in some other way, according to local custom.

HOMILY

18. Then the principal consecrator, while all are sitting, briefly addresses the clergy, people, and the bishop-elect on the duties of a bishop. He may use these words:

Consider carefully the position in the Church to which our brother is about to be raised. Our Lord Jesus Christ, who was sent by the Father to redeem the human race, in turn sent twelve apostles into the world. These men were filled with the power of the Holy Spirit to preach the Gospel and gather every race and people into a single flock to be guided and governed in the way of holiness. Because this service was to continue to the end of time, the apostles selected others to help them. By the laying on of hands which confers the sacrament of orders in its fullness, the apostles passed on the gift of the Holy Spirit which they themselves had received from Christ. In that way, by a succession of bishops unbroken from one generation to the next, the powers conferred in the beginning were handed down, and the work of the Savior lives and grows in our time.

In the person of the bishop, with his priests around him, Jesus Christ, the Lord, who became High Priest for ever, is present among you. Through the ministry of the bishop, Christ himself continues to proclaim the Gospel and to confer the mysteries of faith on those who believe. Through the fatherly action of the bishop, Christ adds new members to his body. Through the bishop's wisdom and prudence, Christ guides you in your earthly pilgrimage toward eternal happiness.

Gladly and gratefully, therefore, receive our brother whom we are about to accept into the college of bishops by the laying on of hands. Respect him as a minister of Christ and a steward of the mysteries of God. He has been entrusted with the task of witnessing to the truth of the Gospel and fostering a spirit of justice and holiness. Remember the words of Christ spoken to the apostles: "Whoever listens to you listens to me; whoever rejects you rejects me, and those who reject me reject the one who sent me."

He then addresses the bishop-elect:

You, dear brother, have been chosen by the Lord. Remember that you are chosen from among men and appointed to act for men and women in relation to God. The title of bishop is one not of honor but of function, and therefore a bishop should strive to serve rather than to rule. Such is the counsel of the Master: the greater should behave as is he were the least, and the leader as if he were the one who serves. Proclaim the message whether it is welcome or unwelcome; correct error with unfailing patience and teaching. Pray and offer sacrifice for the people committed to your care and so draw every kind of grace for them from the overflowing holiness of Christ.

As a steward of the mysteries of Christ in the church entrusted to you, be a faithful overseer and guardian. Since you are chosen by the Father to rule over his family, always be mindful of the Good Shepherd, who knows his sheep and is known by them and who did not hesitate to lay down his life for them.

As a father and a brother, love all those whom God places in your care. Love the priests and deacons who share with you the ministry of Christ. Love the poor and infirm, strangers and the homeless. Encourage the faithful to work with you in your apostolic task; listen willingly to what they have to say. Never relax your concern for those who do not yet belong to the one fold of Christ; they too are commended to you in the Lord. Never forget that in the Catholic Church, made one by the bond of Christian love, you are incorporated into the college of bishops. You should therefore have a constant concern for all the churches and gladly come to the aid and support of churches in need. Attend to the whole flock in which the Holy Spirit appoints you an overseer of the Church of God—in the name of the Father, whose image you personify in the Church—and in the name of his Son, Jesus Christ, whose role of

Teacher, Priest, and Shepherd you undertake—and in the name of the Holy Spirit, who gives life to the Church of Christ and supports our weakness with his strength.

EXAMINATION OF THE CANDIDATE

19. The bishop-elect then rises and stands in front of the principal consecrator, who questions him:

An age-old custom of the Fathers decrees that a bishop-elect is to be questioned before the people on his resolve to uphold the faith and to discharge his duties faithfully.

My brother, are you resolved by the grace of the Holy Spirit to discharge to the end of your life the office the apostles entrusted to us, which we now pass on to you by the laying on of hands?
The bishop-elect replies: I am.

Principal consecrator:
Are you resolved to be faithful and constant in proclaiming the Gospel of Christ?
Bishop-elect: I am.

Principal consecrator:
Are you resolved to maintain the deposit of faith, entire and incorrupt, as handed down by the apostles and professed by the Church everywhere and at all times?
Bishop-elect: I am.

Principal consecrator:
Are you resolved to build up the Church as the body of Christ and to remain united to it within the order of bishops under the authority of the successor of the apostle Peter?
Bishop-elect: I am.

Principal consecrator:
Are you resolved to be faithful in your obedience to the successor of the apostle Peter?
Bishop-elect: I am.

Principal consecrator:

Are you resolved as a devoted father to sustain the people of God and to guide them in the way of salvation in cooperation with the priests and deacons who share your ministry?

Bishop-elect: **I am.**

Principal consecrator:

Are you resolved to show kindness and compassion in the name of the Lord to the poor and to strangers and to all who are in need?

Bishop-elect: **I am.**

Principal consecrator:

Are you resolved as a good shepherd to seek out the sheep who stray and to gather them into the fold of the Lord?

Bishop-elect: **I am.**

Principal consecrator:

Are you resolved to pray for the people of God without ceasing, and to carry out the duties of one who has the fullness of the priesthood so as to afford no grounds for reproach?

Bishop-elect: **I am, with the help of God.**

Principal consecrator:

May God who has begun the good work in you bring it to fulfillment.

INVITATION TO PRAYER

20. Then all stand, and the bishop, without his miter, invites the people to pray:

My dear people, let us pray that almighty God in his goodness will pour out his grace upon this man whom he has chosen to provide for the needs of the Church.

Deacon (except during the Easter season):
Let us kneel.

LITANY OF THE SAINTS

21. The bishop-elect prostrates himself and, except during the Easter season, the rest kneel at their places.

The cantors begin the litany (see Chapter VI); they may add, at the proper place, names of other saints (for example, the patron saint, the titular of the church, the founder of the church, the patron saint of the one to be ordained) or petitions suitable to the occasion.

22. After the litany, the principal consecrator alone stands and, with hands joined sings or says:

Lord,
be moved by our prayers.
Anoint your servant with the fullness of priestly grace,
and bless him with spiritual power in all its richness.

We ask this through Christ our Lord.
℟. Amen.

Deacon: **Let us stand.**

LAYING ON OF HANDS

23. All rise. The principal consecrator and the consecrating bishops stand at their places, facing the people. The bishop-elect rises, goes to the principal consecrator, and kneels before him.

24. The principal consecrator lays his hands upon the head of the bishop-elect, in silence. After him, all the other bishops present do the same.

BOOK OF THE GOSPELS

25. Then the principal consecrator places the open Book of the Gospels upon the head of the bishop-elect; two deacons, standing at either side of the bishop-elect, hold the Book of the Gospels above his head until the prayer of consecration is completed.

PRAYER OF CONSECRATION

26. Next the principal consecrator, with his hands extended over the bishop-elect, sings the prayer of consecration or says it aloud:

God the Father of our Lord Jesus Christ,
Father of mercies and God of all consolation,
you dwell in heaven,
yet look with compassion on all that is humble.
You know all things before they come to be;
by your gracious word
you have established the plan of your Church.

From the beginning
you chose the descendants of Abraham to be your holy
  nation.
You established rulers and priests,
and did not leave your sanctuary without ministers to
  serve you.
From the creation of the world
you have been pleased to be glorified
by those whom you have chosen.

The following part of the prayer is recited by all the consecrating bishops, with hands joined:

So now pour out upon this chosen one
that power which is from you,
the governing Spirit
whom you gave to your beloved Son, Jesus Christ,
the Spirit given by him to the holy apostles,
who founded the Church in every place to be your
  temple
for the unceasing glory and praise of your name.

Then the principal consecrator continues alone:

Father, you know all hearts.
You have chosen your servant for the office of bishop.
May he be a shepherd to your holy flock,
and a high priest blameless in your sight,
ministering to you night and day;
may he always gain the blessing of your favor
and offer the gifts of your holy Church.
Through the Spirit who gives the grace of high priesthood
grant him the power

to forgive sins as you have commanded,
to assign ministries as you have decreed,
and to loose every bond by the authority which you
  gave to your apostles.
May he be pleasing to you by his gentleness and purity
  of heart,
presenting a fragrant offering to you,
through Jesus Christ, your Son,
through whom glory and power and honor are yours
with the Holy Spirit
in your holy Church,
now and for ever.
℟. Amen.

27. After the prayer of consecration, the deacons remove the Book of the Gospels which they have been holding above the head of the new bishop. One of them holds the book until it is given to the bishop. The principal consecrator and the consecrating bishops, wearing their miters, sit.

ANOINTING OF THE BISHOP'S HEAD

28. The principal consecrator puts on a linen gremial, takes the chrism, and anoints the head of the bishop, who kneels before him. He says:

**God has brought you to share the high priesthood
  of Christ,
May he pour out on you the oil of mystical anointing
and enrich you with spiritual blessings.**

The principal consecrator washes his hands.

PRESENTATION OF THE BOOK OF THE GOSPELS

29. He then hands the Book of the Gospels to the newly ordained bishop, saying:

**Receive the Gospel and preach the word of God with
unfailing patience and sound teaching.**

Afterward the deacon takes the Book of the Gospels and returns it to its place.

INVESTITURE WITH RING, MITER, AND PASTORAL
STAFF

30. The principal consecrator places the ring on the ring
finger of the new bishop's right hand, saying:

Take this ring, the seal of your fidelity.
With faith and love protect the bride of God, his holy
Church.

31. Then the principal consecrator places the miter on the
head of the new bishop, in silence.

32. Lastly, he gives the pastoral staff to the bishop, and says:

Take this staff as a sign of your pastoral office:
keep watch over the whole flock
in which the Holy Spirit has appointed you
to shepherd the Church of God.

SEATING OF THE BISHOP

33. All stand. If the ordination takes place at the bishop's
chair and if the new bishop is in his own church, the principal
consecrator invites him to occupy the chair; in that case the
principal consecrator sits at the right of the newly ordained
bishop. If the new bishop is not in his own church, he is
invited by the principal consecrator to take the first place
among the concelebrating bishops.

If the ordination does not take place at the bishop's chair, the
principal consecrator leads the newly ordained bishop to the
chair or to a place prepared for him, and the consecrating
bishops follow them.

KISS OF PEACE

34. The newly ordained then sets aside his staff and receives
the kiss of peace from the principal consecrator and all the
other bishops.

35. After the presentation of the staff, and until the end of
the ordination rite, the following antiphon may be sung with
Psalm 96.

Alleluia, go and teach all people my Gospel, alleluia.

The antiphon is repeated after every two verses. **Glory to the Father** is not said. The psalm is interrupted and the antiphon repeated when all have given the kiss of peace to the new bishop.

Any other appropriate song may be sung.

LITURGY OF THE EUCHARIST

36. The rite for the concelebration of Mass is followed with this change:

37. In Eucharistic Prayer I, the special form of **Father, accept this offering** is said:

**Father, accept this offering
from your whole family
and from the one you have chosen for the order of
    bishops.
Protect the gifts you have given him,
and let him yield a harvest worthy of you.**

[Through Christ our Lord. Amen.]

CONCLUDING RITE

HYMN OF THANKSGIVING AND BLESSING

38. At the conclusion of the prayer after communion, the hymn **Te Deum** is sung, or another hymn similar to it, depending on local custom. Meanwhile, the newly ordained bishop is led by the consecrating bishops through the church, and he blesses the congregation.

After the hymn, the new bishop may stand at the altar or at the chair with staff and miter and address the people briefly.

SOLEMN BLESSING

39. The following blessing may be used in place of the usual blessing. If the newly ordained bishop is the celebrant, he says:

Lord God,
you care for your people with kindness,
you rule them with love.
Give your Spirit of wisdom
to the bishops you have made teachers and pastors.
By advancing in holiness
may the flock become the eternal joy of the
 shepherds.
℟. Amen.

Lord God,
by your power you allot us
the number of our days and the measure of our
 years.
Look favorably upon the service we perform for you,
and give true, lasting peace in our time.
℟. Amen.

Lord God,
now that you have raised me to the order of bishops,
may I please you in the performance of my office.
Unite the hearts of people and bishop,
so that the shepherd may not be without the support of
 his flock,
or the flock without the loving concern of its shepherd.
℟. Amen.

May almighty God bless you,
the Father, and the Son, ✠ and the Holy Spirit.
℟. Amen.

If the principal consecrator presides over the eucharistic
liturgy, he says:

May the Lord bless and keep you.
He chose to make you a bishop for his people:
may you know happiness in this present life
and share unending joy.
℟. Amen.

The Lord has gathered his people and clergy in unity.
By his care and your stewardship

may they be governed happily for many years.
℟. Amen.

May they be obedient to God's law,
free from hardships,
rich in every blessing,
and loyally assist you in your ministry.
May they be blessed with peace and calm in this life
and come to share with you
the fellowship of the citizens of heaven.
℟. Amen.

May almighty God bless you,
the Father, and the Son, ✠ and the Holy Spirit.
℟. Amen.

CHAPTER VI

TEXTS FOR USE IN ORDINATIONS

BIBLICAL READINGS

ADMISSION TO CANDIDACY FOR ORDINATION AS DEACONS AND PRIESTS

The readings are taken in whole or in part from the Mass of the day or from the texts listed below.

READING FROM THE OLD TESTAMENT

1. **Deuteronomy 1:9-14**
Choose wise men from among you and I shall make them your leaders.

2. **Jeremiah 1:4-8** (L 719)
You will go to all the places which I will send you.

3. **Sirach 39:1, 5-8**
He offers his heart to the Lord at dawn to keep the watch.

4. **Isaiah 6:2a, 3-8** (L 76)
Whom shall I send? and who will go for us?

READING FROM THE NEW TESTAMENT

1. **Acts 14:21-23** (L 55)
They appointed presbyters for every church.

2. **1 Corinthians 9:16-19, 22-23** (L 75)
Punishment will come to me if I do not preach the Gospel.

3. **1 Corinthians 12:4-11** (L 67)
One and the same Spirit distributes different gifts as he chooses.

4. **2 Timothy 3:10-12, 14-15**
Continue in what you learned.

RESPONSORIAL PSALM

1. Psalm 16:1-2a and 5, 7-8, 11 (L 721)
℟. (see 5a) **You are my inheritance, O Lord.**

2. Psalm 24:1-2, 3-4ab, 5-6 (L 786)

℟. (see 6) **Lord, this is the people that longs to see your face.**

3. Psalm 98:1, 2-3ab, 3c-4, 5-6 (L 818)

℟. (2b) **The Lord has revealed to the nations his saving power.**

ALLELUIA VERSE AND VERSE BEFORE THE GOSPEL

1. Mark 1:17 (L 723)
**Come, follow me, says the Lord,
and I will make you fishers of men.**

2. Luke 4:18-19 (L 219)
**The Lord sent me to bring Good News to the poor,
and freedom to prisoners.**

3. John 12:26a (L 35)
**If you serve me, follow me, says the Lord;
and where I am, my servant will also be.**

GOSPEL

1. **Matthew 9:35-38** (L 773)
Ask the Lord of the harvest to send laborers to the harvest.

2. **Mark 1:14-20** (L 724)
I will make you into fishers of my people.

3. **Luke 5:1-11** (L 724)
At your word I will lower the nets.

4. **John 1:35-42** (L 743)
Look, there is the Lamb of God. We have found the Messiah.

5. **John 1:45-51** (L 629)
There is a true Israelite in whom there is no deceit.

ORDINATION OF DEACONS, PRIESTS, AND BISHOPS

The readings may be taken in whole or in part from the Mass of the day or from the texts listed below.

Some of the readings are intended for a particular use. The others may be used at any ordination.

According to liturgical tradition, the Old Testament is not read during the Easter season; a preference is given, in the gospel, to the readings from John.

READING FROM THE OLD TESTAMENT (L 769)

1. Numbers 3:5-10a
Gather the tribe of Levi so that they can serve Aaron the priest. [For deacons]

2. Numbers 11:11b-12, 14-17, 24-25a
I will give them your spirit so that they may share with you the burden of this people. [For priests]

3. Isaiah 61:1-3a
The Lord has anointed me and sent me to bring Good News to the poor and to give them the oil of gladness. [For bishops and priests]

4. Jeremiah 1:4-9
You will go to all the places to which I will send you.

READING FROM THE NEW TESTAMENT (L 770)

1. Acts 6:1-7a
They chose seven men filled with the Holy Spirit. [For deacons]

2. Acts 8:26-40
Beginning with this text of Scripture he explained the Good News of Jesus to him. [For deacons]

3. Acts 10:37-43
We are witnesses to everything Jesus did in the countryside around Judea and in Jerusalem.

4. Acts 20:17-18a, 28-32, 36
Keep watch for yourselves and for all the flock of which the Holy Spirit has made you overseers to govern the Church of God. [For bishops and priests]

5. Romans 12:4-8.
Our gifts differ according to the grace given to each of us.

6. 2 Corinthians 4:1-2, 5-7
We are teaching Jesus Christ, but we are your servants for Jesus' sake.

7. 2 Corinthians 5:14-20
He gave us the ministry of reconciliation.

8. Ephesians 4:1-7, 11-13
Unity in the work of service, building up the body of Christ.

9. 1 Timothy 3:8-13
They must be conscientious believers in the mystery of faith.
[For deacons]

10. 1 Timothy 4:12-16
Do not neglect the spiritual gift given you when the elders laid hands on you.
or: **1 Timothy 4:12b-16**
[For bishops]

11. 2 Timothy 1:6-14
Rekindle the gift that God gave you when I laid my hands on you. [For bishops]

12. Hebrews 5:1-10
Christ was acclaimed by God a high priest in the line of Melchizedek.

13. 1 Peter 4:7b-11
As good stewards be responsible for the different graces of God.

14. 1 Peter 5:1-4
Be shepherds of the flock of God which is entrusted to you.

RESPONSORIAL PSALM (L 771)

1. Psalm 23:1-3a, 3b-4, 5, 6
℟. (1) **The Lord is my shepherd; there is nothing I shall want.**

2. Psalm 84:3-4, 5-6a and 8a, 11
℟. (5a) **How happy they who dwell in your house, O Lord.**

3. Psalm 89:21-22, 25 and 27
℟. (2a) **For ever I will sing the goodness of the Lord.**

4. Psalm 96:1-2a, 2b-3, 10
℟. **Go out to the world and teach all nations, alleluia.**

5. Psalm 100:2, 3, 4, 5
℟. (John 15:14) **You are my friends if you do what I command you, says the Lord.**

6. Psalm 110:1, 2, 3, 4
℟. **Priest for ever, like Melchizedek of old, the Lord Christ offered bread and wine.**
or: ℟. (4bc) **You are a priest for ever, in the line of Melchizedek.**

7. Psalm 116:12-13, 17-18
℟. (1 Corinthians 10:16) **Our blessing-cup is a communion with the blood of Christ.**
or: ℟. **Alleluia.**

8. Psalm 117:1, 2
℟. (Mark 16:15) **Go out to all the world, and tell the Good News.**
or: ℟. **Alleluia.**

ALLELUIA VERSE AND VERSE BEFORE THE GOSPEL (L 772)

1. Matthew 28:19-20
Go and teach all people my Gospel.
I am with you always, until the end of the world.

2. Luke 4:18-19
The Lord sent me to bring Good News to the poor,
and freedom to prisoners.

3. John 10:14
I am the good shepherd, says the Lord;
I know my sheep, and mine know me.

4. John 15:15b
I call you my friends, says the Lord,
for I have made known to you all that the Father has told me.

GOSPEL (L 773)

1. **Matthew 5:13-16**
You are the light of the world.

2. **Matthew 9:35-38**
Ask the Lord of the harvest to send laborers to the harvest.

3. **Matthew 10:1-5a**
Proclaim that the kingdom of God is at hand.

4. **Matthew 20:25-28**
Anyone among you who wishes to be first must be your servant.

5. **Luke 10:1-9**
The harvest is rich but the laborers are few.

6. **Luke 12:35-44**
Happy those servants whom the master finds awake when he comes.

7. Luke 22:14-20, 24-30
Do this in memory of me. I come among you as one who serves.

8. John 10:11-16
The good shepherd lays down his life for his sheep.

9. John 12:24-26
Whoever serves me must follow me.

10. John 15:9-17
I shall not call you servants; you are my friends.

11. John 17:6, 14-19
For them I consecrate myself so that they too may be consecrated in truth.

12. John 20:19-23
As the Father has sent me, I send you: receive the Holy Spirit.

13. John 21:15-17
Feed my lambs, feed my sheep.

LITANY OF THE SAINTS

The cantors begin the litany; they may add, at the proper place, names of other saints (for example, the patron saint, the titular of the church, the founder of the church, the patron saints of those to be ordained) or petitions suitable to the occasion.

**Lord, have mercy   Lord, have mercy
Christ, have mercy   Christ, have mercy
Lord, have mercy   Lord, have mercy**

**Holy Mary, Mother of God   pray for us
Saint Michael   pray for us
Holy angels of God   pray for us
Saint John the Baptist   pray for us
Saint Joseph   pray for us
Saint Peter and Saint Paul   pray for us
Saint Andrew   pray for us
Saint John   pray for us
Saint Mary Magdalene   pray for us
Saint Stephen   pray for us
Saint Ignatius   pray for us**

Saint Lawrence   pray for us
Saint Perpetua and Saint Felicity   pray for us
Saint Agnes   pray for us
Saint Gregory   pray for us
Saint Augustine   pray for us
Saint Athanasius   pray for us
Saint Basil   pray for us
Saint Martin   pray for us
Saint Benedict   pray for us
Saint Francis and Saint Dominic   pray for us
Saint Francis Xavier   pray for us
Saint John Vianney   pray for us
Saint Catherine   pray for us
Saint Teresa   pray for us
All holy men and women   pray for us

Lord, be merciful   Lord, save your people
From all evil   Lord, save your people
From every sin   Lord, save your people
From everlasting death   Lord, save your people
By your coming as man   Lord, save your people
By your death and rising to new life   Lord, save your
   people
By your gift of the Holy Spirit   Lord, save your people
Be merciful to us sinners   Lord, hear our prayer
Guide and protect your holy Church   Lord, hear our
   prayer
Keep the pope and all the clergy in faithful service
   to your Church   Lord, hear our prayer
Bring all peoples together in trust and peace
   Lord, hear our prayer
Strengthen us in your service
   Lord, hear our prayer

Bless these chosen men   Lord, hear our prayer
Bless these chosen men and make them holy   Lord,
   hear our prayer
Bless these chosen men, make them holy,
   and consecrate them for their sacred duties   Lord,
   hear our prayer

Bless this chosen man   Lord, hear our prayer
Bless this chosen man and make him holy   Lord, hear
   our prayer
Bless this chosen man, make him holy,
   and consecrate him for his sacred duties   Lord, hear
   our prayer

Jesus, Son of the living God   Lord, hear our prayer
Christ, hear us   Christ, hear us
Lord Jesus, hear our prayer   Lord Jesus, hear our
   prayer

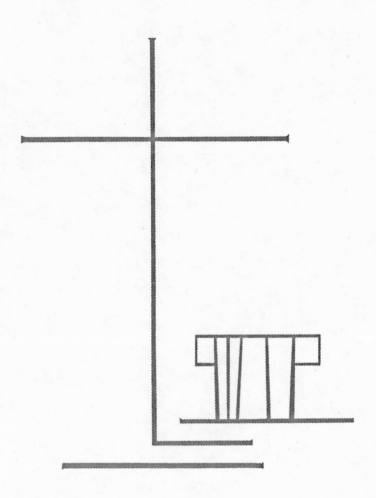

BLESSING OF PERSONS

BLESSING OF PERSONS

CHAPTER I
BLESSING OF AN ABBOT

Introduction (1-11)

Liturgy of the Word (12-15)

Blessing of an Abbot (16-29)

Presentation of the Abbot-Elect (17-18)

Homily (19)

Examination (20)

Invitation to Prayer (21)

Litany of the Saints (22)

Prayer of Blessing (23)

Presentation of the Rule (24)

Presentation of the Pontifical Insignia (25-29)

Liturgy of the Eucharist (30-32)

CHAPTER II
BLESSING OF AN ABBESS

Introduction (1-6)

Liturgy of the Word (7-10)

Blessing of an Abbess (11-21)

Presentation of the Abbess-Elect (12-13)

Homily (14)

Examination (15)

Invitation to Prayer (16)

Litany of the Saints (17)

Prayer of Blessing (18)

CHAPTER IV
RITE OF COMMISSIONING SPECIAL MINISTERS OF
HOLY COMMUNION

A. During Mass (2-6)

B. Outside Mass (7-9)

Rite of Commissioning a Special Minister to Distribute Holy
Communion on a Single Occasion (10-12)

Rite of Distributing Holy Communion by a Special Minister
(13-15)

CHAPTER V
TEXTS FOR USE IN BLESSING OF PERSONS

Readings

Litany of the Saints

CHAPTER I

BLESSING OF AN ABBOT

INTRODUCTION

1. The blessing of an abbot should take place in the presence of a gathering of religious and, if circumstances permit, of the faithful. The blessing should take place on a Sunday or feast day; for pastoral reasons another day may be chosen.

2. The rite of blessing is usually celebrated by the bishop of the place where the monastery is situated. For a good reason, and with the consent of the bishop of the place, the abbot-elect may receive the blessing from another bishop or abbot.

3. Two religious from his monastery assist the abbot-elect.

4. It is desirable that Mass should be concelebrated with the officiating prelate and the abbot-elect by the religious assisting the abbot-elect, the abbots, and other priests present.

5. If the abbot-elect receives the blessing in his own abbey at the hands of another abbot, the officiating abbot may ask the newly blessed abbot to preside over the concelebration of the eucharistic liturgy. Otherwise, the officiating prelate presides, and the new abbot takes the first place among the concelebrants.

6. The officiating prelate and all the concelebrants wear the vestments required for Mass. The abbot-elect wears all the priestly vestments, together with pectoral cross and dalmatic. If the assisting religious do not concelebrate, they wear choir dress or surplice.

7. The blessing of the ring, pastoral staff, and miter ordinarily takes place at a convenient time prior to the actual blessing of the abbot (Appendix II).

8. Besides what is needed for the concelebration of Mass and for communion under both kinds, there should be prepared: a) the Roman Pontifical; b) the Rule; c) the pastoral staff; d)

the ring and the miter for the abbot-elect, if they are to be presented to him.

9. During the liturgy of the word, the officiating prelate should sit in the chair; the abbot-elect should sit between the assisting religious in a suitable place within the sanctuary.

10. The blessing usually takes place at the chair. To enable the faithful to participate more fully, a seat for the officiating prelate may be placed before the altar or in some other suitable place; the seats for the abbot-elect and the religious assisting him should be so arranged that the religious and the faithful may have a complete view of the celebration.

11. When all is ready the procession moves through the church to the altar in the usual way. The minister carrying the Book of the Gospels is followed by the priests who will concelebrate, the abbot-elect with the religious assisting him on either side, and finally the officiating prelate between two deacons.

LITURGY OF THE WORD

12. The liturgy of the word is celebrated in accordance with the rubrics.

13. The readings may be taken, in whole or in part, from the Mass of the day or from the texts for the blessing of an abbot in the Lectionary for Mass (nos. 779-783) and listed in Chapter V.

14. The officiating prelate gives a homily or an address at the appropriate time during the rite of blessing.

15. The profession of faith is not said in this Mass, and the general intercessions are omitted.

BLESSING OF AN ABBOT

16. The rite of blessing begins after the gospel. The officiating prelate, wearing his miter, is seated in the chair prepared for the occasion.

PRESENTATION OF THE ABBOT-ELECT

17. The abbot-elect is escorted by his assistants to the officiating prelate, to whom he makes a sign of reverence.

18. One of the assisting religious addresses the prelate in these or similar words:

Most Reverend Father, in the name of our community we present to you the abbot-elect of our monastery of N., of the Order of N., in the diocese of N. We ask you to bless him as abbot of our monastery.

The prelate asks:
Has he been duly elected?

He replies:
We know and testify that he has.

The prelate replies:
Thanks be to God.

If, however, the abbot is one who has been given jurisdiction over a territory independent of a diocese, the prelate adds, after the question on election:

Have you a mandate from the Holy See?

The religious answers: **We have.**

Prelate: **Let it be read.**

All sit while the mandate is being read. Afterward, all say:
Thanks be to God.

HOMILY

19. All sit while the prelate gives a brief homily to the abbot-elect, the religious and the faithful.

EXAMINATION

20. After the address the abbot-elect rises and stands in front of the prelate, who questions him in these words:

My dear brother, when a man is chosen to stand in the place of Christ and to guide others in the way of the Spirit, it is right that he should be questioned on matters concerning his office and on the qualities he brings

to it. This is the age-old teaching and requirement of our fathers in the spiritual life. Following their wise guidance, I now ask:

Will you persevere in your determination to observe the Rule of Saint N. and will you be diligent in teaching your brothers to do the same, and so encourage them in the love of God, in the life of the Gospel, and in fraternal charity?

The abbot-elect answers: **I will.**

Prelate:
Will you teach your brothers by your constant dedication to monastic life, by sound doctrine, and by the good example of your own deeds rather than by mere words?

Abbot-elect: **I will.**

Prelate:
Will you always be concerned for the spiritual good of those entrusted to your care, and seek to lead your brothers to God?

Abbot-elect: **I will.**

Prelate:
Will you be faithful in watching over the goods of your monastery and prudent in using them for the benefit of your brothers, of the poor, and of the strangers at your gate?

Abbot-elect: **I will.**

Prelate:
Will you always and in all matters be loyal, obedient, and reverent to holy Church and to our Holy Father the Pope and his successors?

Abbot-elect: **I will.**

If the abbot is one who has jurisdiction over a territory, the prelate adds:

Will, you, in cooperation with the priests and deacons who share in your ministry, be a loving father to God's holy people, cherish them, and guide them into the way of salvation?

Abbot-elect: **I will.**

Prelate:
Will you, as a good shepherd, seek out the straying sheep and gather them into the sheepfold of Christ?
Abbot-elect: **I will.**

Prelate:
Will you pray without ceasing for God's holy people, and be blameless in carrying out your duties as a shepherd of souls?
Abbot-elect: **I will.**

Prelate:
May the Lord strengthen your resolve, give you every grace, and keep you always and everywhere in his protection.
All: **Amen.**

INVITATION TO PRAYER
21. Then all stand, and the prelate, without his miter, invites the people to pray:

Dearly beloved, God has chosen N., his servant, to be the leader of his brothers. Let us pray that the Lord will sustain him with his grace.

Deacon (except during the Easter season):
Let us kneel.

LITANY OF THE SAINTS
The abbot-elect kneels at his place and, except during the Easter season, the rest kneel at their places.

The cantors sing the litany (see Chapter V); they may add, at the proper place, names of other saints (for example, the patron saint, the titular of the church, the founder of the church, the patron saint of the abbot-elect) or petitions suitable to the occasion.

22. After the litany the deacon says:
Let us stand.

PRAYER OF BLESSING
23. All stand. The abbot-elect comes before the prelate and kneels. The prelate, with hands extended, says one of the following prayers:

Almighty God and Father,
you sent your only Son into the world
to be the servant of all,
the Good Shepherd who lays down his life for his
 sheep.

Listen to our prayer:
bless ✠ and strengthen N., your servant,
chosen to be abbot of this monastery.
May his manner of life show clearly
that he is what he is called, a father,
so that his teaching will, as a leaven of goodness,
grow in the hearts of his spiritual family.

Let him realize, Lord,
how demanding is the task
to which he now sets his hand,
how heavy the responsibility
of guiding the souls of others,
and of ministering
to the many and various needs of a community.

Let him seek to help his brothers
rather than to preside over them.
Give him a heart full of compassion, wisdom, and zeal,
so that he may not lose even one
of the flock entrusted to his charge.

May he dispose all things with understanding,
so that the members of the monastic family
will steadily make progress
in the love of Christ and of each other,
and run with eager hearts
in the way of your commandments.

Give him the gifts of your Spirit.
Set him on fire with love for your glory
and for the service of your Church,
and may he in turn inflame with zeal
the hearts of his brothers.

In his life and in his teaching
may he set Christ above all things,
and when the day of judgment dawns,

receive him, in the company of his brothers,
into your kingdom.

We ask this through Christ our Lord.
℟. Amen.

Or:

Lord, hear our prayers for your servant N.
He has been chosen to guide this monastic community,
and to stand in the place of Christ your Son
as shepherd of your flock.

Look on him with love,
and strengthen him with every blessing.
Open to him the storehouse of your wisdom,
that he may bring out from it
treasures both old and new.

Guide him in the way of grace and peace,
in the footsteps of your Son,
and reward him at last with the joy of everlasting life.

We ask this through Christ our Lord.
℟. Amen.

Or:

Lord, look with love on your servant N.,
chosen under your providence
to be abbot of this monastery.

Bless ✛ him and make him holy,
so that in every thought and deed
he may seek to please you.
By word and example
may he encourage his brothers
to grow in love of you and of their neighbor.
Though a stranger to the ways of this world,
may he take to heart the needs of all your children,
both of body and of soul.

May he always teach his community
to hold in high esteem
the divine office and sacred reading.
Together with his brothers
may he live the life of the Gospel,

and so enter with them
into the unending joy of heaven.

We ask this through Christ our Lord.
℟. Amen.

Or:
Almighty God and Father,
you sent your Son into the world
to minister to your flock
and to lay down his life for them.

Bless ✠ your servant N.,
chosen to be abbot of this monastery,
and make him holy.

Strengthen him by your grace
for his heavy burden of guiding souls
and of adapting himself to the various needs of those
    he serves.
Give him a heart full of compassion
for the brothers entrusted to his care,
so that he may not lose even one.
And may the Lord, when he comes in glory on the last
    day,
give him the reward of his stewardship.

We ask this through Christ our Lord.
℟. Amen.

PRESENTATION OF THE RULE

24. After the prayer of blessing, the prelate, wearing his miter, sits. The new abbot comes before him and the prelate
gives him the Rule, saying:

Take this Rule
which contains the tradition of holiness
received from our spiritual fathers.
As God gives you strength
and human frailty allows,
use it to guide and sustain your brothers
whom God has placed in your care.

PRESENTATION OF THE PONTIFICAL INSIGNIA

25. The prelate may place the ring on the ring finger of the new abbot's right hand, saying:

Take this ring, the seal of fidelity.
Wear it as the symbol of constancy
and maintain this community (monastic family)
in the bond of brotherly love.

26. Then, in silence, the prelate may put the miter on the new abbot's head.

27. Next he hands the pastoral staff, saying:

Take this shepherd's staff
and show loving care for the brothers
whom the Lord has entrusted to you;
for he will demand an account of your stewardship.

28. All stand. If the blessing has been given by a bishop or outside the new abbot's monastery by another abbot, the new abbot takes the first place among the concelebrants. If the blessing has been given by another abbot in the abbey church of the newly blessed abbot, the latter sits in the chair, and the abbot who has conferred the blessing sits at his right.

If the new abbot has jurisdiction over a territory and has received the blessing in his own church, the prelate invites him to sit in the chair while he sits at his right.

29. Lastly the new abbot puts aside his staff and receives the sign of peace from the prelate who has conferred the blessing and from all the abbots. If circumstances permit, the religious and the priests also exchange the sign of peace with the abbot.

LITURGY OF THE EUCHARIST

30. The rite for the concelebration of Mass is followed.

31. At the end of Mass the blessing is given by the celebrant. If the new abbot is the celebrant, he gives it according to the pontifical rite.

32. After the blessing the **Te Deum** or another appropriate song may be sung. During the singing all return in procession to the sacristy and go their way in peace.

If the new abbot has jurisdiction over a territory, the **Te Deum** or another appropriate song is sung at the end of the prayer after communion. Meanwhile, the new abbot is led by his assistants through the church and he blesses all present.

After the hymn, the new abbot, wearing his miter and holding his staff, may stand at the altar or at his chair and address the people briefly. The Mass concludes in the usual manner.

CHAPTER II

BLESSING OF AN ABBESS

INTRODUCTION

1. The blessing of an abbess should take place in the presence of a gathering of religious and, if circumstances permit, of the faithful. The blessing should take place on a Sunday or feast day; for pastoral reasons another day may be chosen.

2. The rite of blessing is usually performed by the bishop of the place where the monastery is situated. For a good reason, and with the consent of the bishop of the place, the abbess-elect may receive the blessing from another bishop or an abbot.

3. The abbess-elect, assisted by two religious from her monastery, is given a place in the sanctuary, outside the enclosure, so that she may be near the bishop or prelate who gives the blessing, and all present, nuns and faithful, may see the celebration and take part in it.

4. Besides what is needed for the celebration of Mass, there should be prepared: a) the Roman Pontifical; b) the Rule, and, if it is to be presented, the ring; c) a chalice or chalices sufficiently large for communion under both kinds.

5. The blessing usually takes place at the chair. To enable the faithful to participate more fully, a seat for the bishop or prelate who gives the blessing may be placed before the altar or in some other suitable place; the seats for the abbess-elect and the religious assisting her should be so arranged that the nuns and faithful may have a complete view of the celebration.

6. Before the celebration begins the prelate, accompanied by the ministers and clergy, goes to the entrance of the enclosure. The abbess-elect, with the two nuns assisting her, leaves the enclosure and takes her place in the procession to the church immediately in front of the prelate.

LITURGY OF THE WORD

7. The introductory rites and the liturgy of the word are celebrated in accordance with the rubrics.

8. The readings may be taken, in whole or in part, from the Mass of the day or from the texts for the blessing of an abbess in the *Lectionary for Mass* (nos. 779-783) and listed in Chapter V.

9. The officiating prelate gives a homily or an address at the appropriate time during the rite of blessing.

10. The profession of faith is not said in this Mass, and the general intercessions are omitted.

BLESSING OF AN ABBESS

11. The rite of blessing begins after the gospel. The officiating prelate, wearing his miter, is seated in the chair prepared for the occasion.

PRESENTATION OF THE ABBESS-ELECT

12. The abbess-elect is escorted by her assistants to the officiating prelate, to whom she makes a sign of reverence.

13. One of the nuns assisting her addresses the prelate in these or similar words:

Most Reverend Father, in the name of our community we present to you the abbess-elect of our monastery of N., of the Order of N., in the diocese of N. We ask you to bless her as abbess of our monastery.

The prelate asks:
Has she been duly elected?

She replies:
We know and testify that she has.

The prelate replies:
Thanks be to God.

HOMILY

14. All sit while the prelate gives a brief homily to the abbess-elect, the nuns, and the faithful.

EXAMINATION

15. After the address the abbess-elect rises and stands in front of the prelate, who questions her in these words:

Will you persevere in your determination to observe the Rule of Saint N. and will you be diligent in teaching your sisters to do the same, and so encourage them in the love of God, in the life of the Gospel, and in mutual charity?

The abbess-elect replies: **I will.**

Prelate:

Will you always and in all matters be loyal, obedient, and reverent to holy Church and to our Holy Father the Pope and his successors?

Abbess-elect: **I will.**

Prelate:

Will you be obedient to your bishop in the governing of your monastery, in accordance with canon law and the constitutions of your Order?

Abbess-elect: **I will.**

Prelate:

Will you teach your sisters by your constant dedication to the monastic life and by the good example of your own deeds rather than by mere words?

Abbess-elect: **I will.**

Prelate:

Will you encourage your sisters to be faithful to the traditions of the religious life and to extend God's kingdom by the hidden apostolate of the life of contemplation?

Abbess-elect: **I will.**

Prelate:

May the Lord strengthen your resolve, give you every

grace, and keep you always and everywhere in his protection.

All: **Amen.**

INVITATION TO PRAYER

16. Then all stand, and the prelate, without his miter, invites
the people to pray:

**Dearly beloved, God has chosen N. to serve him as the
leader of this monastic community. Let us pray that the
Lord will sustain her with his grace.**

Deacon (except during the Easter season):
Let us kneel.

LITANY OF THE SAINTS

The prelate kneels at his chair; the abbess-elect and all the
others kneel in their places.

Then the cantors sing the litany (see Chapter V); they may
add, at the proper place, names of other saints (for example,
the patron saint, the titular of the church, the founder of the
church, the patron saint of the abbess-elect) or petitions suitable to the occasion.

17. After the litany the deacon says:
Let us stand.

PRAYER OF BLESSING

18. All stand. The abbess-elect comes before the prelate and
kneels. The prelate, with hands extended, says one of the
following prayers:

**Almighty God and Father,
you sent your only Son into the world
to be the servant of all,
the Good Shepherd who lays down his life for his
   sheep.**

**Listen to our prayer:
bless ✠ and sustain N., your servant,
chosen to be abbess of this community.
May her manner of life show clearly
that she is what she is called, a mother.**

Let her seek to help her sisters
rather than to preside over them.

May she dispose all things with understanding,
so that the members of her monastic family
will steadily make progress
in the love of Christ and of each other,
and run with eager hearts
in the way of your commandments.

Give her the gifts of your Spirit.
Set her on fire with love for your glory
and for the service of your Church,
and may she in turn inflame with zeal
the hearts of her sisters.

May she set Christ above all things,
and when the day of judgment dawns,
receive her, in the company of her sisters,
into your kingdom.

We ask this through Christ our Lord.
℟. Amen.

Or:
Lord, hear our prayers for your servant N.,
who has been chosen to guide this monastic community.
Look on her with love,
and strengthen her with every blessing.
Guide her in the way of grace and peace,
in the footsteps of your Son,
and reward her at last with the joy of everlasting life.

We ask this through Christ our Lord.
℟. Amen.

Or:
Lord, look with love on your servant N.,
chosen under your providence
to be abbess of this community.

Bless ✠ her and make her holy,
so that in every thought and deed
she may seek to please you.

By word and example
may she encourage her sisters
to grow in love of you and of their neighbor.

Though a stranger to the ways of this world,
may she take to heart
the needs of all your children,
both of body and of soul.

May she always teach her community
to hold in high esteem
the divine office and sacred reading.
Together with her sisters
may she live the life of the Gospel,
and so enter with them
into the unending joy of heaven.

We ask this through Christ our Lord.
℟. Amen.

Or:
Almighty God and Father,
you sent your Son into the world
to minister to your flock
and to lay down his life for them.

Bless ✛ your servant N.,
chosen to be abbess of this monastery,
and make her holy.
Give her a heart full of compassion
for the sisters entrusted to her care.
And may the Lord, when he comes in glory on the last
    day,
give her the reward of her stewardship.

We ask this through Christ our Lord.
℟. Amen.

PRESENTATION OF THE RULE

19. After the prayer of blessing, the prelate, wearing his miter, sits. The new abbess comes before him and the prelate
gives her the Rule, saying:

**Take this Rule
which contains the traditions of holiness
received from our spiritual fathers.
As God gives you strength
and human frailty allows,
use it to guide and sustain your sisters
whom God has placed in your care.**

PRESENTATION OF THE RING

20. The ring is not presented if the abbess has already received it on the day of her profession and consecration.

If the abbess has not previously received the ring, the prelate may place it on the ring finger of her right hand, saying:

**Take this ring, the seal of fidelity.
Wear it as the symbol of constancy
and maintain this community (monastic family)
in the bond of sisterly love.**

21. Then the abbess gives a sign of peace to the prelate and returns to her place with her two assistants.

CONCLUDING RITE

INSTALLATION

22. After the Mass the **Te Deum** or another appropriate song may be sung. During the singing the prelate leads the abbess to the enclosure. If the prelate is the Ordinary of the place and has immediate jurisdiction over the nuns, he leads her to her place in choir and seats her there, unless the abbess has already been given this sign of her authority immediately after her election.

CHAPTER III

CONSECRATION TO A LIFE OF VIRGINITY

INTRODUCTION

NATURE AND VALUE OF CONSECRATION TO VIRGINITY

1. The custom of consecrating women to a life of virginity flourished even in the early Church. It led to the formation of a solemn rite constituting the candidate a sacred person, a surpassing sign of the Church's love for Christ, and an eschatological image of the world to come and the glory of the heavenly Bride of Christ. In the rite of consecration the Church reveals its love of virginity, begs God's grace on those who are consecrated, and prays with fervor for an outpouring of the Holy Spirit.

PRINCIPAL DUTIES OF THOSE CONSECRATED

2. Those who consecrate their chastity under the inspiration of the Holy Spirit do so for the sake of more fervent love of Christ and of greater freedom in the service of their brothers and sisters.

They are to spend their time in works of penance and of mercy, in apostolic activity and in prayer, according to their state of life and spiritual gifts.

To fulfill their duty of prayer they are strongly advised to celebrate the liturgy of the hours each day, especially morning prayer and evening prayer. In this way, by joining their voices to those of Christ the High Priest and of his Church, they will offer unending praise to the heavenly Father and pray for the salvation of the whole world.

THOSE WHO MAY BE CONSECRATED

3. This consecration may be received by nuns or by women living in the world.

4. In the case of nuns it is required:
a) that they have never married or lived in public or open violation of chastity;

b) that they have made their perpetual profession, either in the same rite or on an earlier occasion;
c) that their religious family uses this rite either by established custom or by new permission of the competent authority.

5. In the case of women living in the world it is required:
a) that they have never married or lived in public or open violation of chastity;
b) that by their age, prudence, and universally approved character they give assurance of perseverance in a life of chastity dedicated to the service of the Church and of their neighbor;
c) that they be admitted to this consecration by the bishop who is the Ordinary of the place.

It is for the bishop to decide on the conditions under which women living in the world are to undertake a life of perpetual virginity.

MINISTER OF THE RITE
6. The minister of the rite of consecration is the bishop who is the Ordinary of the place.

FORM OF THE RITE
7. For the consecration of women living in the world the rite described in section A is to be used.

For the consecration of nuns the rite found in section B is to be followed. This integrates religious profession with the consecration. For a good reason, however, these two rites may be separated, for example, when this is in accordance with long established custom. But care should be taken not to duplicate parts of the rite. The two liturgical services should be so arranged that the rite of religious profession omits any prayer of consecration, retaining only those elements that belong to religious profession. The prayer **Loving Father, chaste bodies** and ritual elements with a nuptial significance (for example, the presentation of the ring) should be reserved for the rite of consecration.

The rite consists of these parts:
a) the calling of the candidates;
b) the homily or address, in which the candidates and the people are instructed on the gift of virginity;

c) the examination in which the bishop asks the candidates about their willingness to persevere in their intention and to receive the consecration;

d) the litany, in which prayer is offered to God the Father and the intercession of the Virgin Mary and all the saints is invoked;

e) the renewal of the intention of chastity (or the making of religious profession);

f) the solemn blessing or consecration, by which the Church asks the heavenly Father to pour out the gifts of the Holy Spirit on the candidates;

g) the presentation of the insignia of consecration, to symbolize a spiritual dedication.

MASS FOR THE CONSECRATION
TO A LIFE OF VIRGINITY

8. It is appropriate to use the ritual Mass for the day of consecration to a life of virginity. On a solemnity or Sundays of Advent, Lent, and Easter the Mass of the day is used, with the special formulas for the eucharistic prayer and the final blessing.

9. Since the liturgy of the word for the rite of consecration to a life of virginity can be a help in understanding the importance and nature of virginity in the Church, it is lawful, when the Mass for the day of consecration to a life of virginity is not permitted, to take one reading from the special lectionary. This may not be done during the Easter triduum, on the solemnities of Christmas, Epiphany, Ascension, Pentecost, Corpus Christi, or on other solemnities of obligation.

10. White vestments are worn for the ritual Mass for the day of consecration.

A. CONSECRATION TO A LIFE OF VIRGINITY FOR WOMEN LIVING IN THE WORLD

INTRODUCTION

1. It is appropriate for the rite of consecration to take place during the octave of Easter, on solemnities, especially those which celebrate the incarnation, on Sundays, or on feasts of the Blessed Virgin Mary or of holy virgins.

2. On a day scheduled close to the day of the rite of consecration, or at least on the day before the consecration, the candidates are presented to the bishop, so that the father of the diocese may begin a pastoral dialogue with his spiritual daughters.

3. It is at the discretion of the bishop and by his authority that women living in the world are admitted to this consecration, and often they take part in the good works of the diocese. It is therefore fitting that the rite of consecration should take place in the cathedral, unless local circumstances or custom suggest otherwise.

4. As occasion offers, and especially to promote an esteem for chastity, to deepen understanding of the Church, and to encourage a greater attendance of the people, the faithful should be notified of the celebration in good time.

5. The Mass of the day or the ritual Mass for the day of consecration is celebrated in accordance with the rubrics (see Introduction, nos. 8-10).

6. The consecration ordinarily takes place at the chair. To enable the faithful to take part more easily, the bishop's chair may be placed in front of the altar. Seats for the candidates should be so arranged in the sanctuary that the faithful may have a complete view of the liturgical rites.

7. For the eucharistic celebration enough bread and wine should be prepared for the ministers, the candidates, their parents, relatives, and friends. If only one chalice is used, it should be sufficiently large.

8. In addition to what is needed for the celebration of Mass, there should be ready: a) the Roman Pontifical; b) veils, rings, or other insignia of bridal consecration to be presented in accordance with local rules or approved customs.

INTRODUCTORY RITES

9. When the people are assembled and everything is ready, the procession moves through the church to the altar in the usual way, while the choir and people sing the entrance song of the Mass. The candidates may join in the procession.

10. It is appropriate for two women—either consecrated themselves or chosen from the laity—to accompany the candidates to the altar.

11. When they come to the sanctuary, all make the customary reverence to the altar. The candidates go to their places in the body of the church and Mass continues.

LITURGY OF THE WORD

12. The liturgy of the word takes place as usual, except for the following:
a) the readings may be taken from the Mass of the day or from the texts listed in Chapter V (see Introduction, nos. 8-9);
b) the profession of faith is not said, even if prescribed by the rubrics of the day;
c) the general intercessions are omitted, since they are included in the litany.

CONSECRATION

CALLING OF THE CANDIDATES

13. After the gospel, if the consecration takes place in front of the altar, the bishop goes to the chair prepared for him and sits.

When candles are not used see no. 15 below.

If candles are used, the choir sings the following antiphon:

Be wise: make ready your lamps.
Behold, the Bridegroom comes;
go out to meet him.

Any other appropriate song may be sung.

The candidates then light their lamps or candles and, accompanied by the two women mentioned above (see no. 10),
approach the sanctuary and stand outside it.

14. Then the bishop calls the candidates; he sings or says
aloud:

Come, listen to me, my children;
I will teach you reverence for the Lord.

The candidates reply by singing this antiphon or some other
appropriate song:

Now with all our hearts we follow you,
we reverence you and seek your presence.
Lord, fulfill our hope:
show us your loving kindness,
the greatness of your mercy.

As they sing the antiphon, the candidates enter the sanctuary
and take up their positions so that everyone may have a complete view of the liturgical rites. They place their candles in a
candelabrum, or give them to the ministers until they are
returned at the end of Mass. They then sit in the places prepared for them.

15. Or, when candles are not used:
[138] The deacon calls each of the candidates by name. Each
candidate, on hearing her name, rises and replies: **Lord, you**
have called me. The candidate may make some other suitable
reply. Then she goes to the sanctuary and stands outside it.

[139] After the calling of the candidates, the bishop invites
them in these or similar words:

Come, daughters,
that through me, his servant,
the Lord may consecrate
the resolution you have formed in your hearts.

The candidates reply by singing this antiphon or some other
appropriate song:

Now with all our hearts we follow you,
we reverence you and seek your presence.
Lord, fulfill our hope:
show us your loving kindness,
the greatness of your mercy.

As they sing the antiphon, the candidates enter the
sanctuary, accompanied by the two women mentioned above
(see no. 10), and take up their positions so that everyone may
have a complete view of the liturgical rites. They then sit in
the places prepared for them.

HOMILY

16. The bishop then gives a short homily to the candidates
and the people on the gift of virginity and its role in the
sanctification of those called to virginity and the welfare of
the whole Church. He does so in these or similar words:

Dear brothers and sisters, today the Church consecrates
these candidates to a life of virginity. They come from
God's holy people, from your own families. They are
your daughters, your sisters, your relatives, joined by
the ties of family or friendship.

God has called them to be more closely united to him-
self and to be dedicated to the service of the Church
and of mankind. Their consecration is a call to greater
fervor in spreading the kingdom of God and in giving
to the world the spirit of Christ. Think of the good they
will accomplish by their prayers and good works, and
the abundant blessings they will obtain from God for
holy Church, for human society, and for your families.

He then addresses the candidates:

And now we speak to you, dear daughters. Our words
are not words of command but encouragement from
the heart. The life you seek to follow has its home in
heaven. God himself is its source. It is he, infinitely
pure and holy, who gives the grace of virginity. Those
to whom he gives it are seen by the Fathers of the
Church as images of the eternal and all-holy God.

When the fullness of time had come, the almighty
Father showed, in the mystery of the incarnation, his
love for this great virtue. In the chaste womb of the
Blessed Virgin Mary, by the power of the Holy Spirit,
the Word was made flesh, in a marriage covenant uniting two natures, human and divine.

Our Lord himself taught us the high calling of such a
life, consecrated to God and chosen for the sake of the
kingdom of heaven. By his whole life, and especially
by his labors, his preaching, and, above all, by his
paschal mystery, he brought his Church into being. He
desired it to be a virgin, a bride, and a mother: a virgin,
to keep the faith whole and entire; a bride, to be one
with him for ever; and a mother, to raise up the family
of the Church.

The Holy Spirit, the Paraclete, through baptism has
already made you temples of God's glory and children
of the Father. Today through our ministry he anoints
you with a new grace and consecrates you to God by a
new title. He gives each one of you the dignity of being
a bride of Christ and binds you to the Son of God in a
covenant to last for ever.

The Church is the bride of Christ. This title of the
Church was given by the fathers and doctors of the
Church to those like you who speak to us of the world
to come, where there is not marrying or giving in marriage. You are a sign of the great mystery of salvation,
proclaimed at the beginning of human history and fulfilled in the marriage covenant between Christ and his
Church.

Make your whole life reflect your vocation and your
dignity. Our holy mother the Church sees in you a
chosen company within the flock of Christ. Through
you the Church's motherhood of grace bears its abundant fruit. Imitate the mother of God; desire to be
called and to be handmaids of the Lord. Preserve the
fullness of your faith, the steadfastness of your hope,
the single-heartedness of your love. Be prudent and
watch: keep the glory of your virginity uncorrupted by

pride. Nourish your love of God by feeding on the body of Christ; strengthen it by self-denial; build it up by study of the Scriptures, by untiring prayer, by works of mercy. Let your thoughts be on the things of God. Let your life be hidden with Christ in God. Make it your concern to pray fervently for the spread of the Christian faith and for the unity of all Christians. Pray earnestly to God for the welfare of the married. Remember also those who have forgotten their Father's goodness and have abandoned his love, so that God's mercy may forgive where his justice must condemn.

Never forget that you are given over entirely to the service of the Church and of all your brothers and sisters. You are apostles in the Church and in the world, in the things of the Spirit and in the things of the world. Let your light then shine before men and women, that your Father in heaven may be glorified, and his plan of making all things one in Christ come to perfection. Love everyone, especially those in need. Help the poor, care for the weak, teach the ignorant, protect the young, minister to the old, bring strength and comfort to widows and all in adversity.

You have renounced marriage for the sake of Christ. Your motherhood will be a motherhood of the spirit, as you do the will of your Father and work with others in a spirit of charity, so that a great family of children may be born, or reborn, to the life of grace.

Your joy and your crown, even here on earth, will be Christ, the Son of the Virgin and the Bridegroom of virgins. He will call you to his presence and into his kingdom, where you will sing a new song as you follow the Lamb of God wherever he leads you.

EXAMINATION

17. After the homily the candidates stand and the bishop questions them in these or similar words:

Are you resolved to persevere to the end of your days in the holy state of virginity and in the service of God and his Church?

Together, all the candidates answer: **I am.**

Bishop:
Are you so resolved to follow Christ in the spirit of the Gospel that your whole life may be a faithful witness to God's love and a convincing sign of the kingdom of heaven?

Candidates: **I am.**

Bishop:
Are you resolved to accept solemn consecration as a bride of our Lord Jesus Christ, the Son of God?

Candidates: **I am.**

Bishop and all present: **Thanks be to God.**

INVITATION TO PRAYER

18. Then all stand, and the bishop, without his miter, invites the people to pray:

Dearly beloved, let us pray to God the almighty Father through his Son, our Lord Jesus Christ, that, by the intercession of the Blessed Virgin Mary and all the saints, he will pour out the Holy Spirit of his love on these servants of his whom he has chosen to be consecrated to his service.

19. Deacon (except during the Easter season):
Let us kneel.

LITANY OF THE SAINTS

Then the bishop, the ministers, the candidates, and the people kneel (except during the Easter season, when all stand). Where it is customary for the candidates to prostrate themselves, this may be done.

20. The cantors then sing the litany (Chapter V). At the proper place they may add the names of other saints who are

specially venerated by the people, or petitions suitable to the occasion.

21. Then the bishop alone rises and, with hands joined, sings or says:

Lord,
hear the prayers of your Church.
Look with favor on your handmaids
whom you have called in your love.
Set them on the way of eternal salvation;
may they seek only what is pleasing to you,
and fulfill it with watchful care.

We ask this through Christ our Lord.
All: **Amen.**

Deacon: **Let us stand.**

All stand.

RENEWAL OF INTENTION

22. Then, if it seems suitable, the candidates offer themselves to God at the hands of the bishop. This may be done, for example, in the following way: the candidates come one by one before the bishop. Each one kneels, places her joined hands between his hands and says:

Father, receive my resolution to follow Christ in a life of perfect chastity which, with God's help, I here profess before you and God's holy people.

If there are many candidates, the bishop may allow all to remain kneeling in their places and to say together:

Father, receive our resolution to follow Christ in a life of perfect chastity which, with God's help, we here profess before you and God's holy people.

23. Another suitable rite, in accordance with local custom, may be substituted.

PRAYER OF CONSECRATION

24. After the renewal of intention, the candidates return to their places in the sanctuary and kneel. The bishop extends

his hands over them, and sings or says the prayer of consecration. The words in brackets may be omitted.

Loving Father,
chaste bodies are your temple;
you delight in sinless hearts.
Our nature was corrupted
when the devil deceived our first parents,
but you have restored it in Christ.
He is your Word, through whom all things were made.
He has made our nature whole again,
and made it possible for mortal people to reflect the
    life of angels.

Lord,
look with favor on your handmaids.
They place in your hands their resolve to live in
    chastity.
You inspire them to take this vow;
now they give you their hearts.
[Only you can kindle this flame of love, and feed its
    brightness,
giving strength and perseverance to our will.
Without you our flesh is weak,
bound by the law of nature,
free with false freedom,
imprisoned by habit,
softened by the spirit of the age.]

You have poured out your grace upon all peoples.
You have adopted as heirs of the new covenant
sons and daughters from every nation under heaven,
countless as the stars.
Your children are born, not of human birth,
nor of man's desire,
but of your Spirit.
Among your many gifts
you give to some the grace of virginity.
Yet the honor of marriage is in no way lessened.
As it was in the beginning,
your first blessing still remains upon this holy union.
Yet your loving wisdom chooses those

who make sacrifice of marriage
for the sake of the love of which it is the sign.
They renounce the joys of human marriage,
but cherish all that it foreshadows.

[Those who choose chastity have looked upon the face
    of Christ,
its origin and inspiration.
They give themselves wholly to Christ,
the Son of the ever-virgin Mary,
and the heavenly Bridegroom of those
who in his honor dedicate themselves to lasting
    virginity.]

Lord,
protect those who seek your help.
They desire to be strengthened by your blessing and
    consecration.
Defend them from the cunning and deceit of the
    enemy.
Keep them vigilant and on their guard;
may nothing tarnish the glory of perfect virginity,
or the vocation of purity which is shared by those who
    are married.

Through the gift of your Spirit, Lord,
give them modesty with right judgment,
kindness with true wisdom,
gentleness with strength of character,
freedom with the grace of chastity.
Give them the warmth of love,
to love you above all others.
Make their lives deserve our praise,
without seeking to be praised.
May they give you glory
by holiness of action and purity of heart.
May they love you and fear you;
may they love you and serve you.

Be yourself their glory, their joy, their whole desire.
Be their comfort in sorrow,
their wisdom in perplexity,

their protection in the midst of injustice,
their patience in adversity,
their riches in poverty,
their food in fasting,
their remedy in time of sickness.

They have chosen you above all things;
may they find all things in possessing you.

We ask this through our Lord Jesus Christ, your Son,
who lives and reigns with you and the Holy Spirit,
one God, for ever and ever.
All: **Amen.**

PRESENTATION OF THE INSIGNIA OF CONSECRATION

One of the following forms, nos. 25 to 29 or nos. 151 to 154, is
used.

25. After the prayer of consecration, the bishop and the
people sit. The newly consecrated stand and, accompanied
by the two consecrated or lay women mentioned above, come
before the bishop. He says once for all of them:

If the veil is given:
Dearest daughters,
receive the veil and the ring
that are the insignia of your consecration.
Keep unstained your fidelity to your Bridegroom,
and never forget that you are bound
to the service of Christ and of his body, the Church.
They all reply together: **Amen.**

26. Or, if the veil is not given:
Receive the ring
that marks you as a bride of Christ.
Keep unstained your fidelity to your Bridegroom,
that you may one day be admitted to the wedding feast
    of everlasting joy.
They all reply together: **Amen.**

27. While the newly consecrated kneel, the bishop gives the
ring to each one and, if customary, the veil and other insignia
of consecration.

Meanwhile, the choir and the people may sing the following antiphon with Psalm 45.

**To you, O Lord, I lift my soul;
come and rescue me, for you are my refuge and my
strength.**

The antiphon is repeated after every two verses. **Glory to the Father** is not said. The psalm is interrupted and the antiphon repeated when the presentation of the insignia is completed.

Any other appropriate song may be sung.

PRESENTATION OF THE LITURGY OF THE HOURS

28. Then, if it seems appropriate, the bishop gives the newly consecrated the book containing the prayer of the Church, saying these or similar words:

**Receive the book of the liturgy of the hours,
the prayer of the Church;
may the praise of our heavenly Father
be always on your lips;
pray without ceasing
for the salvation of the whole world.**
All reply together: **Amen.**

The newly consecrated come before the bishop, who gives each a copy of the liturgy of the hours. After receiving it, they return to their places and remain standing.

---

29. Then, if appropriate, this or some suitable antiphon is sung.

**I am espoused to him whom the angels serve;
sun and moon stand in wonder at his glory.**

If possible, all those newly consecrated sing the antiphon together; otherwise the choir sings it.

Or:
[151] (For the giving of the veil. The rite is omitted if those consecrated have already received the veil canonically.) After the prayer of consecration the bishop and the people sit. The newly consecrated stand and, accompanied by the consecrated or lay women mentioned above, come before the bishop. He gives the veil to each one, saying:

Receive this veil,
by which you are to show
that you have been chosen from other women
to be dedicated to the service of Christ
and of his body, which is the Church.
Each one replies: **Amen.**

After receiving the veil each one returns to her place and remains standing. When all have received their veils, they sing the antiphon:

I will raise my mind and heart to you, O Lord,
that I may be holy in body and in spirit.

The choir may begin the antiphon after the veil has been given to the first or second one. It may be repeated after one or more verses of a suitable psalm or canticle.

[152] (For the giving of the ring.) When all have received the veil, the rings are given in the following way: those consecrated come before the bishop in the same order as before. Then he gives each one her ring, saying:

Receive the ring
that marks you as a bride of Christ.
Keep unstained your fidelity to your Bridegroom,
that you may one day be admitted to the wedding feast
**   of everlasting joy.**
Each one replies: **Amen.**

PRESENTATION OF THE LITURGY OF THE HOURS

[153] Then, if it seems appropriate, the bishop gives the newly consecrated the book containing the prayer of the Church, saying these or similar words:

Receive the book of the liturgy of the hours,
the prayer of the Church;
may the praise of our heavenly Father
be always on your lips;
pray without ceasing
for the salvation of the world.
Each replies: **Amen.**

Each returns to her place.

---

[154] After all have received the insignia of profession, those consecrated sing the antiphon:

**I am espoused to him whom the angels serve;
sun and moon stand in wonder at his glory.**

If appropriate the choir may sing the antiphon after the ring has been given to the first or second person. It may be repeated after one or more verses of a suitable psalm or canticle.

31. After this the newly consecrated return to their places in the sanctuary and the Mass continues.

LITURGY OF THE EUCHARIST

32. During the preparation of the gifts, some of the newly consecrated may bring to the altar the bread, wine, and water for the eucharistic sacrifice.

33. In the eucharistic prayer the offering of those newly consecrated may be mentioned (see Ritual Masses, Consecration to a Life of Virginity).

34. After **The peace of the Lord be always with you**, the bishop gives an appropriate sign of peace to those newly consecrated.

35. After the bishop has received the body and blood of Christ, the newly consecrated come to the altar to receive communion under both kinds.

Their parents, relatives, and friends may also receive communion under both kinds.

CONCLUDING RITE

SOLEMN BLESSING

36. When the prayer after communion has been said, those newly consecrated stand before the altar. The bishop faces them and sings or says one of the following:

**The almighty Father
has poured into your hearts
the desire to live a life of holy virginity.**

May he keep you safe under his protection.
℞. Amen.

May the Lord Jesus Christ,
with whose sacred heart
the hearts of virgins are united,
fill you with his divine love.
℞. Amen.

May the Holy Spirit,
by whom the Virgin Mary conceived her Son,
today consecrate your hearts
and fill you with a burning desire
to serve God and his Church.
℞. Amen.

Finally he blesses the whole congregation:
May almighty God,
the Father, and the Son, ✠ and the Holy Spirit,
bless all of you who have taken part in this celebration.
℞. Amen.

Or [155, 156]:
God inspires all holy desires and brings them
    to fulfillment.
May he protect you always by his grace
so that you may fulfill the duties of your vocation
with a faithful heart.
℞. Amen.

May he make each of you a witness
and sign of his love for all people.
℞. Amen.

May he make those bonds
with which he has bound you to Christ on earth
endure for ever in heavenly love.
℞. Amen.

Finally he blesses the whole congregation:
May almighty God,
the Father, and the Son, ✠ and the Holy Spirit,
bless all of you who have taken part in this celebration.
℞. Amen.

38. After the blessing by the bishop, the newly consecrated may take their candles. The choir and the people sing an appropriate song or a canticle of praise, and the procession is formed as at the beginning.

B. CONSECRATION TO A LIFE OF VIRGINITY TOGETHER WITH RELIGIOUS PROFESSION FOR NUNS

INTRODUCTION

39. It is appropriate for the rite of consecration combined with that of perpetual profession to take place during the octave of Easter, on solemnities, especially those which celebrate the incarnation, on Sundays, or on feasts of the Blessed Virgin Mary, holy virgins or saints distinguished in the living of the religious life.

40. On a day scheduled close to the day of the rite of consecration, or at least on the day before the consecration, the candidates are presented to the bishop, so that the father of the diocese may begin a pastoral dialogue with his spiritual daughters.

41. The consecration ordinarily takes place in the monastery church.

42. Sufficient announcement should be made to the faithful of the date and time so that they may attend in greater numbers.

43. The Mass of the day or the ritual Mass for the day of consecration is celebrated, in accordance with the rubrics (see Introduction, nos. 8-10).

44. The consecration ordinarily takes place at the chair. To enable the faithful to take part more easily, the bishop's chair may be placed in front of the altar. A chair for the superior who is to receive the profession is to be prepared in a suitable place in the sanctuary. Seats for the candidates should be so arranged in the sanctuary that the faithful may have a complete view of the liturgical rites.

45. As the nature of the rite demands, the whole liturgical service should be celebrated with fitting solemnity, but any appearance of lavishness unbecoming to religious poverty should be avoided.

46. For the eucharistic celebration enough bread and wine should be prepared for the ministers, the candidates, their parents, relatives, friends, and fellow religious. If only one chalice is used, it should be sufficiently large.

47. In addition to what is needed for the celebration of Mass, there should be ready: a) the Roman Pontifical; b) veils, rings, or other insignia of consecration or religious profession to be presented in accordance with local rules or customs of the religious family.

INTRODUCTORY RITES

48. When the people are assembled and everything is ready, the procession moves through the church to the altar in the usual way, while the choir and people sing the entrance song of the Mass. The candidates may fittingly join in the procession, accompanied by the superior and novice mistress.

49. When they come to the sanctuary, all make the customary reverence to the altar. The candidates go to their places in the body of the church and Mass continues.

LITURGY OF THE WORD

50. The liturgy of the word takes place as usual, except for the following:
a) the readings may be taken from the Mass of the day or from the texts listed in Chapter V (see Introduction, nos. 8-9);
b) the profession of faith is not said, even if prescribed by the rubrics of the day;
c) the general intercessions are omitted, since they are included in the litany.

CONSECRATION TOGETHER WITH RELIGIOUS PROFESSION

CALLING OF THE CANDIDATES

51. After the gospel, if the consecration takes place in front of the altar, the bishop goes to the chair prepared for him and sits.

When candles are not used see no. 53 below.

If candles are used, the choir sings the following antiphon:

Be wise: make ready your lamps.
Behold, the Bridegroom comes;
go out to meet him.

Any other appropriate song may be sung.

The candidates then light their lamps or candles and, accompanied by the novice mistress and another nun assigned to this task, approach the sanctuary and stand outside it.

52. Then the bishop calls the candidates; he sings or says aloud:

Come, listen to me, my children;
I will teach you reverence for the Lord.

The candidates reply by singing this antiphon or some other appropriate song:

Now with all our hearts we follow you,
we reverence you and seek your presence.
Lord, fulfill our hope:
show us your loving kindness,
the greatness of your mercy.

As they sing the antiphon, the candidates enter the sanctuary and take up their positions so that everyone may have a complete view of the liturgical rites. They place their candles in a candelabrum, or give them to the ministers until they are returned at the end of Mass. They then sit in the places prepared for them.

53. Or, when candles are not used:
[138] The deacon calls each of the candidates by name. Each candidate, on hearing her name, rises and replies: **Lord, you have called me.** The candidate may make some other suitable reply. Then she goes to the sanctuary and stands outside it.

[139] After the calling of the candidates, the bishop invites them in these or similar words:

Come, daughters,
that through me, his servant,

**the Lord may consecrate
the resolution you have formed in your hearts.**

The candidates reply by singing this antiphon or some other appropriate song:

**Now with all our hearts we follow you,
we reverence you and seek your presence.
Lord, fulfill our hope:
show us your loving kindness,
the greatness of your mercy.**

As they sing the antiphon, the candidates enter the sanctuary, accompanied by the two women, and take up their positions so that everyone may have a complete view of the liturgical rites. They then sit in the places prepared for them.

HOMILY

54. The bishop then gives a short homily to the candidates and the people, developing the Scripture readings and the theme of virginity as a gift and religious life as a responsibility, and how it sanctifies those called to it and promotes the good of the Church and the whole human family.

EXAMINATION

55. After the homily the candidates stand; the bishop then questions them on their readiness to dedicate themselves to God and to seek perfect charity, according to the rule or constitutions of the religious community. The questions may be changed or in part omitted, to suit the spirit and character of each religious institute. He uses these or similar words:

Dear sisters (daughters), in baptism you have already died to sin and have been set aside for God's service. Are you now resolved to unite yourself more closely to God by the bond of perpetual profession?
Together, all the candidates answer: **I am.**

Bishop:
Are you resolved to strive steadfastly for perfection in the love of God and of your neighbor by living the Gospel with all your heart and keeping the rule of this religious community?
Candidates: **I am.**

Bishop:
Are you resolved to give yourself to God alone, in solitude and silence, in persevering prayer and willing penance, in humble labor and good works?
Candidates: **I am.**

Are you resolved to accept solemn consecration as a bride of our Lord Jesus Christ, the Son of God?
Candidates: **I am.**

56. At the end of the questions, the bishop confirms the intention of those to be professed in these or similar words:

May God who has begun the good work in you bring it to fulfillment before the day of Christ Jesus.
All: **Amen.**

INVITATION TO PRAYER

57. Then all stand, and the bishop, without his miter, invites the people to pray:

Dearly beloved, let us pray to God the almighty Father through his Son, our Lord Jesus Christ, that, by the intercession of the Blessed Virgin Mary and all the saints, he will pour out the Holy Spirit of his love on these servants of his whom he has chosen to be consecrated to his service.

58. Deacon (except during the Easter season):
Let us kneel.

LITANY OF THE SAINTS

Then the bishop, the ministers, the candidates, and the people kneel (except during the Easter season, when all stand). Where it is customary for the candidates to prostrate themselves, this may be done.

59. The cantors then sing the litany (Chapter V). At the proper place they may add the names of other saints who are specially venerated by the people, or petitions suitable to the occasion.

60. Then the bishop alone rises and, with hands joined, sings or says:

**Lord,
hear the prayers of your Church.
Look with favor on your handmaids
whom you have called in your love.
Set them on the way of eternal salvation;
may they seek only what is pleasing to you,
and fulfill it with watchful care.**

We ask this through Christ our Lord.
All: **Amen.**

Deacon: **Let us stand.**

All stand.

PROFESSION

61. After the litany, if it is the custom of the religious community, two consecrated and professed members of the community come to the chair of the superior and, standing, act as witnesses. Those to be professed come, one by one, to the superior and read the formula of profession, which they themselves have written out beforehand.

62. Then the newly professed may fittingly go to the altar, one by one, to place on it the formula of profession; if it can be done conveniently, each of them should sign the document of profession upon the altar itself. After this, each goes back to her place.

63. Afterward, if it is the practice of the community, the newly professed may stand and sing the following antiphon or another song expressing the spirit of self-giving and joy:

**Uphold me, Lord, according to your promise
and I shall live;
and do not bring to nothing all my hope.**

PRAYER OF CONSECRATION

64. Then the candidates kneel, and the bishop extends his hands over them, and sings or says the prayer of consecration. The words in brackets may be omitted.

Loving Father,
chaste bodies are your temple;
you delight in sinless hearts.
Our nature was corrupted
when the devil deceived our first parents,
but you have restored it in Christ.
He is your Word, through whom all things were made.
He has made our nature whole again,
and made it possible for mortal people to reflect the
    life of angels.

Lord,
look with favor on your handmaids.
They place in your hands their resolve to live in
    chastity.
You inspire them to take this vow;
now they give you their hearts.

[Only you can kindle this flame of love, and feed its
    brightness,
giving strength and perseverance to our will.
Without you our flesh is weak,
bound by the law of nature,
free with false freedom,
imprisoned by habit,
softened by the spirit of the age.]

You have poured out your grace upon all peoples.
You have adopted as heirs of the new covenant
sons and daughters from every nation under heaven,
countless as the stars.
Your children are born, not of human birth,
nor of man's desire,
but of your Spirit.
Among your many gifts
you give to some the grace of virginity.
Yet the honor of marriage is in no way lessened.
As it was in the beginning,
your first blessing still remains upon this holy union.
Yet your loving wisdom chooses those
who make sacrifice of marriage
for the sake of the love of which it is the sign.

They renounce the joys of human marriage,
but cherish all that it foreshadows.

[Those who choose chastity have looked upon the face
   of Christ,
its origin and inspiration.
They give themselves wholly to Christ,
the Son of the ever-virgin Mary,
and the heavenly Bridegroom of those
who in his honor dedicate themselves to lasting
   virginity.]

Lord,
protect those who seek your help.
They desire to be strengthened by your blessing and
   consecration.
Defend them from the cunning and deceit of the
   enemy.
Keep them vigilant and on their guard;
may nothing tarnish the glory of perfect virginity,
or the vocation of purity which is shared by those who
   are married.

Through the gift of your Spirit, Lord,
give them modesty with right judgment,
kindness with true wisdom,
gentleness with strength of character,
freedom with the grace of chastity.
Give them the warmth of love,
to love you above all others.
Make their lives deserve our praise,
without seeking to be praised.
May they give you glory
by holiness of action and purity of heart.
May they love you and fear you;
may they love you and serve you.

Be yourself their glory, their joy, their whole desire.
Be their comfort in sorrow,
their wisdom in perplexity,
their protection in the midst of injustice,
their patience in adversity,

their riches in poverty,
their food in fasting,
their remedy in time of sickness.

They have chosen you above all things; may they find
all things in possessing you.

We ask this through our Lord Jesus Christ, your Son,
who lives and reigns with you and the Holy Spirit,
one God, for ever and ever.
All: **Amen.**

PRESENTATION OF THE INSIGNIA OF CONSECRATION
One of the following forms, nos. 65 to 69 or nos. 151 to 154, is
used.

65. After the prayer of consecration, the bishop and the
people sit. The newly consecrated stand and, accompanied
by the novice mistress and the other nun assigned to this
task, come before the bishop. He says, once for all of them:

If the veil is given:
Dearest daughters,
receive the veil and the ring
that are the insignia of your consecration.
Keep unstained your fidelity to your Bridegroom,
and never forget that you are bound
to the service of Christ and of his body, the Church.
They all reply together: **Amen.**

66. Or, if the veil is not given:
Receive the ring
that marks you as a bride of Christ.
Keep unstained your fidelity to your Bridegroom,
that you may one day be admitted to the wedding feast
    of everlasting joy.
They all reply together: **Amen.**

67. While the newly consecrated kneel, the bishop gives the
ring to each one and, if customary, the veil and other insignia
of consecration.

Meanwhile, the choir and the people may sing the following
antiphon with Psalm 45.

To you, O Lord, I lift my soul;
come and rescue me, for you are my refuge and my
strength.

The antiphon is repeated after every two verses. **Glory to the**
Father is not said. The psalm is interrupted and the antiphon
repeated when the presentation of the insignia is completed.

Any other appropriate song may be sung.

PRESENTATION OF THE LITURGY OF THE HOURS

68. Then, if it seems appropriate, the bishop gives the newly
consecrated the book containing the prayer of the Church,
saying these or similar words:

Receive the book of the liturgy of the hours,
the prayer of the Church;
may the praise of our heavenly Father
be always on your lips;
pray without ceasing
for the salvation of the whole world.
All reply together: **Amen.**

The newly consecrated come before the bishop, who gives
each a copy of the liturgy of the hours. After receiving it, they
return to their places and remain standing.

---

69. Then, if appropriate, this or some other suitable antiphon
is sung.

I am espoused to him whom the angels serve;
sun and moon stand in wonder at his glory.

If possible, all those newly consecrated sing the antiphon
together, otherwise the choir sings it.

Or:
[151] (For the giving of the veil. The rite is omitted if those
consecrated have already received the veil canonically.) After
the prayer of consecration the bishop and the people sit. The
newly consecrated stand and, accompanied by the consecrated or lay women mentioned above, come before the
bishop. He gives the veil to each one, saying:

Receive this veil,
by which you are to show
that you have been chosen from other women
to be dedicated to the service of Christ
and of his body, which is the Church.
Each one replies: **Amen.**

After receiving the veil each one returns to her place and remains standing. When all have received their veils, they sing the antiphon:

I will raise my mind and heart to you, O Lord,
that I may be holy in body and in spirit.

The choir may begin the antiphon after the veil has been given to the first or second one. It may be repeated after one or more verses of a suitable psalm or canticle.

[152] (For the giving of the ring.) When all have received the veil, the rings are given in the following way: those consecrated come before the bishop in the same order as before. Then he gives each one her ring, saying:

Receive the ring
that marks you as a bride of Christ.
Keep unstained your fidelity to your Bridegroom,
that you may one day be admitted to the wedding feast
    of everlasting joy.
Each one replies: **Amen.**

PRESENTATION OF THE LITURGY OF THE HOURS

[153] Then, if it seems appropriate, the bishop gives the newly consecrated the book containing the prayer of the Church, saying these or similar words:

Receive the book of the liturgy of the hours,
the prayer of the Church;
may the praise of our heavenly Father
be always on your lips;
pray without ceasing
for the salvation of the whole world.
Each replies: **Amen.**

Each returns to her place.

---

[154] After all have received the insignia of profession, those consecrated sing the antiphon:

I am espoused to him whom the angels serve; sun and moon stand in wonder at his glory.

If appropriate the choir may sing the antiphon after the ring has been given to the first or second person. It may be repeated after one or more verses of a suitable psalm or canticle.

SIGN OF ACCEPTANCE

70. After this, if it is customary or seems opportune, there may be a ceremony to mark the fact that the newly professed religious have been admitted as lifelong members of the religious family. This can take the form of a suitable statement by the superior or of the sign of peace.

The superior says these or similar words:
We confirm that you are now one with us as members of this religious community of N., sharing all things common with us now and in the future.

The members of the community manifest their assent, saying:
Amen.

Or:
71. The above may be omitted, and the bishop may give the sign of peace. The superior expresses sisterly love for the newly professed by the sign of peace or in some other way, according to the custom of the religious community or monastery. Meanwhile the choir and the people may sing the following antiphon with Psalm 84.

How lovely is your dwelling place, O Lord of power and might.
My soul is longing and fainting for the courts of the Lord.

Any other appropriate song may be sung.

If the sign of peace is given here, it is omitted before communion.

72. After this the newly consecrated return to their places in the sanctuary and the Mass continues.

LITURGY OF THE EUCHARIST

73. During the preparation of the gifts, some of those newly consecrated may bring to the altar the bread, wine, and water for the eucharistic sacrifice.

74. In the eucharistic prayers the offering of those newly consecrated may be mentioned (see Ritual Masses, Consecration to a Life of Virginity).

75. If the sign of peace has not already been given, the bishop now gives it in some suitable form to those newly consecrated.

76. After the bishop has received the body and blood of Christ, the newly consecrated come to the altar to receive communion under both kinds.

Their parents, relatives, friends, and fellow religious may also receive communion under both kinds.

CONCLUDING RITE

SOLEMN BLESSING

77. When the prayer after communion has been said, the newly consecrated stand before the altar. The bishop faces them and sings or says one of the following:

**The almighty Father
has poured into your hearts
the desire to live a life of holy virginity.
May he keep you safe under his protection.
℟. Amen.**

**May the Lord Jesus Christ,
with whose sacred heart
the hearts of virgins are united,
fill you with his divine love.
℟. Amen.**

**May the Holy Spirit,
by whom the Virgin Mary conceived her Son,
today consecrated your hearts**

**and fill you with a burning desire
to serve God and his Church.**
℟. **Amen.**

Finally he blesses the whole congregation:
**May almighty God,
the Father, and the Son, ✠ and the Holy Spirit,
bless all of you who have taken part in this celebration.**
℟. **Amen.**

Or [155, 156]:
**God inspires all holy desires and brings them to ful-
   fillment.
May he protect you always by his grace
so that you may fulfill the duties of your vocation
with a faithful heart.**
℟. **Amen.**

**May he make those bonds
with which he has bound you to Christ on earth
endure for ever in heavenly love.**
℟. **Amen.**

Finally he blesses the whole congregation:
**May almighty God,
the Father, and the Son, ✠ and the Holy Spirit,
bless all of you who have taken part in this celebration.**
℟. **Amen.**

80. After the blessing by the bishop, those newly consecrated
may take their candles. The choir and the people sing an
appropriate song or a canticle of praise, and the procession is
formed as at the beginning.

CHAPTER IV

RITE OF COMMISSIONING SPECIAL MINISTERS OF HOLY COMMUNION

1. Persons authorized to distribute holy communion in special circumstances should be commissioned by the local Ordinary or his delegate[1] according to the following rite. The rite should take place in the presence of the people during Mass or outside Mass.

A. DURING MASS

2. In the homily the celebrant first explains the reason for this ministry and then presents to the people those chosen to serve as special ministers, using these or similar words:

Dear friends in Christ,

Our brothers and sisters N.[*] and N. are to be entrusted with administering the eucharist, with taking communion to the sick, and with giving it as viaticum to the dying.

The celebrant pauses, and then addresses the candidates:

In this ministry, you must be examples of Christian living in faith and conduct; you must strive to grow in holiness through this sacrament of unity and love. Remember that, though many, we are one body because we share the one bread and one cup.

As ministers of holy communion be, therefore, especially observant of the Lord's command to love your neighbor. For when he gave his body as food to his disciples, he said to them: "This is my commandment, that you should love one another as I have loved you."

[1]See instruction *Immensae caritatis* I, nos. 1, 6.
[*]This reference may be modified according to circumstances.

3. After the address the candidates stand before the celebrant, who asks them these questions:

Are you resolved to undertake the office of giving the body and blood of the Lord to your brothers and sisters, and so serve to build up the Church?
℞. **I am.**

Are you resolved to administer the holy eucharist with the utmost care and reverence?
℞. **I am.**

4. All stand. The candidates kneel and the celebrant invites the faithful to pray:

Dear friends in Christ,

Let us pray with confidence to the Father; let us ask him to bestow his blessings on our brothers and sisters, chosen to be ministers of the eucharist:

Pause for silent prayer. The celebrant then continues:

Merciful Father,
creator and guide of your family,
bless ✟ our brothers and sisters N. and N.

May they faithfully give the bread of life
to your people.

Strengthened by this sacrament,
may they come at last
to the banquet of heaven.

We ask this through Christ our Lord.
℞. **Amen.**

5. The general intercessions should include an intention for the newly-commissioned ministers.

6. In the procession at the presentation of gifts, the newly-commissioned ministers carry the vessels with the bread and wine, and at communion may receive the eucharist under both kinds.

B. OUTSIDE MASS

7. When the people are assembled an appropriate song is sung. The celebrant greets the people. There normally follows a short liturgy of the Word. The readings and chants are taken, either in whole or in part, from the liturgy of the day or from those given in Chapter V.

8. The rite continues as above, nos. 2-5.

9. Finally, the celebrant blesses the people and dismisses them in the usual way. The rite concludes with an appropriate song.

RITE OF COMMISSIONING A SPECIAL MINISTER TO DISTRIBUTE HOLY COMMUNION ON A SINGLE OCCASION

10. A person who, in a case of real necessity is authorized to distribute holy communion on a single occasion[1] should normally be commissioned according to the following rite.

11. During the breaking of the bread and the commingling, the person who is to distribute holy communion comes to the altar and stands before the celebrant. After the **Lamb of God** the priest blesses him/her with these words:

**Today you are to distribute
the body and blood of Christ
to your brothers and sisters.
May the Lord bless ✛ you, N.
℟. Amen.**

12. When the priest has himself received communion in the usual way, he gives communion to the minister of the eucharist. Then he gives him/her the paten or other vessel with the hosts. They then go to give communion to the people.

[1]See instruction *Immensae caritatis* I, nos. 2, 6.

RITE OF DISTRIBUTING HOLY COMMUNION BY A SPECIAL MINISTER

13. A special minister of holy communion should wear the vestments customary in the country, or clothing in keeping with this sacred ministry.

14. In distributing holy communion during Mass, the minister holds the host slightly raised and says:

The body of Christ.

The communicant answers: **Amen,** and receives it.

After all have received communion, the minister of the eucharist cleanses his/her fingers over the paten and, if necessary, washes them and then returns to his/her place.

15. In distributing holy communion outside Mass, the special minister is to follow the rite given in the Roman Ritual: Holy Communion and Worship of the Eucharist outside Mass.

CHAPTER V

TEXTS FOR USE IN BLESSING OF PERSONS

BIBLICAL READINGS

BLESSING OF AN ABBOT OR ABBESS

The readings are taken in whole or in part from the Mass of the day or from the texts listed below.

READING FROM THE OLD TESTAMENT (L 779)

1. **Proverbs 2:1-9**
Incline your heart to understanding.

2. **Proverbs 4:7-13**
I will point out to you the way of wisdom.

READING FROM THE NEW TESTAMENT (L 780)

1. **Acts 2:42-47**
All those who believed were equal and held everything in common.

2. **Ephesians 4:1-6**
Do all you can to preserve the unity of the Spirit in the bond of peace.

3. **Colossians 3:12-17**
Love one another: that is the bond of perfection.

4. **Hebrews 13:1-2, 7-8, 17-18**
Be obedient and behave honorably. Pray for us.

5. **I Peter 5:1-4**
Be the shepherds of those entrusted to you. .

RESPONSORIAL PSALM (L 781)

1. Psalm 1:1-2, 3, 4 and 6
℟. (Psalm 40:5a) **Happy are they who hope in the Lord.**

2. Psalm 34:2-3, 4-5, 10-11, 12-13
℟. (12) **Listen to me, my children: I will teach you to honor the Lord.**

3. Psalm 92:2-3, 5-6, 13-14, 15-16
℟. (see 2a) **Lord, it is good to give thanks to you.**

ALLELUIA VERSE AND VERSE BEFORE THE GOSPEL
(L 782)

1. Matthew 23:9a, 10b
**You have one Father, your Father in heaven;
you have one teacher, the Lord Jesus Christ!**

2. Colossians 3:15
**May the peace of Christ rule in your hearts,
that peace to which all of you are called as one body.**

GOSPEL (L 783)

1. **Matthew 23:8-12**
The greater among you must be your servant.

2. **Luke 12:35-44**
The master will place him at the head of his household.

3. **Luke 22:24-27**
I am here among you as one who serves.

CONSECRATION TO A LIFE OF VIRGINITY

The readings are taken in whole or in part from the Mass of
the day or from the texts listed below.

READING FROM THE OLD TESTAMENT (L 784)

1. **Genesis 12:1-4a**
Leave your country, your family, and come.

2. **1 Samuel 3:1-10**
Speak, Lord, your servant is listening.

3. **1 Kings 19:4-9a, 11-15a**
Go out and stand on the mountain before the Lord.

4. **1 Kings 19:16b, 19-21**
Elisha left and followed Elijah.

5. **Song of Songs 2:8-14**
Rise, my love, and come.

6. **Song of Songs 8:6-7**
Love is as strong as death.

7. **Isaiah 44:1-5**
One shall say, I am the Lord's.

8. Isaiah 61:9-11
I exult for joy in the Lord.

9. Jeremiah 31:31-37
A new covenant.

10. Hosea 2:14, 19-20 (Hebrew: 16, 21-22)
I will betroth you to myself for ever.

READING FROM THE NEW TESTAMENT (L 785)

1. Acts 2:42-47
All those who believed were equal and held everything in common.

2. Acts 4:32-35
One heart and one soul.

3. Romans 6:3-11
Let us walk in newness of life.

4. Romans 12:1-13
Offer your bodies as a living, holy sacrifice, truly pleasing to God.

5. 1 Corinthians 1:22-31
To many, preaching a crucified Christ is madness; to us, it is the power of God.

6. 1 Corinthians 7:25-35
An unmarried woman can devote herself to the Lord's work.

7. Ephesians 1:3-14
The Father chose us in Christ to be holy and spotless in love.

8. Philippians 2:1-4
Be united in your convictions and in your love.

9. Philippians 3:8-14
I look on everything as useless if only I can know Christ.

10. Colossians 3:1-4
Let your thoughts be on heavenly things, not on the things that are of the earth.

11. Colossians 3:12-17
Above everything, have love for each other because that is the bond of perfection.

12. Thessalonians 4:1-3a, 7-12
What God wants is for you to be holy.

13. **1 Peter 1:3-9**
You have not seen the Christ, yet you love him.

14. **1 John 4:7-16**
As long as we love one another, God will live in us.

15. **Revelation 3:14b, 20-22**
I will share a meal side by side with him.

16. **Revelation 22:12-14, 16-17, 20**
Come, Lord Jesus!

RESPONSORIAL PSALM

1. Psalm 24:1-2, 3-4ab, 5-6
℟. (6) **Lord, this is the people that longs to see your face.**

2. Psalm 27:1, 4, 5, 8b-9abc, 9d and 11
℟. (8b) **I long to see your face, O Lord.**

3. Psalm 33:2-3, 4-5, 11-12, 13-14, 18-19, 20-21
℟. (12b) **Happy the people the Lord has chosen to be his own.**

4. Psalm 34:2-3, 4-5, 6-7, 8-9
or: Psalm 34:10-11, 12-13, 14-15, 17 and 19
℟. (2a) **I will bless the Lord at all times.**
or: ℟. (9a) **Taste and see the goodness of the Lord.**

5. Psalm 40:2 and 4ab, 7-8a, 8b-9, 10, 12
℟. (8a and 9a) **Here am I, Lord: I come to do your will.**

6. Psalm 45:11-12, 14-15, 16-17
℟. (Matthew 25:6) **The bridegroom is here; let us go out to meet Christ the Lord.**

7. Psalm 63:2, 3-4, 5-6, 8-9
℟. (2b) **My soul is thirsting for you, O Lord my God.**

8. Psalm 84:3, 4, 5-6a and 8a, 11, 12
℟. (2) **How lovely is your dwelling place, Lord, mighty God!**

9. Psalm 100:2, 3, 4, 5
℟. (2c) **Come with joy into the presence of the Lord.**

ALLELUIA VERSE AND VERSE BEFORE THE GOSPEL
(L 787)

1. Psalm 133:1
See how good it is, how pleasant, that all live together in unity.

2. Matthew 11:25
Blessed are you, Father, Lord of heaven and earth;
you have revealed to little ones the mysteries of the king-
dom.

3. John 13:34
I give you a new commandment:
love one another as I have loved you.

4. John 15:5
I am the vine and you are the branches, says the Lord:
those who live in me, and I in them, will bear much fruit.

5. 2 Corinthians 8:9
Jesus Christ was rich but he became poor,
to make you rich out of his poverty.

6. Galatians 6:14
My only glory is the cross of our Lord Jesus Christ,
which crucifies the world to me and me to the world.

7. Philippians 3:8-9
I count all things worthless but this;
to gain Jesus Christ and to be found in him.

GOSPEL (L 788)

1. **Matthew 11:25-30**
You have hidden these things from the learned and clever
and revealed them to children.

2. **Matthew 16:24-27**
Anyone who loses his life for my sake will find it.

3. **Matthew 19:3-12**
There are some persons who choose to remain unmarried for
the sake of the kingdom of heaven.

4. **Matthew 19:16-26**
If you wish to be perfect, go and sell everything you have and
come, follow me.

5. **Matthew 25:1-13**
Look, the bridegroom is coming; go out and meet him.

6. **Mark 3:31-35**
Whoever does the will of God is my brother, my sister, and
my mother.

7. Mark 10:24b-30
We have left everything and have followed you.

8. Luke 1:26-38
I am the handmaid of the Lord.

9. Luke 9:57-62
Once the hand is laid on the plow, no one who looks back is fit for the kingdom of God.

10. Luke 10:38-42
Jesus accepts the hospitality of Martha and praises the attentiveness of Mary.

11. Luke 11:27-28
Happy are they who hear the word of God and keep it.

12. John 12:24-26
If a grain of wheat falls on the ground and dies, it yields a rich harvest.

13. John 15:1-8
All who remain in me, with me in them, bear fruit in plenty.

14. John 15:9-17
You are my friends if you do what I command you.

15. John 17:20-26
I want those you have given me to be with me where I am.

COMMISSIONING SPECIAL MINISTERS IN THE RITE OUTSIDE MASS

READINGS FROM THE OLD TESTAMENT

1. Genesis 14:18-20 (L 170)
Melchisedech brought bread and wine.

2. Exodus 16:2-4, 12-15 (L 114)
I will rain bread from heaven upon you.

3. Exodus 24:3-8 (L 169)
This is the blood of the covenant that the Lord has made with you.

4. Deuteronomy 8:2-3, 14b-16a (L 168)
He gave you food which you and your fathers did not know.

5. **1 Kings 19:4-8** (L 117)
Strengthened by the food, he walked to the mountain of the Lord.

6. **Proverbs 9:1-6** (L 120)
Come and eat my bread, drink the wine I have prepared.

READINGS FROM THE NEW TESTAMENT

1. **Acts 2:42-47** (L 44)
All who believed shared everything in common.

2. **Acts 10:34a, 37-43** (L 43)
We have eaten and drunk with him after his resurrection from the dead.

3. **1 Corinthians 10:16-17** (L 168)
Though we are many, we form a single body because we share this one loaf.

4. **1 Corinthians 11:23-26** (L 40)
Until the Lord comes, every time you eat this bread and drink this cup, you proclaim his death.

5. **Hebrews 9:11-15** (L 169)
The blood of Christ will purify our inner selves.

RESPONSORIAL PSALMS

1. Psalm 23:1-3a, 3b-4, 5-6 (L 31)
℟. (1) **The Lord is my shepherd; there is nothing I shall want.**

2. Psalm 34:2-3, 4-5, 6-7 (L 33)
℟. (9a) **Taste and see the goodness of the Lord.**

3. Psalm 78:3, 4bc, 23-24, 25, 54 (L 114)
℟. (24b) **The Lord gave them bread from heaven.**

4. Psalm 145:10-11, 15-16, 17-18 (L 111)
℟. (16) **The hand of the Lord feeds us; he answers all our needs.**

5. Psalm 147:12-13, 14-15, 19-20 (L 906)
℟. (John 6:59b) **Whoever eats this bread will live for ever.**

ALLELUIA VERSE AND VERSE BEFORE THE GOSPEL

1. John 6:57 (L 908)
Whoever eats my flesh and drinks my blood will live in me and I in him, says the Lord.

2. John 6:58 (L 908)
As the living Father sent me, and I live because of the Father, so whoever feeds on me lives because of me.

3. John 6:35
The Lord says: I am the bread of life. Anyone who comes to me will never be hungry; anyone who believes in me will never thirst.

4. John 6:51-52 (L 168)
I am the living bread from heaven, says the Lord; anyone who eats this bread will live for ever.

GOSPEL

1. **Mark 14:12-16, 22-26 (L 169)**
This is my body. This is my blood.

2. **Luke 9:11b-17 (L 170)**
They all ate and were filled.

3. **Luke 24:13-35 (L 47)**
They had recognized him in the breaking of the bread.

4. **John 6:1-15 (L 111)**
He distributed to those who were seated as much as they wanted.

5. **John 6:24-35 (L 114)**
Anyone who comes to me will never be hungry; anyone who believes in me will never thirst.

6. **John 6:41-52 (L 117)**
I am the living bread that came down from heaven.

7. **John 6:51-59 (L 168)**
My flesh is real food and my blood is real drink.

8. **John 21:1-14 (L 265)**
Jesus came and took the bread and gave it to them.

LITANY OF THE SAINTS

BLESSING OF AN ABBOT OR ABBESS

The cantors begin the litany; they may add, at the proper place, names of other saints (for example, the patron saint, the titular of the church, the founder of the church, the patron saint of the abbot-elect or abbess-elect) or petitions suitable to the occasion.

Lord, have mercy   Lord, have mercy
Christ, have mercy   Christ, have mercy
Lord, have mercy   Lord, have mercy

Holy Mary, Mother of God   pray for us
Saint Michael   pray for us
Holy angels of God   pray for us
Saint John the Baptist   pray for us
Saint Joseph   pray for us
Saint Peter and Saint Paul   pray for us
Saint Andrew   pray for us
Saint John   pray for us
Saint Mary Magdalene   pray for us
Saint Stephen   pray for us
Saint Ignatius   pray for us
Saint Lawrence   pray for us
Saint Perpetua and Saint Felicity   pray for us
Saint Agnes   pray for us
Saint Gregory   pray for us
Saint Augustine   pray for us
Saint Athanasius   pray for us
Saint Basil   pray for us
Saint Martin   pray for us
Saint Anthony   pray for us
Saint Benedict   pray for us
Saint Columban   pray for us
Saint Bede   pray for us
Saint Romuald   pray for us
Saint Bruno   pray for us

Saint Bernard   pray for us
Saint Francis   pray for us
Saint Dominic   pray for us
Saint Scholastica   pray for us
Saint Clare   pray for us
Saint Teresa   pray for us
All holy men and women   pray for us

Lord, be merciful   Lord, save your people
From all evil   Lord, save your people
From every sin   Lord, save your people
From everlasting death   Lord, save your people
By your coming as man   Lord, save your people
By your death and rising to a new life   Lord, save your
 people
By your gift of the Holy Spirit   Lord, save your people
Be merciful to us sinners   Lord, hear our prayer
Guide and protect your holy Church   Lord, hear our
 prayer
Keep the pope and all the clergy in faithful service
 to your Church   Lord, hear our prayer
Bring all peoples together in trust and peace
 Lord, hear our prayer
Give all who profess the counsels of the Gospel a
 deeper share in the work of redemption   Lord,
 hear our prayer
Grant that all religious communities may live and grow
 in the love of Christ and the spirit of their found-
 ers   Lord, hear our prayer
Strengthen us in your service   Lord, hear our prayer
Bless and sustain your servant, chosen to be abbot (ab-
 bess)   Lord, hear our prayer
Jesus, Son of the living God   Lord, hear our prayer
Christ, hear us   Christ hear us
Lord Jesus, hear our prayer   Lord Jesus, hear our
 prayer

CONSECRATION TO A LIFE OF VIRGINITY

The cantors begin the litany. At the proper place they may add the names of other saints who are specially venerated by the people or petitions suitable to the occasion.

Lord, have mercy   Lord, have mercy
Christ, have mercy   Christ, have mercy
Lord, have mercy   Lord, have mercy

Holy Mary   pray for us
Mother of God   pray for us
Most honored of all virgins   pray for us
Saint Michael   pray for us
Holy angels of God   pray for us
Saint John the Baptist   pray for us
Saint Joseph   pray for us
Saint Peter and Saint Paul   pray for us
Saint John   pray for us
Saint Mary Magdalene   pray for us
Saint Stephen and Saint Lawrence   pray for us
Saint Perpetua and Saint Felicity   pray for us
Saint Agnes   pray for us
Saint Maria Goretti   pray for us
Saint Athanasius   pray for us
Saint Ambrose   pray for us
Saint Augustine   pray for us
Saint Jerome   pray for us
Saint Benedict   pray for us
Saint Dominic and Saint Francis   pray for us
Saint Macrina   pray for us
Saint Scholastica   pray for us
Saint Clare and Saint Catherine   pray for us
Saint Teresa of Avila   pray for us
Saint Rose of Lima   pray for us
Saint Louise Marillac   pray for us
Saint Margaret Mary Alacoque   pray for us
All holy men and women   pray for us

Lord, be merciful   Lord, save your people
From all evil   Lord, save your people
From every sin   Lord, save your people
From everlasting death   Lord, save your people
By your coming as man   Lord, save your people
By your death and rising to new life   Lord, save your people
By your gift of the Holy Spirit   Lord, save your people
Be merciful to us sinners   Lord, hear our prayer
Give to your servant Pope N., and to all other bishops, the grace of growing daily in the likeness of Christ, Bridegroom of the Church   Lord, hear our prayer
Maintain and foster in your Church love for holy virginity   Lord, hear our prayer
Strengthen in Christ's faithful people hope of a glorious resurrection and of the life of the world to come   Lord, hear our prayer
Give to all nations true harmony and peace   Lord, hear our prayer
Increase in holiness and in number those who follow the counsels of the Gospel   Lord, hear our prayer
Reward a hundredfold the parents of your handmaids for the sacrifice they have made   Lord, hear our prayer
Bless these handmaids, make them holy, and consecrate them to your service   Lord, hear our prayer
Jesus, Son of the living God   Lord, hear our prayer
Christ, hear us   Christ, hear us
Lord Jesus, hear our prayer   Lord Jesus, hear our prayer

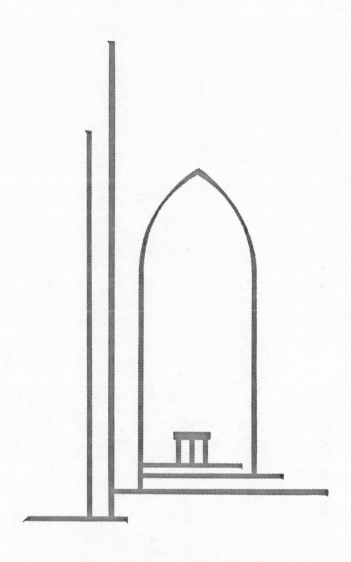

DEDICATION OF A CHURCH

AND AN ALTAR

DEDICATION OF A CHURCH AND AN ALTAR

Decree

CHAPTER III
DEDICATION OF A CHURCH ALREADY IN
GENERAL USE FOR SACRED CELEBRATIONS

Introduction (1-2)

Rite of Dedication (3-40)

Introductory Rites (3-12)
Entrance into the Church (3-7)
Blessing and Sprinkling of Water (8-10)
Hymn (11)
Opening Prayer (12)

Liturgy of the Word (13-16)

Prayer of Dedication and the Anointings (17-31)
Invitation to Prayer (17)
Litany of the Saints (18-20)
Depositing of the Relics (21)
Prayer of Dedication (22)
Anointing of the Altar and Walls of the Church (23-25)
Incensation of the Altar and the Church (26-28)
Lighting of the Altar and the Church (29-31)

Liturgy of the Eucharist (32-40)
Prayer over the Gifts (34)
Eucharistic Prayer (35-36)
[Inauguration of the Blessed Sacrament Chapel (36)]
Prayer after Communion (38)
Blessing and Dismissal (39-40)

CHAPTER IV
DEDICATION OF AN ALTAR

Introduction (1-30)

Nature and Dignity of the Altar (1-5)

Building of an Altar (6-11)

CHAPTER V
BLESSING OF A CHURCH

Introduction (1-7)

Rite of Blessing (8-28)

Introductory Rites (8-15)
  Entrance into the Church (8-9)
  Blessing and Sprinkling of Water (10-13)
  Hymn (14)
  Opening Prayer (15)

Liturgy of the Word (16-19)

Blessing of the Altar (20-22)

Liturgy of the Eucharist (23-26)
  Blessing and Dismissal (27-28)

CHAPTER VI
BLESSING OF AN ALTAR

Introduction (1-7)

Rite of Blessing (8-13)

CHAPTER VII
BLESSING OF A CHALICE AND PATEN

Introduction (1-4)

Rite of Blessing within Mass (5-14)

Rite of Blessing outside Mass (15-23)

CHAPTER VIII
LITANY OF THE SAINTS

SACRED CONGREGATION FOR
THE SACRAMENTS AND
DIVINE WORSHIP

Prot. no. CD 300/77

DECREE

The rite for the dedication of a church and an altar is properly considered among the most solemn liturgical services. A church is the place where the Christian community is gathered to hear the word of God, to offer prayers of intercession and praise to God, and above all to celebrate the holy mysteries; and it is the place where the holy sacrament of the eucharist is kept. Thus it stands as a special kind of image of the Church itself, which is God's temple built from living stones. And the altar of a church, where the holy people of God gathers to take part in the Lord's sacrifice and to be refreshed by the heavenly meal, stands as a sign of Christ himself, who is the priest, the victim, and the altar of his own sacrifice.

These rites, found in the second book of the Roman Pontifical, were revised and simplified in 1961. Nevertheless it appeared necessary to revise the rites again and to adapt them to contemporary conditions in view of the purpose and the norms of the liturgical restoration that the Second Vatican Council set in motion and fostered.

Pope Paul VI has by his authority approved this rite of *Dedication of a Church and an Altar*, prepared by the Congregation for the Sacraments and Divine Worship. He has ordered it to be published and prescribed that it replace the rites now contained in the second book of the Roman Pontifical.

This congregation, by mandate of the supreme pontiff, therefore publishes this rite of *Dedication of a Church and an Altar*. In the Latin version it will take effect, as soon as it appears; in the vernaculars it will take effect, after the translations have been confirmed and approved by the Apostolic See, on the day determined by the conferences of bishops.

Anything to the contrary notwithstanding.

From the office of the Congregation for the Sacraments and Divine Worship, May 29, 1977, Pentecost.

James R. Cardinal Knox
Prefect

✠ Antonio Innocenti
Titular Archbishop of Eclano
Secretary

CHAPTER I

LAYING OF A FOUNDATION STONE
OR COMMENCEMENT OF WORK
ON THE BUILDING OF A CHURCH

INTRODUCTION

1. When the building of a new church begins, it is desirable
to celebrate a rite to ask God's blessing on the work which is
to be undertaken and to remind the people that the structure
built of stone will be a visible sign of the living Church, God's
building, which is formed of the people themselves.[1]

In accordance with liturgical tradition, this rite consists of the
blessing of the site of the new church and the blessing and the
laying of the foundation stone. If there is to be no foundation
stone because of the particular style or plan of the building,
the rite of the blessing of the site of the new church should
still be celebrated to dedicate the beginning of this work to
God.

2. The rite for the laying of a foundation stone or for beginning a new church may be celebrated on any day except during the Easter triduum. However, insofar as possible a day
should be chosen which would be convenient for the participation of the people.

3. It is appropriate that the rite be celebrated by the bishop of
the diocese. If he cannot do this, he shall entrust the function
to another bishop or a priest, especially to one who is his
associate and assistant in the pastoral care of the diocese or of
the community for which the new church is to be built.

4. Notice of the day and hour of the celebration should be
given to the people in good time. The parish priest (pastor) or
others concerned should instruct them in the meaning of the
rite and the reverence to be shown towards the church which
is to be built for them.

[1]See 1 Corinthians 3:9, Second Vatican Council, const. on the Church, no.
6:*AAS* 57 (1965) 8-9.

It is also desirable that the people be asked to assist generously and willingly in the building of the church.

5. Insofar as possible, the area for the erection of the church should be marked out well. It should be possible to walk around it conveniently.

6. In the place where the altar will be located, a wooden cross of appropriate height is placed.

7. For the celebration of the rite the following should be prepared:
—*The Roman Pontifical;*
—*The Lectionary;*
—a chair for the bishop;
—depending upon the circumstances, the foundation stone, which is traditionally rectangular, and a cornerstone, together with cement and the tools for placing the stone in the foundation;
—a vessel of holy water and a sprinkler;
—a censer, incense boat, and spoon;
—a cross to be carried in the procession and torches for the ministers.

Speaking equipment should be so arranged that the assembly may clearly hear the readings, prayers, and instructions.

8. For the celebration of the rite the vestments are white or of some festive color. The following should be prepared:
—for the bishop: alb, stole, cope, miter, and pastoral staff;
—for the priest, when he presides over the celebration: alb, stole, and cope;
—for the deacons: albs, stoles, and, if opportune, dalmatics;
—for other ministers: albs or other lawfully approved dress.

RITE OF BLESSING

APPROACH TO THE CONSTRUCTION SITE

9. The assembly of the people and the approach to the construction site take place, according to circumstances of time and place, in one of the two ways described below.

A. First Form: Procession

10. At a convenient hour the people assemble in a suitable place, from which they will go in procession to the site.

11. The bishop, in his vestments and with the miter and pastoral staff, proceeds with the ministers to the place where the people are assembled. Putting aside the pastoral staff and miter he greets the people, saying:

The grace of our Lord Jesus Christ
and the love of God
and the fellowship of the Holy Spirit
be with you all.
R̷. And also with you.

Other suitable words taken preferably from sacred Scripture may be used.

12. Then the bishop briefly instructs the people on their participation in the celebration and explains to them the meaning of the rite.

13. When the bishop has finished the instruction, he says:

Let us pray.

All pray in silence for a brief period. The bishop then continues:

Lord,
you built a holy Church,
founded upon the apostles
with Jesus Christ its cornerstone.

Grant that your people,
gathered in your name,
may fear and love you
and grow as the temple of your glory.

May they always follow you,
until, with you at their head,
they arrive at last in your heavenly city.

We ask this through Christ our Lord.
R̷. Amen.

14. When the bishop has finished the prayer, he receives the miter and pastoral staff, and, should the occasion demand, the deacon says:

Let us go forth in peace.

The procession takes place in the usual way: the crossbearer leads between two servers with lighted torches; the clergy follow, then the bishop with the assisting deacons and other ministers, and lastly, the congregation. As the procession proceeds the following anthiphon is sung with Psalm 84.

My soul is yearning for the courts of the Lord (alleluia).

Another appropriate song may be sung.

Then the reading of the word of God takes place as described below in nos. 18-22.

B. Second Form: Station at the Construction Site of the New Church

15. If the procession cannot take place or seems inappropriate, the people assemble at the construction site of the new church. When the people are assembled the following acclamation is sung.

Eternal peace be yours.
Let the Father's peace unite you in his love.

Abiding peace be yours.
Let the Word be peace to those who bear his name.

Lasting peace be yours.
Let the Spirit's peace comfort all the world.

Another appropriate song may be sung.

Meanwhile, the bishop, in his vestments and with miter and pastoral staff, approaches the people. Putting aside the pastoral staff and miter, he greets the people, saying:

The grace of our Lord Jesus Christ
and the love of God
and the fellowship of the Holy Spirit
be with you all.
℟. And also with you.

Other suitable words taken preferably from sacred Scripture may be used.

16. Then the bishop briefly instructs the people on their participation in the celebration and explains to them the meaning of the rite.

17. When the bishop has finished the instruction, he says:

Let us pray.

All pray in silence for a brief period. The bishop then continues:

Lord,
you built a holy Church,
founded upon the apostles
with Jesus Christ its cornerstone.

Grant that your people,
gathered in your name,
may fear and love you
and grow as the temple of your glory.

May they always follow you,
until, with you at their head,
they arrive at last in your heavenly city.

We ask this through Christ our Lord.
℟. Amen.

READING OF THE WORD OF GOD

18. Then one or more relevant passages of sacred Scripture are read, chosen especially from those in *The Lectionary* (nos. 704 and 706) for the rite of the dedication of a church, with an appropriate intervening responsorial psalm or another appropriate song. However, it is in keeping with the occasion, especially if a foundation stone is used in the rite, to read one of the following passages.

19. READINGS FROM SACRED SCRIPTURE

1. **1 Kings 5:2-18**
At the king's orders they quarried huge stones, special stones, for the laying of the temple foundations.

2. **Isaiah 28:16-17**
See how I lay in Zion a stone of witness, a precious cornerstone, a foundation stone.

3. **Acts 4:8-12**
Jesus, the one you crucified, has proved to be the keystone.

4. **1 Corinthians 10:1-6**
And that rock was Christ.

20. RESPONSORIAL PSALMS

1. Psalm 24:1-2, 3-4ab, 5-6
℟. (2 Chronicles 7:16a) **I have chosen and sanctified this place.**

2. Psalm 42:3, 5bcd; Psalm 43:3-4
℟. (See Psalm 43:3) **Lord, may your truth lead me to your holy mountain.**

3. Psalm 87:1-3, 4-6, 6-7
℟. (See 1) **The city of God is founded on the holy mountains.**

4. Psalm 100:2, 3, 5
℟. (See Ezechiel 37:27) **I will make my dwelling place among the people.**

5. Psalm 118:1-2, 16ab-17, 22-23
℟. (See 1 Corinthians 3:11) **There is no other foundation than Christ Jesus.**

21. GOSPEL

1. **Matthew 7:21-29**
A house built on rock and a house built on sand.

2. **Matthew 16:13-18**
On this rock I will build my Church.

3. **Mark 12:1-12**
It was the stone rejected by the builders that became the keystone.

4. **Luke 6:46-49**
He laid the foundation on rock.

22. When the readings are finished the homily is given, in which the biblical readings are elucidated and the significance of the rite explained: Christ is the cornerstone of the Church, and the temple that is going to be built by the living Church of the community of believers will be at once the house of God and the house of God's people.

23. After the homily, according to the custom of the place, the document of the blessing of the foundation stone and of the beginning of the building of the church may be read; it is signed by the bishop and by representatives of those who are going to work on the building of the church, and together with the stone, is enclosed in the foundations.

BLESSING OF THE SITE OF THE NEW CHURCH

24. When the homily is finished, the bishop takes off the miter, rises, and blesses the site of the new church, saying:

Let us pray.

Lord,
you fill the entire world with your presence
that your name may be hallowed through all the earth.

Bless all those
who have worked or contributed
to provide this site (property, land)
on which a church will be built.

Today may they rejoice in a work just begun,
soon may they celebrate the sacraments in your temple,
and in time to come may they praise you for ever in
heaven.

We ask this through Christ our Lord.
℟. Amen.

25. Then the bishop puts on the miter and sprinkles the site of the new church with holy water. To do this he may stand in the middle of the site or go in procession around the foundations with the ministers; in the latter case the following antiphon is sung with Psalm 48.

The walls of Jerusalem will be made of precious
stones, and its towers built with gems (alleluia).

Another appropriate song may be sung.

BLESSING AND LAYING OF THE FOUNDATION STONE

26. When the site has been blessed, if a foundation stone is to be laid, it is blessed and placed in position as described below in nos. 27-29; otherwise the conclusion of the rite takes place immediately as indicated in nos. 30-31.

27. The bishop goes to the place where the foundation stone is to be laid and, taking off the miter, blesses the stone, saying:

Let us pray.

Father,
the prophet Daniel spoke of your Son,
as a stone wondrously hewn from a mountain.

The apostle Paul spoke of him,
as a stone firmly founded.

Bless ✠ this foundation stone
to be laid in Christ's name.

You appointed him
the beginning and the end of all things.

May this work begin, continue,
and be brought to fulfillment in him,
for he is Lord for ever and ever.
℟. Amen.

Then the bishop may sprinkle the stone with holy water and incense it. Afterward he receives the miter again.

28. When he has finished, the bishop lays the stone on the foundations in silence or, if he wishes, saying these or similar words:

With faith in Jesus Christ
we lay this stone
on which a church will rise.

May it be a place of sacrament
and a source of grace
to the glory of the Father
who with the Son and Holy Spirit
lives and reigns for ever and ever.
℟. Amen.

29. A stone mason then fixes the stone in with mortar. Meanwhile, if the occasion demands, the following antiphon is sung.

The house of the Lord is firmly built on solid rock (alleluia).

Another appropriate song may be sung.

CONCLUDING RITE

30. When the singing is finished, the bishop takes off the miter, and invites the people to pray the general intercessions, in these or similar words:

Brothers and sisters, now that we have laid the cornerstone of our new church, let us pray to God, our Father.

All pray in silence for a brief period.

That he may transform into a living temple of his glory all whom he has gathered here and who look upon Christ as the cornerstone of their faith, let us pray to the Lord:
℟. **Bless and watch over your Church, O Lord.**

That God in his power may overcome the division and sin which separate his people so that they may ultimately worship as one, let us pray to the Lord: ℟.

That he may ground upon the bedrock of his Church the faith of all those who have undertaken the work on this building, let us pray to the Lord: ℟.

That those who are prevented from building places of worship may bear witness to the Lord by conducting themselves as living temples of glory and faith, let us pray to the Lord: ℟.

That all here present may be cleansed by his divine power and come to share in the celebration of his holy mysteries, let us pray to the Lord: ℟.

Then the bishop may introduce the Lord's Prayer in these or similar words:

Let us join the voice of the Church with that of Christ in praying to the Father using those words which the Son has given us. And so, with one voice, let us say:

Our Father . . .

The bishop continues immediately:

**God of love,
we praise your holy name,
for you have made us your temple by baptism
and inspire us to build on earth
churches dedicated to your worship.**

**Look favorably upon your children,
for they have come with joy
to begin work on this new church.**

**Enable them to grow into the temple of your glory,
until, shaped anew by your grace,
they are gathered by your hand into your heavenly city.**

**We ask this through Christ our Lord.
℟. Amen.**

31. When the bishop has received the miter and pastoral staff, he blesses the people in the usual way.

The deacon dismisses them, saying:
**Go in peace.
℟. Thanks be to God.**

CHAPTER II

DEDICATION OF A CHURCH

INTRODUCTION

NATURE AND DIGNITY OF CHURCHES

1. Through his death and resurrection, Christ became the true and perfect temple[1] of the New Covenant, and gathered together a people to be his own.

This holy people, unified through the unity of the Father, Son, and Holy Spirit, is the Church,[2] that is, the temple of God built of living stones, where the Father is worshiped in spirit and in truth.[3]

Rightly, then, from early times the name "church" has also been given to the building in which the Christian community gathers to hear the word of God, to pray together, to celebrate the sacraments, and to participate in the eucharist.

2. Because the church is a visible building, it stands as a special sign of the pilgrim Church on earth and reflects the Church dwelling in heaven.

When a church is erected as a building destined solely and permanently for assembling the people of God and for carrying out sacred functions, it is fitting that it be dedicated to God with a solemn rite, in accordance with the ancient custom of the Church.

3. A church, as its nature requires, should be suitable for sacred celebrations. It should be dignified, evincing a noble beauty, not just costly display, and it should stand as a sign and symbol of heavenly things. The general plan of the sacred building should be such that it reflects in some way the whole assembly. It should allow for the distribution of all in due order and facilitate each one's proper function.

---

[1]See John 2:21.
[2]See Saint Cyprian, *The Lord's Prayer*, 23: PL 4, 553; Second Vatican Council, const. on the Church, no. 4: *AAS* 57 (1965) 7.
[3]See John 4:23.

Moreover, in what concerns the sanctuary, the altar, the chair, the lectern, and the place for the reservation of the blessed sacrament, the norms of the General Instruction of *The Roman Missal* are to be followed.[4]

Also, those norms must be carefully observed which concern things and places destined for the celebration of other sacraments, especially baptism and penance.[5]

TITULAR OF A CHURCH AND THE RELICS OF THE SAINTS TO BE PLACED IN IT

4. When a church is to be dedicated it must have a titular. Churches may have for their titular: the Blessed Trinity, our Lord Jesus Christ invoked according to a mystery of his life or a title already accepted in the sacred liturgy, the Holy Spirit, the Blessed Virgin Mary, likewise invoked according to some appellation already accepted in the sacred liturgy, one of the angels, or, finally, a saint inscribed in the Roman Martyrology or in an Appendix duly approved; but not a blessed, without an indult of the Apostolic See. A church should have one titular only, unless it is a question of saints who are inscribed together in the Calendar.

5. It is fitting that the tradition of the Roman liturgy should be preserved of placing relics of martyrs or other saints beneath the altar.[6] However, the following should be noted:
a) Relics intended for deposition should be of such a size that they can be recognized as parts of human bodies. Hence excessively small relics of one or more saints must not be deposited.
b) The greatest care must be taken to determine whether relics intended for deposition are authentic. It is better for an altar to be dedicated without relics than to have relics of doubtful credibility placed beneath it.
c) A reliquary must not be placed on the altar or in the table of the altar but beneath the table of the altar, as the design of the altar may allow.

[4]See *The Roman Missal*, General Instruction, nos. 253, 257, 258, 259-267, 271, 272, 276-277. See Roman Ritual, *Holy Communion and Worship of the Eucharist outside Mass*, nos. 6 and 9-11.
[5]See Roman Ritual, *Rite of Baptism for Children*, no. 25; *Rite of Penance*, no. 12.
[6]See *The Roman Missal*, General Instruction, no. 266.

CELEBRATION OF THE DEDICATION

MINISTER OF THE RITE

6. Since the bishop has been entrusted with the care of the particular Church, it is his responsibility to dedicate to God new churches built in his diocese.

If he cannot himself preside at the rite, he shall entrust this function to another bishop, especially to one who is his associate and assistant in the pastoral care of the community for which the church has been built; or, in altogether special circumstances, to a priest, to whom he shall give a special mandate.

CHOICE OF DAY

7. A day should be chosen for the dedication of the new church when as many of the people as possible can participate, especially Sunday. Since the theme of the dedication pervades this rite throughout, the dedication of a new church may not take place on days on which it is totally improper to disregard the mystery then commemorated: the Easter triduum, Christmas, Epiphany, Ascension, Pentecost, Ash Wednesday, the weekdays of Holy Week, and All Souls.

MASS OF THE DEDICATION

8. The celebration of the eucharist is inseparably bound up with the rite of the dedication of a church; so when a church is dedicated the liturgical texts of the day are omitted and texts proper to the rite are used for both the liturgy of the word and the liturgy of the eucharist.

9. It is fitting that the bishop should concelebrate the Mass with the priests who take part with him in the rite of dedication and with those who have been given the task of directing the parish or the community for which the church has been built.

OFFICE OF THE DEDICATION

10. The day on which a church is dedicated is kept as a solemnity in the church which is dedicated.

The office is that of the dedication of a church. The office begins with Evening Prayer I. When the rite of the depositing of relics takes place, it is highly recommended to keep a vigil at the relics of the martyr or saint which are to be placed under the altar; the best way of doing this is to have the Office of Readings taken from the Commons or from the appropriate Proper. But to encourage the participation of the people, the vigil, while observing what is normative,[7] may be suitably adapted.

PARTS OF THE RITE

A. Entrance into the Church

11. The rite of the dedication begins with the entrance into the church; this may take place in three ways; that way is to be used which seems to suit best the circumstances of time and place.

—*The procession* to the church to be dedicated: all assemble in a nearby church or other suitable place, from which the bishop, the ministers, and the congregation proceed to the church to be dedicated, praying and singing.

—*The solemn entrance:* if the procession cannot take place or seems inopportune, the community gathers at the entrance of the church.

—*The simple entrance:* the congregation assembles in the church itself; the bishop, the concelebrants, and the ministers come out from the sacristy in the usual way.

Two rites are most significant in the entrance into the new church:
a) The handing over of the church: representatives of those who have been involved in the building of the church hand it over to the bishop.
b) The sprinkling of the church: the bishop blesses water and with it sprinkles the people, who are the spiritual temple, then the walls of the church, and finally, the altar.

B. Liturgy of the Word

12. Three readings are used in the liturgy of the word. The texts are chosen from those in *The Lectionary* (nos. 704 and 706) for the rite of the dedication of a church.

In the first reading, even during the Easter Season, the passage of Nehemiah is always read which recounts the assembl-

---

[7]See *The Liturgy of the Hours*, General Instruction, nos. 70-73.

ing of the people of Jerusalem in the presence of Ezra the scribe to hear the proclamation of the law of God (Nehemiah 8:1-4a; 5-6, 8-10).

13. After the readings the bishop gives the homily, in which he explains the biblical readings and the meaning of the dedication of a church.

The profession of faith is said. The general intercessions are omitted since in their place the litany of the saints is sung.

C. Prayer of Dedication and the Anointing of the Church and the Altar

14. After the singing of the litany, if this is to be done, the relics of a martyr are deposited to denote the fact that the sacrifice of the members has its source in the sacrifice of the Head.[8] When relics of a martyr are not available, relics of another saint may be deposited in the altar.

15. The celebration of the eucharist is the most important rite, and the only necessary one, for the dedication of a church. Nevertheless, in accordance with the common tradition of the Church, both East and West, a special prayer of dedication is also said. This prayer declares the intention of dedicating the church to the Lord for all times and it asks for his blessing.

16. The rites of the anointing, incensation, covering, and lighting of the altar express in visible signs several aspects of that invisible work which the Lord accomplishes through the Church in its celebration of the divine mysteries, especially the eucharist.

a) The anointing of the altar and the walls of the church:
—In virtue of the anointing with chrism the altar becomes a symbol of Christ who, before all others, is and is called "The Anointed One"; for the Father anointed him with the Holy

---

[8]See *The Roman Missal*, Common of Martyrs 8, prayer over the gifts; Saint Ambrose, Epistula 22:13: PL 16, 1023: "Let the triumphant victims occupy the place where Christ is victim: he, however, who suffered for all, upon the altar; they, who have been redeemed by his sufferings, beneath the altar"; see Ps. Maximus of Turin, *Sermo* 78: PL 57, 689-690; Book of Revelation 6:9: "I saw underneath the altar the souls of all the people who had been killed on account of the word of God, for witnessing to it."

Spirit and constituted him the High Priest who on the altar of his body would offer the sacrifice of his life for the salvation of all;

—The anointing of the church signifies that it is given over entirely and perpetually to Christian worship. Twelve anointings are made in accordance with liturgical tradition, or, where it is more convenient, four signifying that the church is an image of the holy city of Jerusalem.

b) Incense is burned on the altar to signify that the sacrifice of Christ, which is there perpetuated in mystery, ascends to God as an odor of sweetness, and also as a sign that the prayers of the people rise up pleasing and acceptable, reaching to the throne of God.[9]

The incensation of the nave of the church indicates that the dedication makes it a house of prayer, but the People of God are incensed first, for it is the living temple in which each faithful member is a spiritual altar.[10]

c) The covering of the altar indicates that the Christian altar is the altar of the eucharistic sacrifice and the table of the Lord; standing around it priests and people, in one and the same action but with a difference of function, celebrate the memorial of the death and resurrection of Christ and partake in the Lord's Supper. For this reason the altar is prepared as the table of the sacrificial banquet and adorned as for a feast. Thus the decoration of the altar clearly signifies that it is the Lord's table at which all God's people meet with joy to be refreshed with divine food, namely the body and blood of Christ sacrificed.

d) The lighting of the altar, which is followed by the lighting of the church, teaches us that Christ is "a light to enlighten the nations,"[11] whose brightness shines out in the Church and through it upon the whole human family.

D. Celebration of the Eucharist

17. When the altar has been prepared, the bishop celebrates the eucharist, which is the principal and the most ancient part of the whole rite.[12] The celebration of the eucharist is in the

[9]See Book of Revelation 8:3-4.
[10]See Romans 12:1.
[11]Luke 2:32.
[12]See Pope Vigilius, *Epistula ad Profuturum episcopum*, IV: PL 84, 832.

closest harmony with the rite of the dedication of a church:
—for when the eucharistic sacrifice is celebrated, the end for
which the church was built and the altar erected is attained
and manifested by particularly clear signs;
—furthermore, the eucharist, which sanctifies the hearts of
those who receive it, in a sense consecrates the altar and the
place of celebration, as the ancient Fathers of the Church
assert more than once: "This altar is an object of wonder: by
nature it is stone, but it is made holy when it receives the
body of Christ";[13]
—finally, the bond whereby the dedication of a church is
closely linked with the celebration of the eucharist is likewise
evident from the fact that the proper preface of the Mass is, as
it were, an integral part of the rite of the dedication of a
church.

ADAPTATION OF THE RITE

ADAPTATION WITHIN THE COMPETENCE
OF THE CONFERENCES OF BISHOPS

18. Conferences of bishops can adapt this rite, as they see fit,
to the character of each region, but in such a way that nothing
detracts from its dignity and solemnity.

However, the following should be observed:
a) the celebration of the Mass with its proper preface and the
prayer of dedication must never be omitted;
b) rites which have a special meaning and force from liturgical
tradition (see above no. 16) must be retained, unless weighty
reasons stand in the way, but the wording may be suitably
adapted if necessary.

With regard to adaptations, the competent ecclesiastical authority is to consult the Holy See and with its consent introduce adaptations.[14]

DECISIONS WITHIN THE COMPETENCE
OF THE MINISTERS

19. It is for the bishop and for those who are in charge of the
celebration of the rite:

---

[13]Saint John Chrysostom, *Homilia XX in II Cor.*, 3: PG 61, 540.
[14]See Second Vatican Council, const. on the liturgy, no. 40: *AAS* 56 (1964)
111.

—to decide the way in which the entrance into the church is to take place (see above, no. 11);
—to determine the way in which the new church is to be handed over to the bishop (see above, no. 11);
—to judge the suitability of depositing relics of the saints. Here it is primarily the spiritual good of the community that must be looked to and what is laid down in no. 5 is to be observed.

It is for the rector of the church to be dedicated, helped by those who assist him in the pastoral work, to decide and prepare everything concerning the readings, chants, and other pastoral aids to foster the fruitful participation of the people and to promote a dignified celebration.

PASTORAL PREPARATION

20. In order that the people may take part fully in the rite of dedication, the rector of the church to be dedicated and others experienced in the pastoral ministry are to instruct them on the importance and value, spiritual, ecclesial, and missionary, of the celebration.

Accordingly, the people are to be instructed about the various parts of the church and their use, the rite of the dedication, and the chief liturgical symbols employed in it. Thus fully understanding the meaning of the dedication of a church through its rites and prayers, they may take an active, intelligent, and devout part in the sacred action.

REQUISITES FOR THE DEDICATION OF A CHURCH

21. For the celebration of the rite the following should be prepared:

a) In the place where the station is held:
—*The Roman Pontifical;*
—a cross to be carried in the procession;
—if relics of the saints are to be carried in procession, the items indicated in no. 24a.

b) In the sacristy or in the sanctuary or in the nave of the church to be dedicated according as each situation requires:
—*The Roman Missal;*
—*The Lectionary;*
—a vessel of water and a sprinkler;
—vessels of holy chrism;
—towels for wiping the table of the altar;
—if it is to be used, a waxed linen cloth or a waterproof linen cover of the same size as the altar;
—a basin and a jug of water, towels, and all that is needed for washing the bishop's hands and those of the priests after they have anointed the walls of the church;
—a linen gremial;
—a brazier for burning incense or aromatic spices; or grains of incense and small candles to burn on the altar;
—a censer, incense boat, and spoon;
—a chalice, corporal, purificators, and hand towel;
—bread, wine, and water for the celebration of Mass;
—an altar cross, unless there is already a cross in the sanctuary, or the cross which is carried in the entrance procession is placed near the altar;
—a linen cloth and candles;
—flowers, if opportune.

22. It is praiseworthy to keep the ancient custom of placing crosses made of stone, brass, or other suitable material or having the crosses carved on the walls of the church. Thus twelve or four crosses should be provided according to the number of anointings (see above no. 16) and suitably distributed on the walls of the church at a convenient height. A small bracket should be fitted beneath each cross into which is fixed a small candlestick with a candle to be lighted.

23. For the Mass of the dedication the vestments are white or of some festive color. The following should be prepared:
—for the bishop: alb, stole, chasuble, miter, pastoral staff, and pallium, if this is used by the bishop;
—for the concelebrating priests: the vestments for concelebrating Mass;
—for the deacons: albs, stoles, and if opportune, dalmatics;
—for other ministers: albs or other lawfully approved dress.

24. If relics of the saints are to be placed beneath the altar, the following should be prepared:

a) In the place where the station is held:
—a reliquary containing the relics, placed between flowers and lights. If the simple entrance takes place, the reliquary may be placed in a suitable part of the sanctuary before the rite begins;
—for the deacons who will carry the relics to be deposited: albs, red stoles if the relics are those of a martyr, or white in other cases, and, if available, dalmatics. If the relics are carried by priests, then in place of dalmatics chasubles should be prepared.

Relics may also be carried by other ministers vested in albs or other lawfully approved dress.

b) In the sanctuary:
—a small table on which the reliquary is placed during the first part of the dedication rite.

c) In the sacristy:
—pitch or cement to seal the cover of the aperture. In addition, a stone mason should be at hand to close the aperture containing the relics at the proper time.

25. A record of the dedication of the church is to be made out in duplicate, signed by the bishop, the rector of the church, and representatives of the local community; one copy is to be kept in the diocesan archives, the other in the archives of the church. Where, however, the depositing of relics takes place, a third copy of the record should be made, to be placed in the reliquary, if opportune.

Mention should be made in the record of the day, month, and year of the church's dedication, the name of the bishop who performed the rite, also the title of the church, and the names of the martyrs or saints, as the case may be, whose relics have been deposited beneath the altar.

Moreover, in a suitable place in the church, an inscription should be placed on which is recorded the day, month, and year when the dedication took place, the title of the church, and the name of the bishop who celebrated the rite.

ANNIVERSARY OF THE DEDICATION

A. ANNIVERSARY OF THE DEDICATION OF THE CATHEDRAL CHURCH

26. In order that the importance and dignity of a particular church may stand out with greater clarity, the anniversary of its cathedral church's dedication is to be celebrated, with the rank of a solemnity in the cathedral church itself, with the rank of a feast in the other churches of the diocese, on the day on which the dedication of the church recurs.[15] If this day is always impeded, the celebration is assigned to the next free day.

It is desirable that on the anniversary the bishop should concelebrate the eucharist in the cathedral church with the chapter of canons or senate of priests, and with the participation of as many of the people as possible.

B. ANNIVERSARY OF THE DEDICATION OF A PARTICULAR CHURCH

27. The anniversary of a church's dedication is celebrated with the rank of a solemnity.[16]

RITE OF DEDICATION

INTRODUCTORY RITES

ENTRANCE INTO THE CHURCH

28. The entry into the church to be dedicated is made, according to circumstances of time and place, in one of the three ways described below.

A. First Form: Procession

29. The door of the church to be dedicated should be closed. At a convenient hour the people assemble in a neighboring church or other suitable place from which the

---

[15]See Roman Calendar, Table of Liturgical Days, I 4b and II 8b.
[16]*Ibid.*, I 4b.

procession may proceed to the church. The relics of the martyrs or saints, if they are to be placed beneath the altar, are prepared in the place where the people assemble.

30. The bishop, the concelebrating priests, the deacons, and ministers, each in appropriate vestments, proceed to the place where the people are assembled. Putting aside the pastoral staff and miter, the bishop greets the people, saying:

The grace and peace of God
be with all of you
in his holy Church.
℟. And also with you.

Other suitable words preferably from sacred Scripture may be used.

Then the bishop addresses the people in these or similar words:

Brothers and sisters in Christ, this is a day of rejoicing: we have come together to dedicate this church by offering within it the sacrifice of Christ.

May we open our hearts and minds to receive his word with faith; may our fellowship born in the one font of baptism and sustained at the one table of the Lord, become the one temple of his Spirit, as we gather round his altar in love.

31. When he has finished addressing the people, the bishop receives the miter and pastoral staff and the procession to the church to be dedicated begins. No lights are used apart from those which surround the relics of the saints, nor is incense used either in the procession or in the Mass before the rite of the incensation and the lighting of the altar and the church (see below, nos. 66-71.) The crossbearer leads the procession; the ministers follow; then the deacons or priests with the relics of the saints, ministers, or the faithful accompanying them on either side with lighted torches; then the concelebrating priests; then the bishop with two deacons; and lastly, the congregation.

32. As the procession proceeds, the following antiphon is sung with Psalm 122.

Let us go rejoicing to the house of the Lord.

Another appropriate song may be sung.

33. At the threshold of the church the procession comes to a halt. Representatives of those who have been involved in the building of the church (members of the parish or of the diocese, contributors, architects, workers) hand over the building to the bishop, offering him according to place and circumstances either the legal documents for possession of the building, or the keys, or the plan of the building, or the book in which the progress of the work is described and the names of those in charge of it and the names of the workers recorded. One of the representatives addresses the bishop and the community in a few words, pointing out, if need be, what the new church expresses in its art and in its own special design.

If the door is closed, the bishop then calls upon the priest to whom the pastoral care of the church has been entrusted to open the door.

34. When the door is unlocked, the bishop invites the people to enter the church in these or similar words:

Go within his gates giving thanks, enter his courts with songs of praise.

Then, preceded by the crossbearer, the bishop and the assembly enter the church. As the procession enters, the following antiphon is sung with Psalm 24.

Lift high the ancient portals. The King of glory enters.

Another appropriate song may be sung.

35. The bishop, without kissing the altar, goes to the chair; the concelebrants, deacons, and ministers go to the places assigned to them in the sanctuary. The relics of the saints are placed in a suitable part of the sanctuary between lighted torches. Water is then blessed with the rite described below, nos. 48-50.

B. Second Form: Solemn Entrance

36. If the procession cannot take place or seems inappropriate, the people assemble at the door of the church to be dedicated, where the relics of the saints have been placed beforehand.

37. Preceded by the crossbearer, the bishop and the con-celebrating priests, the deacons, and the ministers, each in appropriate vestments, approach the church door, where the people are assembled. The door of the church should be closed, and the bishop, concelebrants, deacons, and ministers should approach it from outside.

38. Putting aside the pastoral staff and miter, the bishop greets the people, saying:

The grace and peace of God
be with all of you
in his holy Church.
℟. **And also with you.**

Other suitable words taken preferably from sacred Scripture may be used.

Then the bishop addresses the people in these or similar words:

Brothers and sisters in Christ, this is a day of rejoicing: we have come together to dedicate this church by offering within it the sacrifice of Christ.

May we open our hearts and minds to receive his word with faith; may our fellowship born in the one font of baptism and sustained at the one table of the Lord, become the one temple of his Spirit, as we gather round his altar in love.

39. When the bishop has finished addressing the people, he puts on the miter and, if it seems appropriate, the following antiphon is sung with Psalm 122.

Let us go rejoicing to the house of the Lord.

Another appropriate song may be sung.

40. Then representatives of those who have been involved in the building of the church (members of the parish or of the diocese, contributors, architects, workers) hand over the building to the bishop, offering him according to place and circumstances either the legal documents for possession of the building, or the keys, or the plan of the building, or the book in which the progress of the work is described and the

names of those in charge of it and the names of the workers recorded. One of the representatives addresses the bishop and the community in a few words, pointing out, if need be, what the new church expresses in its art and in its own special design.

If the door is closed, the bishop then calls upon the priest to whom the pastoral care of the church has been entrusted to open the door.

41. The bishop takes the pastoral staff and invites the people to enter the church in these or similar words:

Go within his gates giving thanks, enter his courts with songs of praise.

Then, preceded by the crossbearer, the bishop and the assembly enter the church. As the procession enters, the following antiphon is sung with Psalm 24.

Lift high the ancient portals. The King of glory enters.

Another appropriate song may be sung.

42. The bishop, without kissing the altar, goes to the chair; the concelebrants, deacons, and ministers go to the places assigned to them in the sanctuary. The relics of the saints are placed in a suitable part of the sanctuary between lighted torches. Water is then blessed with the rite described below, in nos. 48-50.

C. Third Form: Simple Entrance

43. If the solemn entrance cannot take place, the simple entrance is used. When the people are assembled, the bishop and the concelebrating priests, the deacons, and the ministers, each in appropriate vestments, preceded by the crossbearer, go from the sacristy through the main body of the church to the sanctuary.

44. If there are relics of the saints to be placed beneath the altar, these are brought in the entrance procession to the sanctuary from the sacristy or the chapel where since the vigil they have been exposed for the veneration of the people. For a just cause, before the celebration begins, the relics may be placed between lighted torches in a suitable part of the sanctuary.

45. As the procession proceeds, the entrance antiphon is sung with Psalm 122.

God in his holy dwelling, God who has gathered us together in his house: he will strengthen and console his people.

Or:

Let us go rejoicing to the house of the Lord.

Another appropriate song may be sung.

46. When the procession reaches the sanctuary, the relics of the saints are placed between lighted torches in a suitable place. The concelebrating priests, the deacons, and the ministers go to the places assigned to them; the bishop, without kissing the altar, goes to the chair. Then, putting aside the pastoral staff and miter, he greets the people, saying:

**The grace and peace of God
be with all of you
in his holy Church.
℟. And also with you.**

Other suitable words taken preferably from sacred Scripture may be used.

47. Then representatives of those who have been involved in the building of the church (members of the parish or of the diocese, contributors, architects, workers) hand over the building to the bishop, offering him according to place and circumstances either the legal documents for possession of the building, or the keys, or the plan of the building, or the book in which the progress of the work is described and the names of those in charge of it and the names of the workers recorded. One of the representatives addresses the bishop and the community in a few words, pointing out, if need be, what the new church expresses in its art and in its own special design.

BLESSING AND SPRINKLING OF WATER

48. When the entrance rite is completed, the bishop blesses water with which to sprinkle the people as a sign of repentance and as a reminder of their baptism, and to purify the walls and the altar of the new church. The ministers bring the vessel with the water to the bishop who stands at the chair. The bishop invites all to pray, in these or similar words:

Brothers and sisters in Christ, in this solemn rite of dedication, let us ask the Lord our God to bless this water created by his hand.

It is a sign of our repentance, a reminder of our baptism, and a symbol of the cleansing of these walls and this altar.

May the grace of God help us to remain faithful members of his Church, open to the Spirit we have received.

All pray in silence for a brief period. The bishop then continues:

God of mercy,
you call every creature to the light of life,
and surround us with such great love
that when we stray
you continually lead us back to Christ our head.

For you have established an inheritance of such mercy,
that those sinners, who pass through water made
sacred,
die with Christ and rise restored
as members of his body
and heirs of his eternal covenant.

Bless ✠ this water;
sanctify it.

As it is sprinkled upon us and throughout this church
make it a sign of the saving waters of baptism,
by which we become one in Christ, the temple of your
Spirit.

May all here today,
and all those in days to come,
who will celebrate your mysteries in this church,
be united at last in the holy city of your peace.

We ask this in the name of Jesus the Lord.
℟. Amen.

49. The bishop, accompanied by the deacons, passes through the main body of the church, sprinkling the people and the walls with the holy water; then, when he has returned to the sanctuary, he sprinkles the altar. Meanwhile the following antiphon is sung.

I saw water flowing from the right side of the temple, alleluia. I brought God's life and his salvation, and the people sang in joyful praise: alleluia, alleluia.

Or, during Lent:
I will pour clean water over you and wash away all your defilement. A new heart will I give you, says the Lord.

Another appropriate song may be sung.

50. After the sprinkling the bishop returns to the chair and, when the singing is finished, standing with hands joined, says:

**May God, the Father of mercies,
dwell in this house of prayer.
May the grace of the Holy Spirit cleanse us,
for we are the temple of his presence.
℟. Amen.**

HYMN
51. Then the **Gloria** is sung.

OPENING PRAYER
52. When the hymn is finished, the bishop, with hands joined, says:

**Lord,
fill this place with your presence,
and extend your hand
to all those who call upon you.**

**May your word here proclaimed
and your sacraments here celebrated
strengthen the hearts of all the faithful.**

We ask this through our Lord Jesus Christ, your Son,
who lives and reigns with you and the Holy Spirit,
one God, for ever and ever.
℟. Amen.

LITURGY OF THE WORD

53. The proclamation of the word of God is fittingly carried
out in this way: two readers, one of whom carries *The Lectionary*, and the psalmist come to the bishop. The bishop,
standing with the miter on, takes *The Lectionary*, shows it to
the people, and says:

May the word of God always be heard in this place,
as it unfolds the mystery of Christ before you
and achieves your salvation within the Church.
℟. Amen

Then the bishop hands *The Lectionary* to the first reader. The
readers and the psalmist proceed to the lectern, carrying *The
Lectionary* for all to see.

54. The readings are arranged in this way:
a) The first reading is always taken from the Book of
Nehemiah 8:1-4a, 5-6, 8-10, followed by the singing of
Psalm 19B:8-9, 10, 15 with the response:

℟. **Your words, Lord, are spirit and life.**

b) The second reading and the gospel are taken from the texts
in *The Lectionary* (nos. 701-706) for the rite of the dedication
of a church. Neither lights nor incense are carried at the gospel.

55. After the gospel the bishop gives the homily, in which he
explains the biblical readings and the meaning of the rite.

56. The profession of faith is said. The general intercessions
are omitted since in their place the litany of the saints is sung.

PRAYER OF DEDICATION AND THE ANOINTINGS

INVITATION TO PRAYER

57. Then all stand, and the bishop, without his miter, invites the people to pray in these or similar words:

Let us ask the saints to support our prayers to God the Father almighty, who has made the hearts of his people faithful temples of his Spirit.

Deacon (except on Sundays and during the Easter season):

Let us kneel.

LITANY OF THE SAINTS

58. Then the litany of the saints is sung, with all responding. On Sundays and also during the Easter season, all stand; on other days, all kneel.

59. The cantors begin the litany (Chapter VIII); they add, at the proper place, names of other saints (the titular of the church, the patron saint of the place, and the saints whose relics are to be deposited, if this is to take place) and petitions suitable to the occasion.

60. When the litany is finished, the bishop, standing with hands extended, says:

**Lord,
may the prayers of the Blessed Virgin Mary
and of all the saints
make our prayers acceptable to you.**

**May this building,
which we dedicate to your name,
be a house of salvation and grace
where Christians gathered in fellowship
may worship you in spirit and truth
and grow together in love.**

**Grant this through Christ our Lord.
℟. Amen.**

If it is applicable, the deacon says:

Let us stand.

All rise. The bishop receives the miter.

When there is no depositing of the relics of the saints, the bishop immediately says the prayer of dedication as indicated in no. 62 below.

DEPOSITING OF THE RELICS

61. Then, if relics of the martyrs or other saints are to be placed beneath the altar, the bishop approaches the altar. A deacon or priest brings them to the bishop, who places them in a suitably prepared aperture. Meanwhile one of the following antiphons is sung with Psalm 15.

Saints of God, you have been enthroned at the foot of God's altar; pray for us to the Lord Jesus Christ.

Or:

The bodies of the saints lie buried in peace, but their names will live on for ever (alleluia).

Another appropriate song may be sung.

Meanwhile a stone mason closes the aperture and the bishop returns to the chair.

PRAYER OF DEDICATION

62. Then the bishop, standing without miter at the chair or near the altar, with hands extended, says:

Father in heaven,
source of holiness and true purpose,
it is right that we praise and glorify your name.

For today we come before you,
to dedicate to your lasting service
this house of prayer, this temple of worship,
this home in which we are nourished by your word and
your sacraments.

Here is reflected the mystery of the Church.

The Church is fruitful,
made holy by the blood of Christ:
a bride made radiant with his glory,
a virgin splendid in the wholeness of her faith,
a mother blessed through the power of the Spirit.

The Church is holy,
your chosen vineyard:
its branches envelop the world,
its tendrils, carried on the tree of the cross,
reach up to the kingdom of heaven.

The Church is favored,
the dwelling place of God on earth:
a temple built of living stones,
founded on the apostles
with Jesus Christ its corner stone.

The Church is exalted,
a city set on a mountain:
a beacon to the whole world,
bright with the glory of the Lamb,
and echoing the prayers of her saints.

Lord,
send your Spirit from heaven
to make this church an ever-holy place,
and this altar a ready table for the sacrifice of Christ.

Here may the waters of baptism
overwhelm the shame of sin;
here may your people die to sin
and live again through grace as your children.

Here may your children,
gathered around your altar,
celebrate the memorial of the Paschal Lamb,
and be fed at the table
of Christ's word and Christ's body.

Here may prayer, the Church's banquet,
resound through heaven and earth
as a plea for the world's salvation.

Here may the poor find justice,
the victims of oppression, true freedom.

From here may the whole world
clothed in the dignity of the children of God,
enter with gladness your city of peace.

We ask this through our Lord Jesus Christ, your Son,
who lives and reigns with you and the Holy Spirit,
one God, for ever and ever.
℟. Amen.

ANOINTING OF THE ALTAR
AND THE WALLS OF THE CHURCH

63. Then the bishop, removing the chasuble if necessary and
putting on a linen gremial, goes to the altar with the deacons
and other ministers, one of whom carries the chrism. The
bishop proceeds to anoint the altar and the walls of the
church as described in no. 64 below.

If the bishop wishes to associate some of the concelebrating
priests with him in the anointing of the walls, after the anointing of the altar, he hands them vessels of sacred chrism and
goes with them to complete the anointings.

However, the bishop may give the task of anointing the walls
to the priests alone; in that case, he hands the vessel of sacred
chrism to them after he has anointed the altar.

64. The bishop, standing before the altar, says:

We now anoint this altar and this building.
May God in his power make them holy,
visible signs of the mystery of Christ and his Church.

Then he pours chrism on the middle of the altar and on each
of its four corners, and it is recommended that he anoint the
entire table of the altar with this.

When the altar has been anointed, the bishop anoints the
walls of the church, signing with chrism the suitably distributed twelve or four crosses. He may have the assistance
of two or four priests.

If the anointing of the walls is given to the priests, after the
bishop has anointed the altar, they anoint the walls of the
church signing the crosses with chrism.

Meanwhile one of the following antiphons is sung with Psalm
84.

See the place where God lives among his people; there
the Spirit of God will make his home among you; the

temple of God is holy and you are that temple (alleluia).

Or:

Holy is the temple of the Lord, it is God's handiwork, his dwelling place.

Another appropriate song may be sung.

65. When the altar and walls have been anointed, the bishop returns to the chair, sits, and washes his hands. Then the bishop takes off the gremial and puts on the chasuble. The priests also wash their hands after they have anointed the walls.

INCENSATION OF THE ALTAR AND THE CHURCH

66. After the rite of anointing, a brazier is placed on the altar for burning incense or aromatic gums. The bishop puts incense into the brazier, saying:

Lord,
may our prayer ascend as incense in your sight.
As this building is filled with fragrance
so may your Church fill the world
with the fragrance of Christ.

67. Then the bishop puts incense into some censers and incenses the altar; he returns to the chair, is incensed, and then sits. Ministers, walking through the church, incense the people and the walls.

68. Meanwhile one of the following antiphons is sung with Psalm 138.

An angel stood by the altar of the temple, holding a golden censer.

Or:

From the hand of the angel, clouds of incense rose in the presence of the Lord.

Another appropriate song may be sung.

LIGHTING OF THE ALTAR AND THE CHURCH

69. After the incensation, a few ministers wipe the table of the altar with cloths, and if need be, cover it with a waterproof linen. They then cover the altar with a cloth, and, if opportune, decorate it with flowers. They arrange in a suitable manner the candles needed for the celebration of Mass, and, if need be, the cross.

70. Then the bishop gives to the deacon a lighted candle, and says:

**Light of Christ,
shine forth in the Church
and bring all nations
to the fullness of truth.**

Then the bishop sits. The deacon goes to the altar and lights the candles for the celebration of the eucharist.

71. Then the festive lighting takes place: all the candles, including those at the places where the anointings were made, and the other lamps are lit as a sign of rejoicing. Meanwhile the following antiphon is sung with the canticle of Tobias.

Your light will come, Jerusalem; upon you the glory of the Lord will dawn and all nations will walk in your light, alleluia.

Or, during Lent:

Jerusalem, city of God, you will shine with the light of God's splendor; all people on earth will pay you homage.

CANTICLE OF TOBIAS
(Vg. 13:10, 13-14ab; 14c-15; 17)

**Bless the Lord, all you saints of the Lord.
Rejoice and give him thanks.**

(Repeat antiphon)

**Jerusalem, city of God,
you will shine with the light of God's splendor;**

all people on earth will pay you homage.
Nations will come from afar,
bearing gifts for the King of heaven;
in you they will worship the Lord.

(Repeat antiphon)

Nations will consider your land holy,
for in you they will call upon the great name of the
** Lord.**
You will exult and rejoice over the children of the
** righteous,**
for they will be gathered together to praise the Lord.

(Repeat antiphon)

Another appropriate song may be sung, especially one in
honor of Christ, the light of the world.

LITURGY OF THE EUCHARIST

72. The deacons and the ministers prepare the altar in the
usual way. Then some of the congregation bring bread, wine,
and water for the celebration of the Lord's sacrifice. The
bishop receives the gifts at the chair. While the gifts are being
brought, the following antiphon may be sung:

Lord God, in the simplicity of my heart I have joyously
offered all things to you; with great joy I have looked
upon your chosen people, Lord God, I have obeyed
your will (alleluia).

Another appropriate song may be sung.

73. When all is ready, the bishop goes to the altar, removes
the miter, and kisses the altar. The Mass proceeds in the
usual way; however, neither the gifts nor the altar are incensed.

PRAYER OVER THE GIFTS

74. With hands extended, the bishop sings or says:

Lord,
accept the gifts of a rejoicing Church.

May your people,
who are gathered in this sacred place,
arrive at eternal salvation
through the mysteries in which they share.

Grant this through Christ our Lord.
℟. **Amen.**

EUCHARISTIC PRAYER

75. Eucharistic Prayer I or III is said, with the following preface, which is an integral part of the rite of the dedication of a church. With hands extended the bishop sings or says:

The Lord be with you.
℟. **And also with you.**

Lift up your hearts.
℟. **We lift them up to the Lord.**

Let us give thanks to the Lord our God.
℟. **It is right to give him thanks and praise.**

Father, all-powerful and ever-living God,
we do well always and everywhere to give you thanks.

The whole world is your temple,
shaped to resound with your name.
Yet you also allow us to dedicate to your service
places designed for your worship.

With hearts full of joy
we consecrate to your glory
this work of our hands, this house of prayer.

Here is foreshadowed the mystery of your true temple;
this church is the image on earth of your heavenly city:

For you made the body of your Son
born of the Virgin,
a temple consecrated to your glory,
the dwelling place of your godhead in all its fullness.

You have established the Church as your holy city,
founded on the apostles,
with Jesus Christ its cornerstone.

You continue to build your Church with chosen stones,
enlivened by the Spirit,
and cemented together by love.

In that holy city you will be all in all for endless ages,
and Christ will be its light for ever.

Through Christ we praise you, Lord,
with all the angels and saints in their song of joy:

Holy, holy, holy Lord, God of power and might,
heaven and earth are full of your glory.
    Hosanna in the highest.
Blessed is he who comes in the name of the Lord.
    Hosanna in the highest.

76. In Eucharistic Prayer I the special form of **Father, accept this offering** is said:

Father,
accept this offering
from your whole family,
and from your servants
who with heart and hand
have given and built this church
as an offering to you (in honor of N.).
Grant us your peace in this life,
save us from final damnation,
and count us among those you have chosen.

77. In the intercessions of Eucharistic Prayer III, after the words, **with . . . the entire people your Son has gained for you,** the following is said:

Father,
accept the prayers of those who dedicate this church to
    you.

May it be a place of salvation and sacrament
where your Gospel of peace is proclaimed
and your holy mysteries celebrated.

Guided by your word and secure in your peace

may your chosen people now journeying through life
arrive safely at their eternal home.

There may all your children
now scattered abroad
be settled at last in your city of peace.

78. While the bishop is receiving the body of Christ the
communion song begins. One of the following antiphons is
sung with Psalm 128.

My house shall be called a house of prayer, says the
Lord: in it all who ask shall receive, all who seek shall
find, and all who knock shall have the door opened to
them (alleluia).

Or:
May the children of the Church be like olive branches
around the table of the Lord (alleluia).

Another appropriate song may be sung.

If there is no inauguration of the blessed sacrament chapel,
the Mass proceeds as below, no.83.

INAUGURATION OF THE
BLESSED SACRAMENT CHAPEL

79. The inauguration of a chapel where the blessed sacrament is to be reserved, is carried out appropriately in this
way: after the communion the pyx containing the blessed
sacrament is left on the table of the altar. The bishop goes to
the chair, and all pray in silence for a brief period. Then the
bishop says the following prayer after communion:

Let us pray.

Pause for silent prayer, if this has not preceded.

Lord,
through these gifts
increase the vision of your truth in our minds.

May we always worship you in your holy temple,
and rejoice in your presence with all your saints.

Grant this through Christ our Lord.
℟. Amen.

80. When the prayer is completed, the bishop returns to the altar, genuflects, and incenses the blessed sacrament. Afterward, when he has received the humeral veil, he takes the pyx, which he covers with the veil itself. Then a procession is formed in which, preceded by the crossbearer and with lighted torches and incense, the blessed sacrament is carried through the main body of the church to the chapel of reservation. As the procession proceeds, the following antiphon is sung with Psalm 147:12-20.

Praise the Lord, Jerusalem.

Another appropriate song may be sung.

81. When the procession comes to the chapel of reservation, the bishop places the pyx on the altar or in the tabernacle, the door of which remains open. Then he puts incense in the censer, kneels, and incenses the blessed sacrament. Finally, after a brief period during which all pray in silence, the deacon puts the pyx in the tabernacle or closes the door. A minister lights the lamp, which will burn perpetually before the blessed sacrament.

82. If the chapel where the blessed sacrament is reserved can be seen clearly by the congregation, the bishop immediately imparts the blessing of the Mass (see below, no. 84). Otherwise the procession returns to the sanctuary by the shorter route and the bishop imparts the blessing either at the altar or at the chair.

PRAYER AFTER COMMUNION

83. If there is no inauguration of the blessed sacrament chapel, when the communion of the congregation is finished, the bishop says:

Let us pray.

Pause for silent prayer, if this has not preceded.

Lord,
through these gifts
increase the vision of your truth in our minds.

May we always worship you in your holy temple,
and rejoice in your presence with all your saints.

Grant this through Christ our Lord.
℟. **Amen.**

BLESSING AND DISMISSAL

84. The bishop receives the miter and says:

The Lord be with you.
℟. **And also with you.**

Then the deacon, if appropriate, gives the invitation to the people in these or similar words:

Bow your heads and pray for God's blessing.

Then the bishop extends his hands over the people and blesses them, saying:

The Lord of earth and heaven
has assembled you before him this day
to dedicate this house of prayer.
May he fill you with the blessings of heaven.
℟. **Amen.**

God the Father wills that all his children
scattered through the world
become one family in his Son.
May he make you his temple,
the dwelling place of his Holy Spirit.
℟. **Amen.**

May God free you from every bond of sin,
dwell within you and give you joy.
May you live with him for ever
in the company of all his saints.
℟. **Amen.**

The bishop takes the pastoral staff and continues:

May almighty God bless you,
the Father, and the Son, ✠ and the Holy Spirit.
℟. **Amen.**

85. Finally the deacon dismisses the people in the usual way.

CHAPTER III

DEDICATION OF A CHURCH ALREADY IN GENERAL USE FOR SACRED CELEBRATIONS

INTRODUCTION

1. In order to bring out the full force of the symbolism and the significance of the rite, the opening of a new church and its dedication should take place at one and the same time. For this reason, as was said before, care should be taken that, as far as possible, Mass is not celebrated in a new church before it is dedicated (see Chapter II, nos. 8, 15, 17).

When, however, churches are dedicated in which it has already been customary to celebrate the sacred mysteries, the rite which is set out in this chapter must be used.

Moreover, in churches such as these an obvious distinction is made between those which have been built recently, the dedication of which is more clearly desirable, and those which have been standing for a long time; that the latter be dedicated it is necessary:
—that the altar has not been dedicated, since it is rightly forbidden both by custom and by liturgical law to dedicate a church without dedicating the altar, for the dedication of the altar is a principal part of the whole rite;
—that there is something new or greatly changed in it which affects the building, for example, the church has been completely restored or its juridical status, for example, it has been raised to the rank of a parish church.

2. All the directions given in the Introduction to Chapter II pertain also to this rite, unless they are clearly seen to be contrary to the situation which this rite envisages, or other directions are given.

This rite differs chiefly from that described in Chapter II in these ways:
a) The rite of opening the doors of the church (see Chapter II, no. 34 or no. 41) is omitted, since the church is already open to the community; consequently the entrance takes the form of the simple entrance (see Chapter II, nos. 43-47). However,

if it is a question of dedicating a church which has been closed for a long time and is now being opened again for sacred celebrations, the rite can be carried out, since in this case it retains its force and significance;

b) the rite of handing over the church to the bishop (see Chapter II, no. 33 or 40 or 47), as circumstances dictate, is either observed or omitted or so adapted that it respects the state of the church to be dedicated (for example, it will be suitably observed in the dedication of a church built recently; it will be omitted in the dedication of an old church where nothing has been changed in the structure of the building; it will be adapted in the dedication of an old church completely restored);

c) the rite of sprinkling the walls of the church with holy water (see Chapter II, nos. 48-50), purificatory by its very nature, is omitted;

d) those things which are special to the first proclamation of the word of God (see Chapter II, no. 53) are omitted, and the liturgy of the word takes place in the usual way. Instead of Nehemiah 8:1-4a, 5-6, 8-10 with Psalm 19B:8-9, 10, 15 and its responsory (see Chapter II, no. 54a), another suitable reading is chosen.

RITE OF DEDICATION

INTRODUCTORY RITES

ENTRANCE INTO THE CHURCH

3. When the people are assembled, the bishop and the celebrating priests, the deacons, and the ministers, each in appropriate vestments, preceded by the crossbearer, go from the sacristy through the main body of the church to the sanctuary.

4. If there are relics of the saints to be placed beneath the altar, these are brought in the entrance procession to the sanctuary from the sacristy or the chapel where since the vigil they have been exposed for the veneration of the people. For a just cause, before the celebration begins, the relics may be placed between lighted torches in a suitable part of the sanctuary.

5. As the procession proceeds, the entrance antiphon is sung with Psalm 122.

God in his holy dwelling, God who has gathered us together in his house: he will strengthen and console his people.

Or:

Let us go rejoicing to the house of the Lord.

Another appropriate song may be sung.

6. When the procession reaches the sanctuary, the relics of the saints are placed between lighted torches in a suitable place. The concelebrating priests, the deacons, and the ministers go the places assigned to them; the bishop, without kissing the altar, goes to the chair. Then putting aside the pastoral staff and miter, greets the people, saying:

**The grace and peace of God
be with all of you
in his holy Church.
℟. And also with you.**

Other suitable words taken preferably from sacred Scripture may be used.

7. If circumstances dictate that the church is to be handed over to the bishop (see Introduction, no. 2b), representatives of those who have been involved in the building of the church (members of the parish or of the diocese, contributors, architects, workers) hand over the building to the bishop, offering him either the legal documents for possession of the building, or the keys, or the plan of the building, or the book in which the progress of the work is described and the names of those in charge of it and the names of the workers recorded. One of the representatives addresses the bishop and the community in a few words, pointing out, if need be, what the church expresses in its art and in its own special design.

BLESSING AND SPRINKLING OF WATER

8. When the entrance rite is completed, the bishop blesses water with which to sprinkle the people as a sign of repentance and as a reminder of their baptism. The ministers return the vessel with the water to the bishop who stands at the chair. The bishop invites all to pray, in these or similar words:

Brothers and sisters in Christ in this solemn rite of dedication let us ask the Lord our God to bless this water, created by his hand.

It is a sign of our repentance and a reminder of our baptism.

May the grace of God help us to remain faithful members of his Church, open to the Spirit we have received.

All pray in silence for a brief period. The bishop then continues:

God of mercy,
you call every creature to the light of life,
and surround us with such great love
that when we stray
you continually lead us back to Christ our head.

For you have established an inheritance of such mercy,
that those sinners, who pass through water made
    sacred,
die with Christ and rise restored
as members of his body
and heirs of his eternal covenant.

Bless ✝ this water;
sanctify it.

As it is sprinkled upon us and throughout this church
make it a sign of the saving waters of baptism,
by which we become one in Christ, the temple of your
    Spirit.

May all here today,
and all those in days to come,
who will celebrate your mysteries in this church
be united at last in the holy city of your peace.

We ask this in the name of Jesus the Lord.
℟. Amen.

9. The bishop, accompanied by the deacons, sprinkles the people with holy water; then if the altar is completely new he sprinkles it too. Meanwhile the following antiphon is sung.

I saw water flowing from the right side of the temple, alleluia. It brought God's life and his salvation, and the people sang in joyful praise: alleluia, alleluia.

Or, during Lent:
I will pour clean water over you and wash away all your defilement. A new heart will I give you, says the Lord.

Another appropriate song may be sung.

10. After the sprinkling the bishop returns to the chair and, when the singing is finished, standing with hands joined, says:

May God, the Father of mercies,
dwell in this house of prayer.
May the grace of the Holy Spirit cleanse us,
for we are the temple of his presence.
℟. Amen.

HYMN
11. Then the **Gloria** is sung.

OPENING PRAYER
12. When the hymn is finished, the bishop, with hands joined, says:

Let us pray.

All pray in silence for a brief period. Then the bishop, with hands extended, says:

Lord,
fill this place with your presence,
and extend your hand
to all those who call upon you.

May your word here proclaimed
and your sacraments here celebrated
strengthen the hearts of all the faithful.

We ask this through our Lord Jesus Christ, your Son,
who lives and reigns with you and the Holy Spirit,
one God, for ever and ever.
℟. Amen.

LITURGY OF THE WORD

13. The bishop sits and receives the miter; the people also are seated. Then the liturgy of the word takes place; the readings are taken from the texts in *The Lectionary* (nos. 701 and 706) for the rite of the dedication of a church.

14. Neither lights nor incense are carried at the gospel.

15. After the gospel the bishop gives the homily, in which he explains the biblical readings and the meaning of the rite.

16. The profession of faith is said. The general intercessions are omitted since in their place the litany of the saints is sung.

PRAYER OF DEDICATION AND THE ANOINTINGS

INVITATION TO PRAYER

17. Then all stand, and the bishop, without his miter, invites the people to pray in these or similar words:

Let us ask the saints to support our prayers to God the Father almighty, who has made the hearts of his people faithful temples of his Spirit.

Deacon (except on Sundays and during the Easter season):

Let us kneel.

LITANY OF THE SAINTS

18. Then the litany of the saints is sung, with all responding. On Sundays and also during the Easter season, all stand; on other days, all kneel.

19. The cantors begin the litany (see Chapter VIII); they add, at the proper place, names of other saints (the titular of the church, the patron saint of the place, and the saints whose relics are to be deposited, if this is to take place) and petitions suitable to the occasion.

20. When the litany is finished, the bishop, standing with hands extended, says:

Lord,
may the prayers of the Blessed Virgin Mary

and of all the saints
make our prayers acceptable to you.

May this building,
which we dedicate to your name,
be a house of salvation and grace
where Christians gathered in fellowship
may worship you in spirit and truth
and grow together in love.

Grant this through Christ our Lord.
℟. Amen.

If it is applicable, the deacon says:

Let us stand.

All rise. The bishop receives the miter.

When there is no depositing of the relics of the saints, the
bishop immediately says the prayer of dedication as indicated
in no. 22 below.

DEPOSITING OF THE RELICS

21. Then, if relics of the matyrs or other saints are to be
placed beneath the altar, the bishop approaches the altar. A
deacon or priest brings them to the bishop, who places them
in a suitably prepared aperture. Meanwhile one of the following antiphons is sung with Psalm 15.

Saints of God, you have been enthroned at the foot of
God's altar; pray for us to the Lord Jesus Christ.

Or:

The bodies of the saints lie buried in peace, but their
names will live on forever (alleluia).

Another appropriate song may be sung.

Meanwhile a stone mason closes the aperture and the bishop
returns to the chair.

PRAYER OF DEDICATION

22. Then the bishop, standing without miter at the chair or
near the altar, with hands extended, says:

Father in heaven,
source of holiness and true purpose,
it is right that we praise and glorify your name.

For today we come before you,
to dedicate to your lasting service
this house of prayer, this temple of worship,
this home in which we are nourished by your word and
   your sacraments.

Here is reflected the mystery of the Church.

The Church is fruitful,
made holy by the blood of Christ:
a bride made radiant with his glory,
a virgin splendid in the wholeness of her faith,
a mother blessed through the power of the Spirit.

The Church is holy,
your chosen vineyard:
its branches envelop the world,
its tendrils, carried on the tree of the cross,
reach up to the kingdom of heaven.

The Church is favored,
the dwelling place of God on earth:
a temple built of living stones,
founded on the apostles
with Jesus Christ its corner stone.

The Church is exalted,
a city set on a mountain:
a beacon to the whole world,
bright with the glory of the Lamb,
and echoing the prayers of her saints.

Lord,
send your Spirit from heaven
to make this church an ever-holy place,
and this altar a ready table for the sacrifice of Christ.

Here may the waters of baptism
overwhelm the shame of sin;

here may your people die to sin
and live again through grace as your children.

Here may your children,
gathered around your altar,
celebrate the memorial of the Paschal Lamb,
and be fed at the table
of Christ's word and Christ's body.

Here may prayer, the Church's banquet,
resound through heaven and earth
as a plea for the world's salvation.

Here may the poor find justice,
the victims of oppression, true freedom.

From here may the whole world
clothed in the dignity of the children of God,
enter with gladness your city of peace.

We ask this through our Lord Jesus Christ, your Son,
who lives and reigns with you and the Holy Spirit,
one God, for ever and ever.
℟. Amen.

ANOINTING OF THE ALTAR
AND THE WALLS OF THE CHURCH

23. Then the bishop, removing the chasuble if necessary and putting on a linen gremial, goes to the altar with the deacons and other ministers, one of whom carries the chrism. The bishop proceeds to anoint the altar and the walls of the church as described in no. 24 below.

If the bishop wishes to associate some of the concelebrating priests with him in the anointing of the walls, after the anointing of the altar, he hands them vessels of sacred chrism and goes with them to complete the anointings.

However, the bishop may give the task of anointing the walls to the priests alone; in that case, he hands the vessels of sacred chrism to them after he has anointed the altar.

24. The bishop, standing before the altar says:

We now anoint this altar and this building.
May God in his power make them holy,
visible signs of the mystery of Christ and his Church.

Then he pours chrism on the middle of the altar and on each of its four corners, and it is recommended that he anoint the entire table of the altar with this.

When the altar has been anointed, the bishop anoints the walls of the church, signing with chrism the suitably distributed twelve or four crosses. He may have the assistance of two or four priests.

If the anointing of the walls is given to the priests, after the bishop has anointed the altar, they anoint the walls of the church signing the crosses with chrism.

Meanwhile one of the following antiphons is sung with Psalm 84.

See the place where God lives among his people; there the Spirit of God will make his home among you; the temple of God is holy and you are that temple (alleluia).

Or:
Holy is the temple of the Lord, it is God's handiwork, his dwelling place.

Another appropriate song may be sung.

25. When the altar and walls have been anointed, the bishop returns to the chair, sits, and washes his hands. Then the bishop takes off the gremial and puts on the chasuble. The priests also wash their hands after they have anointed the walls.

INCENSATION OF THE ALTAR AND THE CHURCH

26. After the rite of anointing, the brazier is placed on the altar for burning incense or aromatic gums. The bishop puts incense into the brazier, saying:

Lord,
may our prayer ascend as incense in your sight.

**As this building is filled with fragrance
so may your Church fill the world
with the fragrance of Christ.**

27. Then the bishop puts incense into some censers and incenses the altar; he returns to the chair, is incensed, and then sits. Ministers, walking through the church, incense the people and the walls.

28. Meanwhile one of the following antiphons is sung with Psalm 138.

An angel stood by the altar of the temple, holding a golden censer.

Or:

From the hand of the angel, clouds of incense rose in the presence of the Lord.

Another appropriate song may be sung.

LIGHTING OF THE ALTAR AND THE CHURCH

29. After the incensation, a few ministers wipe the table of the altar with cloths, and, if need be, cover it with a waterproof linen. They then cover the altar with a cloth, and, if opportune, decorate it with flowers. They arrange in a suitable manner the candles needed for the celebration of Mass, and, if need be, the cross.

30. Then the bishop gives to the deacon a lighted candle and says:

**Light of Christ,
shine forth in the Church
and bring all nations
to the fullness of truth.**

Then the bishop sits. The deacon goes to the altar and lights the candles for the celebration of the eucharist.

31. Then the festive lighting takes place: all the candles, including those at the places where the anointings were made, and the other lamps are lit as a sign of rejoicing. Meanwhile the following antiphon is sung with the canticle of Tobias.

Your light will come, Jerusalem; upon you the glory of the Lord will dawn and all nations will walk in your light, alleluia.

Or, during Lent:
Jerusalem, city of God, you will shine with the light of God's splendor; all people on earth will pay you homage.

CANTICLE OF TOBIAS
(Vg. 13:10; 13-14ab; 14c-15; 17)

**Bless the Lord, all you saints of the Lord.
Rejoice and give him thanks.**

(Repeat antiphon)

**Jerusalem, city of God,
you will shine with the light of God's splendor;
all people on earth will pay you homage.
Nations will come from afar,
bearing gifts for the King of heaven;
in you they will worship the Lord.**

(Repeat antiphon)

**Nations will consider your land holy,
for in you they will call upon the great name of the
   Lord.
You will exult and rejoice over the children of the
   righteous,
for they will be gathered together to praise the Lord.**

(Repeat antiphon)

Another appropriate song may be sung, especially one in honor of Christ, the light of the world.

LITURGY OF THE EUCHARIST

32. The deacons and the ministers prepare the altar in the usual way. Then some of the congregation bring bread, wine, and water for the celebration of the Lord's sacrifice. The bishop receives the gifts at the chair. While the gifts are being brought, the following antiphon may be sung:

Lord God, in the simplicity of my heart I have joyously offered all things to you; with great joy I have looked upon your chosen people; Lord God, I have obeyed your will (alleluia).

Another appropriate song may be sung.

33. When all is ready, the bishop goes to the altar, removes the miter, and kisses the altar. The Mass proceeds in the usual way; however, neither the gifts nor the altar are incensed.

PRAYER OVER THE GIFTS

34. With hands extended, the bishop sings or says:

Lord,
accept the gifts of a rejoicing Church.

May your people,
who are gathered in this sacred place,
arrive at eternal salvation
through the mysteries in which they share.

Grant this through Christ our Lord.
℟. Amen.

EUCHARISTIC PRAYER

35. Eucharist Prayer I or III is said, with the following preface. With hands extended the bishop sings or says:

The Lord be with you.
℟. And also with you.

Lift up your hearts.
℟. We lift them up to the Lord.

Let us give thanks to the Lord our God.
℟. It is right to give him thanks and praise.

Father of holiness and power,
we give you thanks and praise
through Jesus Christ, your Son.
For you have blessed this work of our hands
and your presence makes it a house of prayer;

nor do you ever refuse us welcome
when we come in before you as your pilgrim people.

In this house you realize the mystery of your dwelling
     among us:
for in shaping us here as your holy temple
you enrich your whole Church,
which is the very body of Christ,
and thus bring closer to fulfillment
the vision of your peace,
the heavenly city of Jerusalem.

And so, with all your angels and saints,
who stand in your temple of glory,
we praise you and give you thanks, as we sing:

Holy, holy, holy Lord, God of power and might,
heaven and earth are full of your glory.
     Hosanna in the highest.
Blessed is he who comes in the name of the Lord.
     Hosanna in the highest.

36. While the bishop is receiving the body of Christ the
communion song begins. One of the following antiphons is
sung with Psalm 128.

My house shall be called a house of prayer, says the
Lord: in it all who ask shall receive, all who seek shall
find, and all who knock shall have the door opened to
them (alleluia).

Or:
May the children of the Church be like olive branches
around the table of the Lord (alleluia).

Another appropriate song may be sung.

The inauguration of the blessed sacrament chapel proceeds as
in Chapter II, nos. 79-82.

PRAYER AFTER COMMUNION
38. If there is no inauguration of the blessed sacrament
chapel, when the communion of the congregation is finished,
the bishop says:

Let us pray.

Pause for silent prayer, if this has not preceded.

Lord,
through these gifts
increase the vision of your truth in our minds.

May we always worship you in your holy temple,
and rejoice in your presence with all your saints.

Grant this through Christ our Lord.
℟. Amen.

BLESSING AND DISMISSAL

39. The bishop receives the miter and says:

The Lord be with you.
℟. And also with you.

Then the deacon, if appropriate, gives the invitation to the people in these or similar words:

Bow your heads and pray for God's blessing.

Then the bishop extends his hands over the people and blesses them, saying:

The Lord of earth and heaven
has assembled you before him this day
to dedicate this house of prayer.
May he fill you with the blessings of heaven.
℟. Amen.

God the Father wills that all his children
scattered through the world
become one family in his Son.
May he make you his temple,
the dwelling place of his Holy Spirit.
℟. Amen.

May God free you from every bond of sin,
dwell within you and give you joy.
May you live with him for ever
in the company of all his saints.
℞. Amen.

The bishop takes the pastoral staff and continues:

May almighty God bless you,
the Father, and the Son, ✛ and the Holy Spirit.
℞. Amen.

40. Finally the deacon dismisses the people in the usual way.

CHAPTER IV

DEDICATION OF AN ALTAR

INTRODUCTION

NATURE AND DIGNITY OF THE ALTAR

1. The ancient Fathers of the Church, meditating on the word of God, did not hesitate to assert that Christ was the victim, priest, and altar of his own sacrifice.[1] For in the Letter to the Hebrews, Christ is presented as the high priest who is also the living altar of the heavenly temple;[2] and in the Book of Revelation our Redeemer appears as a Lamb which has been sacrificed,[3] whose offering is taken by the holy angel to the altar in heaven.[4]

THE CHRISTIAN IS ALSO A SPIRITUAL ALTAR

2. Since Christ, Head and Teacher, is the true altar, his members and disciples are also spiritual altars on which the sacrifice of a holy life is offered to God. This is the teaching of the Fathers: Saint Ignatius of Antioch asks the Romans quite plainly: "Grant me only this favor: let my blood be spilled in sacrifice to God, while there is still an altar ready";[5] Saint Polycarp exhorts widows to lead a life of holiness, for "they are God's altar."[6] Among others, Saint Gregory the Great echoes these words when he says: "What is God's altar if not the soul of those who lead good lives? . . . Rightly then, the heart of the just is said to be the altar of God."[7]

Or according to another idea frequently used by the writers of the Church: Christians who give themselves to prayer, who offer petitions to God and present sacrifices of supplication, are the living stones from which the Lord Jesus builds the Church's altar.[8]

---

[1]See Saint Epiphanius, *Panarium II, I, Haeresis* 55: PG 41, 979; Saint Cyril of Alexandria, *De adoratione in spiritu et veritate*, IX: PG 68, 647.
[2]See Hebrews 4:14; 13:10.
[3]See Book of Revelation 5:6.
[4]See *The Roman Missal*, Order of Mass, no. 96.
[5]*Ad Romanos* 2:2: ed. F. X. Funk, p. 255.
[6]*Ad Philippenses* 4:3: ed. F. X. Funk, p. 301.
[7]*Homiliarum in Ezechielem* II, 10, 19: PL 76, 1069.
[8]See Origen, *In librum Iesu Nave*, Homily IX, I: SC 71, pp. 244 and 246.

ALTAR, TABLE OF THE SACRIFICE
AND THE PASCHAL MEAL

3. When Christ the Lord instituted a memorial of the sacrifice he was about to offer the Father on the altar of the cross in the form of a sacrificial banquet, he made holy the table where the community would come to celebrate their Passover. Therefore the altar is the table of the sacrifice and the banquet in which the priest, representing Christ the Lord, accomplishes what the Lord himself did and what he handed on to his disciples to do in his memory. The Apostle clearly intimates this: "The blessing cup that we bless is a communion with the blood of Christ, and the bread that we break is a communion with the body of Christ. The fact that there is only one loaf means that, though there are many of us, we form a single body because we all have a share in this one loaf."⁹

ALTAR, SIGN OF CHRIST

4. Everywhere, according to circumstances, the Church's children can celebrate the memorial of Christ and take their place at the Lord's table. However, it is in keeping with the eucharistic mystery that the Christian people should erect a permanent altar for the celebration of the Lord's Supper, something that has been done from the earliest times.

The Christian altar is by its very nature a table of sacrifice and at the same time a table of the paschal banquet:
—a unique altar on which the sacrifice of the cross is perpetuated in mystery throughout the ages until Christ comes;
—a table at which the Church's children assemble to give thanks to God and receive the body and blood of Christ.

In every church, then, the altar "is the center of the thanksgiving perfected in the eucharist"¹⁰ and the focal point around which the Church's other rites are, in a certain manner, arranged.¹¹

Because it is at the altar that the memorial of the Lord is celebrated and his body and blood given to the people, the Church's writers see in the altar a sign of Christ himself—hence they affirm: "The altar is Christ."

⁹See 1 Corinthians 10:16-17.
¹⁰*The Roman Missal*, General Instruction, no. 259.
¹¹See Pius XII, encyclical letter *Mediator Dei: AAS* 39 (1947) 529.

ALTAR, HONOR OF THE MARTYRS

5. The entire dignity of an altar consists in this: the altar is the table of the Lord. It is not, then, the bodies of the martyrs that render the altar glorious; it is the altar that renders the burial place of the martyrs glorious. However, as a mark of respect for the bodies of the martyrs and other saints, and as a sign that the sacrifice of the members has its source in the sacrifice of the Head,[12] it is fitting that altars should be constructed over their tombs, or their relics placed beneath altars, so that "the triumphant victims may occupy the place where Christ is victim: he, however, who suffered for all, upon the altar; they, who have been redeemed by his sufferings, beneath the altar."[13] This arrangement would seem to recall in a certain manner the spiritual vision of the apostle John in the Book of Revelation: "I saw underneath the altar the souls of all the people who had been killed on account of the word of God, for witnessing to it."[14] Although all the saints are rightly called Christ's witnesses, the witness of blood has a special significance, which is given complete and perfect expression by depositing only martyrs' relics beneath the altar.

BUILDING OF AN ALTAR

6. It is desirable that in every church there should be a fixed altar and that in other places set apart for sacred celebrations there should be either a fixed or a movable altar.

An altar is considered fixed if it is attached to the floor so that it cannot be moved. It is a movable altar if it can be transferred from place to place.[15]

7. In new churches it is better to erect one altar only, so that in the one assembly of the people of God the one altar may signify our one savior Jesus Christ and the one eucharist of the Church.

But in a chapel, if possible separated to a certain extent from the main body of the church, where the tabernacle for the reservation of the blessed sacrament is situated, another altar

---

[12]See *The Roman Missal*, Common of Martyrs 8, prayer over the gifts.
[13]Saint Ambrose, *Epistula* 22, 13: PL 16, 1023; see Ps. Maximus of Turin, *Sermo*, 78: PL 57, 689-690.
[14]Book of Revelation 6:9.
[15]See *The Roman Missal*, General Instruction, nos. 265, 261.

may be erected where Mass can be celebrated on weekdays with a small assembly of the people.

The erection of several altars in a church merely for the sake of adornment must be entirely avoided.

8. The altar should be constructed away from the wall so that the priest can easily walk around it and celebrate Mass facing the people. "It should be placed in a central position which draws the attention of the whole congregation."[16]

9. In accordance with the received custom of the Church and the biblical symbolism connected with an altar, the table of a fixed altar should be of stone, indeed natural stone. But any becoming, solid, and skillfully constructed material, with the approval of the conference of bishops, may be used in erecting an altar.

The supports or pedestal for upholding the table may be made from any sort of material provided it is becoming and durable.[17]

10. The altar is dedicated to the one God by its very nature, for the eucharistic sacrifice is offered to the one God. It is in this sense that the Church's practice of dedicating altars to God in honor of the saints must be understood. Saint Augustine expresses it well: "It is not to any of the martyrs, but to the God of the martyrs, though in memory of the martyrs, that we raise our altars."[18]

This should be made clear to the people. In new churches statues and pictures of saints may not be placed over the altar.

Likewise relics of saints should not be placed on the table of the altar when they are exposed for the veneration of the people.

11. It is fitting that the tradition of the Roman liturgy should be preserved of placing relics of martyrs or other saints beneath the altar.[19] However, the following should be noted:

[16]*Ibid.*, no. 262.
[17]See *ibid.*, no. 263.
[18]*Contra Faustum*, XX, 21: PL 42, 384.
[19]See *The Roman Missal*, General Instruction, no. 266.

a) Relics intended for deposition should be of such a size that they can be recognized as parts of human bodies. Hence excessively small relics of one or more saints must not be deposited.

b) The greatest care must be taken to determine whether relics intended for deposition are authentic. It is better for an altar to be dedicated without relics than to have relics of doubtful credibility placed beneath it.

c) A reliquary must not be placed on the altar or in the table of the altar but beneath the table of the altar, as the design of the altar may allow.

When the rite of the depositing of relics takes place, it is highly recommended to keep a vigil at the relics of the martyr or saint, in accordance with the provisions of Chapter II, no. 10.

CELEBRATION OF THE DEDICATION

MINISTER OF THE RITE

12. Since the bishop has been entrusted with the care of the particular Church, it is his responsibility to dedicate to God new altars built in his diocese.

If he cannot himself preside at the rite, he shall entrust the function to another bishop, especially to one who is his associate and assistant in the pastoral care of the community for which the new altar has been erected; or, in altogether special cirumstances, to a priest, to whom he shall give a special mandate.

CHOICE OF DAY

13. Since an altar becomes sacred principally by the celebration of the eucharist, in order to respect this truth, care should be taken that Mass is not celebrated on a new altar before it has been dedicated, so that the Mass of dedication may also be the first eucharist celebrated on the altar.

14. A day should be chosen for the dedication of a new altar when as many of the people as possible can participate, especially Sunday, unless pastoral considerations suggest otherwise. However, the rite of the dedication of an altar may not

be celebrated during the Easter triduum, Ash Wednesday, the weekdays of Holy Week, and All Souls.

MASS OF THE DEDICATION

15. The celebration of the eucharist is inseparably bound up with the rite of the dedication of an altar. The texts for the dedication of an altar are used. On Christmas, the Epiphany, the Ascension, Pentecost, and on the Sundays of Advent, Lent, and Easter, the Mass of the day is used, with the exception of the prayer over the gifts and the preface which are closely interwoven with the rite itself.

16. It is fitting that the bishop should concelebrate the Mass with the priests present, especially with those who have been given the task of directing the parish or the community for which the altar has been erected.

PARTS OF THE RITE

A. Introductory Rites

17. The introductory rites of the Mass of the dedication of an altar take place in the usual way apart from the fact that, in place of the penitential rite, the bishop blesses water and with it sprinkles the people and the new altar.

B. Liturgy of the Word

18. It is commendable to have three readings in the liturgy of the word, chosen, according to the rubrical norm, either from the liturgy of the day (see above, no. 15) or from those in *The Lectionary* (nos. 704 and 706) for the rite of the dedication of an altar.

19. After the readings the bishop gives the homily, in which he explains the biblical readings and the meaning of the dedication of an altar.

The profession of faith is said. The general intercessions are omitted since in their place the litany of the saints is sung.

C. Prayer of Dedication and the Anointing of the Altar

20. After the singing of the litany, if this is to be done, the relics of martyrs or other saints are placed beneath the altar; this is to signify that all who have been baptized in the death

of Christ, especially those who have shed their blood for the Lord, share in Christ's passion (see above, no. 5).

21. The celebration of the eucharist is the most important rite, and the only necessary one, for the dedication of an altar. Nevertheless, in accordance with the common tradition of the Church, both East and West, a special prayer of dedication is also said. This prayer declares the intention of dedicating the altar to the Lord for all times and it asks for his blessing.

22. The rites of the anointing, incensation, covering, and lighting of the altar express in visible signs several aspects of that invisible work which the Lord accomplishes through the Church in its celebration of the divine mysteries, especially the eucharist.

a) The anointing of the altar: in virtue of the anointing with chrism the altar becomes a symbol of Christ who, before all others, is and is called "The Anointed One"; for the Father anointed him with the Holy Spirit and constituted him the High Priest who on the altar of his body would offer the sacrifice of his life for the salvation of all.

b) Incense is burned on the altar to signify that the sacrifice of Christ, which is there perpetuated in mystery, ascends to God as an odor of sweetness, and also as a sign that the prayers of the people rise up pleasing and acceptable, reaching to the throne of God.[20]

c) The covering of the altar indicates that the Christian altar is the altar of the eucharistic sacrifice and the table of the Lord; standing around it priests and people, in one and the same action but with a difference of function, celebrate the memorial of the death and resurrection of Christ and partake in the Lord's Supper. For this reason the altar is prepared as the table of the sacrificial banquet and adorned as for a feast. Thus people meet with joy to be refreshed with divine food, namely the body and blood of Christ sacrificed.

---

[20]See Book of Revelation 8:3-4: An angel "who had a golden censer, came and stood at the altar. A large quantity of incense was given to him to offer with the prayers of all the saints on the golden altar that stood in front of the throne; and so from the angel's hand the smoke of the incense went up in the presence of God and with it the prayers of the saints."

d) The lighting of the altar teaches us that Christ is "a light to enlighten the nations,"[21] whose brightness shines out in the Church and through it upon the whole human family.

D. Celebration of the Eucharist

23. When the altar has been prepared, the bishop celebrates the eucharist, which is the principal and the most ancient part of the whole rite.[22] The celebration of the eucharist is in the closest harmony with the rite of the dedication of an altar:

—for when the eucharistic sacrifice is celebrated, the end for which the altar was erected is attained and manifested by particularly clear signs;

—furthermore, the eucharist, which sanctifies the hearts of those who receive it, in a sense consecrates the altar, as the ancient Fathers of the Church assert more than once: "This altar is an object of wonder: by nature it is stone, but it is made holy when it receives the body of Christ";[23]

—finally, the bond whereby the dedication of an altar is closely linked with the celebration of the eucharist is likewise evident from the fact that the proper preface of the Mass is, as it were, an integral part of the rite of the dedication of an altar.

ADAPTATION OF THE RITE

ADAPTATIONS WITHIN THE COMPETENCE OF THE CONFERENCES OF BISHOPS

24. Conferences of bishops can adapt this rite, as they see fit, to the character of each region, but in such a way that nothing detracts from its dignity and solemnity.

However, the following should be observed:

a) the celebration of the Mass with its proper preface and the prayer of dedication must never be omitted;

[21]Luke 2:32.
[22]See Pope Vigilius, *Epistula ad Profuturum episcopum*, IV: PL 84, 832.
[23]Saint John Chrysostom, *Homilia XX in II Cor.*, 3: PG 61, 540.

b) rites which have a special meaning and force from liturgical tradition (see above, no. 22) must be retained, unless weighty reasons stand in the way, but the wording may be suitably adapted if necessary.

With regard to adaptations, the competent ecclesiastical authority is to consult the Holy See and with its consent introduce adaptations.[24]

DECISIONS WITHIN THE COMPETENCE OF THE MINISTERS

25. It is for the bishop and for those who are in charge of the celebration of the rite to judge the suitability of depositing relics of the saints; in so doing, they are to observe what is laid down in no. 11 above and they are to be guided primarily by the spiritual good of the community and a proper sense of liturgy.

It is for the rector of the church in which the altar is to be dedicated, helped by those who assist him in the pastoral work, to decide and prepare everything concerning the readings, chants, and other pastoral aids to foster the fruitful participation of the people and to promote a dignified celebration.

PASTORAL PREPARATION

26. The people are not only to be informed in good time about the dedication of a new altar; they are to be properly prepared to take an active part in the rite. Accordingly, they should be taught what each rite means and how it is carried out. For the purpose of giving this instruction, what is said above about the nature and dignity of an altar and the meaning and import of the rites may be of use. In this way the people will be imbued with a due and proper love for the altar.

REQUISITES FOR THE DEDICATION OF AN ALTAR

27. For the celebration of the rite the following should be prepared:

[24]See Second Vatican Council, const. on the liturgy, n. 40: *AAS* 56 (1964) 111.

—*The Roman Missal;*
—*The Lectionary;*
—*The Roman Pontifical;*
—a cross and *The Book of the Gospels* to be carried in the procession;
—a vessel of water and a sprinkler;
—a vessel of holy chrism;
—towels for wiping the table of the altar;
—if it is to be used, a waxed linen cloth or a waterproof linen cover of the same size as the altar;
—a basin and a jug of water, towels, and all that is needed for washing the bishop's hands;
—a linen gremial;
—a brazier for burning incense or aromatic spices; or grains of incense and small candles to burn on the altar;
—a censer, incense boat, and spoon;
—a chalice, corporal, purificators, and hand towel;
—bread, wine, and water for the celebration of Mass;
—an altar cross, unless there is already a cross in the sanctuary, or the cross which is carried in the entrance procession is placed near the altar;
—a linen cloth and candles;
—flowers, if opportune.

28. For the Mass of the dedication the vestments are white or of some festive color. The following should be prepared:
—for the bishop: alb, stole, chasuble, miter, pastoral staff, and pallium, if this is used by the bishop;
—for the concelebrating priests: the vestments for concelebrating Mass;
—for the deacons: albs, stoles, and if opportune, dalmatics;
—for other ministers: albs or other lawfully approved dress.

29. If relics of the saints are to be placed beneath the altar, the following should be prepared:

a) In the place from which the procession begins:
—a reliquary containing the relics, placed between flowers and lights. But as circumstances dictate, the reliquary may be placed in a suitable part of the sanctuary before the rite begins;
—for the deacons who will carry the relics to be deposited: albs, red stoles if the relics are those of a martyr, or white in other cases, and, if available, dalmatics. If the relics are car-

ried by priests, then in place of dalmatics chasubles should be prepared.

Relics may also be carried by other ministers vested in albs or other lawfully approved dress.

b) In the sanctuary:
—a small table on which the reliquary is placed during the first part of the dedication rite.

c) In the sacristy:
—pitch or cement to seal the cover of the aperture. In addition, a stone mason should be at hand to close the aperture containing the relics at the proper time.

30. It is fitting to observe the custom of enclosing a parchment in the reliquary on which is recorded the day, month, and year of the dedication of the altar, the name of the bishop who celebrated the rite, the title of the church, and the names of the martyrs or saints whose relics are deposited beneath the altar.

A record of the dedication is to be made out in duplicate, signed by the bishop, the rector of the church, and representatives of the local community; one copy is to be kept in the diocesan archives, the other in the archives of the church.

RITE OF DEDICATION

INTRODUCTORY RITES

ENTRANCE INTO THE CHURCH

31. When the people are assembled, the bishop and the concelebrating priests, the deacons, and the ministers, each in appropriate vestments, preceded by the crossbearer, go from the sacristy through the main body of the church to the sanctuary.

32. If there are relics of the saints to be placed beneath the altar, these are brought in the entrance procession to the sanctuary from the sacristy or the chapel where since the vigil they have been exposed for the veneration of the people. For a just cause, before the celebration begins, the relics may be

placed between lighted torches in a suitable part of the sanctuary.

33. As the procession proceeds, the entrance antiphon is sung with Psalm 43.

O God, our shield, look with favor on the face of your anointed; one day within your courts is better than a thousand elsewhere (alleluia).

Or:
I will go to the altar of God, the God of my joy.

Another appropriate song may be sung.

34. When the procession reaches the sanctuary, the relics of the saints are placed between lighted torches in a suitable place. The concelebrating priests, the deacons, and the ministers go to the places assigned to them; the bishop, without kissing the altar, goes to the chair. Then, putting aside the pastoral staff and miter, he greets the people, saying:

The grace and peace of God
be with all of you
in his holy Church.
℟. And also with you.

Other suitable words taken preferably from sacred Scripture may be used.

BLESSING AND SPRINKLING OF WATER

35. When the entrance rite is completed, the bishop blesses water with which to sprinkle the people as a sign of repentance and as a reminder of their baptism, and to purify the altar. The ministers bring the vessel with the water to the bishop who stands at the chair. The bishop invites all to pray, in these or similar words:

Brothers and sisters in Christ, this is a day of rejoicing: we have come together to dedicate this altar by offering the sacrifice of Christ.

May we respond to these holy rites, receive God's word with faith, share at the Lord's table with joy, and raise our hearts in hope.

Gathered around this one altar we draw nearer to Christ, the living stone, in whom we become God's holy temple.

But first let us ask God to bless this gift of water. As it is sprinkled upon us and upon this altar, may it be a sign of our repentance and a reminder of our baptism.

All pray in silence for a brief period. The bishop then continues:

God of mercy,
you call every creature to the light of life,
and surround us with such great love
that when we stray
you continually lead us back to Christ our head.

For you have established an inheritance of such mercy,
that those sinners, who pass through water made
    sacred,
die with Christ to rise restored
as members of his body
and heirs of his eternal covenant.

Bless ✠ this water;
sanctify it.

As it is sprinkled upon us and upon this altar
make it a sign of the saving waters of baptism,
by which we become one in Christ, the temple of your
    Spirit.

May all here today,
and all those in days to come,
who will celebrate your mysteries on this altar,
be united at last in the holy city of your peace.

We ask this in the name of Jesus the Lord.
℟. Amen.

36. When the invocation over the water is finished, the bishop, accompanied by the deacons, passes through the main body of the church, sprinkling the people with the holy water; then, when he has returned to the sanctuary, he sprinkles the altar. Meanwhile the following antiphon is sung.

I saw water flowing from the right side of the temple, alleluia. It brought God's life and his salvation, and the people sang in joyful praise: alleluia, alleluia.

Or, during Lent:
I will pour clean water over you and wash away all your defilement. A new heart will I give you, says the Lord.

Another appropriate song may be sung.

37. After the sprinkling the bishop returns to the chair and, when the singing is finished, standing with hands joined says:

May God, the Father of mercies,
to whom we dedicate this altar on earth,
forgive us our sins
and enable us to offer
an unending sacrifice of praise
on his altar in heaven.
℟. Amen.

HYMN
38. Then the **Gloria** is sung.

OPENING PRAYER
39. When the hymn is finished, the bishop, with hands joined, says:

Let us pray.

All pray in silence for a brief period. Then the bishop, with hands extended, says:

Lord,
you willed that all things be drawn to your Son,
mounted on the altar of the cross.
Bless those who dedicate this altar to your service.

May it be the table of our unity,
a banquet of plenty,
and a source of the Spirit,
in whom we grow daily as your faithful people.

We ask this through our Lord Jesus Christ, your Son, who lives and reigns with you and the Holy Spirit, one God, for ever and ever.
℟. **Amen.**

LITURGY OF THE WORD

40. In the liturgy of the word everything takes place in the usual way. The readings and the gospel are taken, in accordance with the rubrics, either from the text in *The Lectionary* (nos. 704 and 706) for the rite of dedication of an altar or from the Mass of the day.

41. After the gospel the bishop gives the homily, in which he explains the biblical readings and the meaning of the rite.

42. The profession of faith is said. The general intercessions are omitted since in their place the litany of the saints is sung.

PRAYER OF DEDICATION AND THE ANOINTINGS

INVITATION TO PRAYER

43. Then all stand, and the bishop, without his miter, invites the people to pray in these or similar words:

Let our prayers go forth to God the Father through Jesus Christ, his Son, with whom are joined all the saints who have shared in his suffering and now sit at his table of glory.

Deacon (except on Sundays and during the Easter season):

Let us kneel.

LITANY OF THE SAINTS

44. Then the litany of the saints is sung, with all responding. On Sundays and also during the Easter season, all stand; on other days, all kneel.

45. The cantors begin the litany (Chapter VIII); they add, at the proper place, names of other saints (the titular of the church, the patron saint of the place, and the saints whose

relics are to be deposited, if this is to take place) and petitions suitable to the occasion.

46. When the litany is finished, the bishop, standing with hands extended, says:

**Lord,
may the prayers of the Blessed Virgin Mary
and of all the saints
make our prayers acceptable to you.**

**May this altar be the place
where the great mysteries of redemption are accomplished:
a place where your people offer their gifts,
unfold their good intentions,
pour out their prayers,
and echo every meaning of their faith and devotion.**

**Grant this through Christ our Lord.
℟. Amen.**

If it is applicable, the deacon says:

Let us stand.

All rise. The bishop receives the miter.

When there is no depositing of the relics of the saints, the bishop immediately says the prayer of dedication as indicated in no. 48 below.

DEPOSITING OF THE RELICS

47. Then, if relics of the martyrs or other saints are to be placed beneath the altar, the bishop approaches the altar. A deacon or priest brings them to the bishop, who places them in a suitably prepared aperture. Meanwhile one of the following antiphons is sung with Psalm 15.

Saints of God, you have been enthroned at the foot of God's altar; pray for us to the Lord Jesus Christ.

Or:

The bodies of the saints lie buried in peace, but their names will live on for ever (alleluia).

Another appropriate song may be sung.

Meanwhile a stone mason closes the aperture and the bishop returns to the chair.

PRAYER OF DEDICATION

48. Then the bishop, standing without miter at the chair or near the altar, with hands extended, says:

Father,
we praise you and give you thanks,
for you have established the sacrament of true worship
by bringing to perfection in Christ
the mystery of the one true altar
prefigured in those many altars of old.

Noah,
the second father of the human race,
once the waters fell and the mountains peaked again,
built an altar in your name.
You, Lord, were appeased by his fragrant offering
and your rainbow bore witness
to a covenant refounded in love.

Abraham,
our father in faith,
wholeheartedly accepted your word
and constructed an altar on which to slay
Isaac, his only son.
But you, Lord, stayed his hand
and provided a ram for his offering.

Moses,
mediator of the old law,
built an altar
on which was cast the blood of a lamb:
so prefiguring the altar of the cross.

All this Christ has fulfilled in the paschal mystery:
as priest and victim he freely mounted the tree of the
cross
and gave himself to you, Father, as the one perfect
oblation.

In his sacrifice the new covenant is sealed,
in his blood sin is engulfed.

Lord, we therefore stand before you in prayer.

Bless this altar built in the house of the Church,
that it may ever be reserved for the sacrifice of Christ,
and stand for ever as the Lord's table,
where your people will find nourishment and strength.

Make this altar a sign of Christ
from whose pierced side flowed blood and water,
which ushered in the sacraments of the Church.

Make it a table of joy,
where the friends of Christ may hasten
to cast upon you their burdens and cares
and take up their journey restored.

Make it a place of communion and peace,
so that those who share the body and blood of your Son
may be filled with his Spirit
and grow in your life of love.

Make it a source of unity and friendship,
where your people may gather as one
to share your spirit of mutual love.

Make it the center of our praise and thanksgiving
until we arrive at the eternal tabernacle,
where, together with Christ,
high priest and living altar,
we will offer you an everlasting sacrifice of praise.

We ask this thorugh our Lord Jesus Christ, your Son,
who lives and reigns with you and the Holy Spirit,
one God, for ever and ever.
℟. Amen.

ANOINTING OF THE ALTAR

49. When the above is finished, the bishop, removing the
chasuble if necessary and putting on a linen gremial, goes to

the altar with the deacon or another minister, one of whom carries the chrism. Standing before the altar, the bishop says:

We now anoint this altar.
May God in his power make it holy,
a visible sign of the mystery of Christ,
who offered himself for the life of the world.

Then he pours chrism on the middle of the altar and on each of its four corners, and it is recommended that he anoint the entire table of the altar with this.

50. During the anointing, outside the Easter Season, the following antiphon is sung (see below, no. 51) with Psalm 45.

God, your God, has anointed you with the oil of gladness.

Another appropriate song may be sung.

51. During the Easter Season the following antiphon is sung with Psalm 118.

The stone which the builders rejected has become the keystone of the building, alleluia.

Another appropriate song may be sung.

52. When the altar has been anointed, the bishop returns to the chair, sits, and washes his hands. Then the bishop takes off the gremial and puts on the chasuble.

INCENSATION OF THE ALTAR

53. After the rite of anointing, a brazier is placed on the altar for burning incense or aromatic gums. The bishop puts incense into the brazier, saying:

Lord,
may our prayer ascend as incense in your sight.
As this building is filled with fragrance
so may your Church fill the world
with the fragrance of Christ.

Then the bishop puts incense into the censer and incenses the altar; he returns to the chair, is incensed, and then sits. A minister incenses the people. Meanwhile one of the following antiphons is sung with Psalm 138.

An angel stood by the altar of the temple, holding a golden censer.

Or:

From the hand of the angel, clouds of incense rose in the presence of the Lord.

Another appropriate song may be sung.

LIGHTING OF THE ALTAR

54. After the incensation, a few ministers wipe the table of the altar with cloths, and, if need be, cover it with a waterproof linen. They then cover the altar with a cloth, and, if opportune, decorate it with flowers. They arrange in a suitable manner the candles needed for the celebration of Mass, and, if need be, the cross.

55. Then the bishop gives to the deacon a lighted candle, and says:

**Light of Christ,
shine on this altar
and be reflected by those
who share at this table.**

Then the bishop sits. The deacon goes to the altar and lights the candles for the celebration of the eucharist.

56. Then the festive lighting takes place: as a sign of rejoicing all the lamps around the altar are lit. Meanwhile the following antiphon is sung.

In you, O Lord, is the fountain of life; in your light we shall see light.

Another appropriate song may be sung, especially one in honor of Christ, the light of the world.

LITURGY OF THE EUCHARIST

57. The deacons and the ministers prepare the altar in the usual way. Then some of the congregation bring bread, wine, and water for the celebration of the Lord's sacrifice. The bishop receives the gifts at the chair. While the gifts are being brought, one of the following antiphons may be sung.

If you are bringing your gift to the altar, and there you remember that your neighbor has something against you, leave your gift in front of the altar; go at once and make peace with your neighbor, and then come back and offer your gift, alleluia.

Or:

Moses consecrated the altar to the Lord and offered sacrifices and burnt offerings; he made an evening sacrifice of sweet fragrance to the Lord God in the sight of the children of Israel.

Another appropriate song may be sung.

58. When all is ready, the bishop goes to the altar, removes the miter, and kisses the altar. The Mass proceeds in the usual way; however, neither the gifts nor the altar are incensed.

PRAYER OVER THE GIFTS

59. With hands extended, the bishop sings or says:

**Lord,
send your Spirit upon this altar
to sanctify these gifts;
may he prepare our hearts
to receive them worthily.**

**Grant this through Christ our Lord.
℟. Amen.**

EUCHARISTIC PRAYER

60. Eucharistic Prayer I or III is said, with the following preface, which is an integral part of the rite of the dedication of an altar:

**The Lord be with you.
℟. And also with you.**

**Lift up your hearts.
℟. We lift them up to the Lord.**

**Let us give thanks to the Lord our God.
℟. It is right to give him thanks and praise.**

Father, all-powerful and ever-living God,
we do well always and everywhere to give you thanks
through Jesus Christ our Lord.

True priest and true victim,
he offered himself to you
on the altar of the cross
and commanded us to celebrate
that same sacrifice,
until he comes again.

Therefore your people have built this altar
and have dedicated it to your name
with grateful hearts.

This is truly a sacred place.

Here the sacrifice of Christ is offered in mystery,
perfect praise is given to you,
and our redemption is made continually present.

Here is prepared the Lord's table,
at which your children,
nourished by the body of Christ,
are gathered into a Church, one and holy.

Here your people drink of the Spirit,
the stream of living water,
flowing from the rock of Christ.
They will become, in him,
a worthy offering and a living altar.

We praise you, Lord,
with all the angels and saints in their song of joy:

Holy, holy, holy Lord, God of power and might,
heaven and earth are full of your glory.
Hosanna in the highest.
Blessed is he who comes in the name of the Lord.
Hosanna in the highest.

61. While the bishop is receiving the body of Christ the
communion song begins. One of the following antiphons is
sung with Psalm 128.

Even the sparrow finds a home and the swallow a nest wherein she places her young: near to your altars, O Lord of Hosts, my King and my God.

Or:

May the children of the Church be like olive branches around the table of the Lord (alleluia).

Another appropriate song may be sung.

PRAYER AFTER COMMUNION

62. Then, standing at the chair or at the altar, the bishop sings or says:

Let us pray.

Pause for silent prayer, if this has not preceded.

**Lord,
may we always be drawn
to this altar of sacrifice.**

**United in faith and love,
may we be nourished by the body of Christ
and transformed into his likeness,
who lives and reigns with you and the Holy Spirit,
one God, for ever and ever.
℟. Amen.**

BLESSING AND DISMISSAL

63. The bishop receives the miter and says:

**The Lord be with you.
℟. And also with you.**

Then the deacon, if appropriate, gives the invitation to the people in these or similar words:

Bow your heads and pray for God's blessing.

Then the bishop extends his hands over the people and blesses them, saying:

May God, who has given you the dignity
of a royal priesthood,
strengthen you in your holy service
and make you worthy to share in his sacrifice.
℟. Amen.

May he, who invites you to the one table
and feeds you with the one bread,
make you one in heart and mind.
℟. Amen.

May all to whom you proclaim Christ
be drawn to him
by the example of your love.
℟. Amen.

The bishop takes the pastoral staff and continues:

May almighty God bless you,
the Father, and the Son, ✛ and the Holy Spirit.
℟. Amen.

64. Finally the deacon dismisses the people in the usual way.

CHAPTER V

BLESSING OF A CHURCH

INTRODUCTION

1. It is desirable that sacred buildings of churches which are destined for the celebration of divine mysteries in a stable manner should be dedicated to God. Such a dedication takes place according to the rite of dedication described in Chapters II and III, which is distinguished by the wealth of its rites and symbols.

It is fitting that private oratories, chapels, or sacred buildings which, because of special circumstances, are destined for divine worship only for a time, should be blessed according to the rite which is described below.

2. As to the liturgical procedure, the choice of a titular, and the pastoral preparation of the people, what is said in the Introduction to Chapter II, nos. 4-5, 7, 20, after suitable adjustments have been made, is to be observed.

A church or an oratory is blessed by the bishop of the diocese or by a priest delegated by him.

3. A church or an oratory may be blessed on any day, apart from the Easter triduum. Insofar as possible a day should be chosen when as many of the people as possible can participate, especially Sunday, unless pastoral considerations suggest otherwise.

4. On days mentioned in the list of liturgical days, nos. 1-4, the Mass of the day is said; but on other days either the Mass of the day or the Mass of the titular of the church or oratory may be said.

5. For the rite of the blessing of a church or an oratory all things necessary for the celebration of Mass are prepared. But the altar, even though it has been blessed or dedicated, should remain uncovered until the beginning of the Liturgy of the Eucharist. Furthermore in a suitable place in the sanctuary the following should be prepared:

—a vessel of water and a sprinkler;
—a censer, incense boat, and spoon;
—*The Roman Pontifical*;
—an altar cross, unless there is already a cross in the sanctuary, or the cross, which is carried in the entrance procession is placed near the altar;
—a linen cloth and candles;
—flowers, if opportune.

6. If, together with the blessing of the church, the altar is to be consecrated, all those things should be prepared which are mentioned in Chapter IV, no. 27, and in no. 29, if relics of the saints are to be deposited beneath the altar.

7. For the Mass of the blessing of a church the vestments are white or of some festive color. The following should be prepared:
—for the bishop: alb, stole, chasuble, miter, pastoral staff;
—for a priest: the vestments for celebrating Mass;
—for the concelebrating priests: the vestments of concelebrating Mass;
—for the deacons: albs, stoles, and, if opportune, dalmatics;
—for other ministers: albs or other lawfully approved dress.

RITE OF BLESSING

INTRODUCTORY RITES

ENTRANCE INTO THE CHURCH
8. When the people are assembled, while the entrance song is being sung, the bishop and the concelebrating priests, the deacons, and the ministers, each in appropriate vestments, preceded by the crossbearer, go from the sacristy through the main body of the church to the sanctuary.

When the procession arrives at the sanctuary, the bishop without kissing or incensing the altar, goes immediately to the chair; the others go to the places assigned to them.

9. The bishop puts aside the pastoral staff and miter, and when the singing is finished, he greets the people, saying:

**The grace and peace of God
be with all of you
in his holy Church.**
℟. **And also with you.**

Other suitable words taken preferably from sacred Scripture
may be used.

BLESSING AND SPRINKLING OF WATER

10. Then the bishop blesses water with which to sprinkle the
people as a sign of repentance and as a reminder of their
baptism, and to purify the walls of the new church or oratory.
The ministers bring the vessel with the water to the bishop
who stands at the chair. The bishop invites all to pray, in
these or similar words:

**Brothers and sisters in Christ, this is a day of rejoicing.
For we have come together to offer this new church to
God.**

**We ask that he bless us with his grace and, by his
power, bless this gift of water.**

**As it is sprinkled upon us and throughout this new
church, may it become a sign of our repentance, a reminder of our baptism, and a symbol of the cleansing
of these walls.**

**But first let us call to mind that we ourselves, who are
bound here in faith and love, are the living Church, set
in the world, as a sign and witness of God's love for
all.**

11. All pray in silence for a brief period. The bishop then
continues:

**God of mercy,
you call every creature to the light of life,
and surround us with such great love
that when we stray
you continually lead us back to Christ our head.**

For you have established an inheritance of such mercy,
that those sinners, who pass through water made
   sacred,
die with Christ and rise restored
as members of his body
and heirs of his eternal covenant.

Bless ✠ this water;
sanctify it.

As it is sprinkled upon us and throughout this church
make it a sign of the saving waters of baptism,
by which we become one in Christ, the temple of your
   Spirit.

May all here today
and all those in days to come,
who will celebrate your mysteries in this church,
be united at last in the holy city of your peace.

We ask this in the name of Jesus the Lord.
℟. Amen.

12. When the invocation over the water is finished, the
bishop, accompanied by the deacons, passes through the
main body of the church, sprinkling the people and the walls
with the holy water; then, when he has returned to the
sanctuary, he sprinkles the altar, unless it is already blessed
or dedicated (see above, no. 5). Meanwhile the following
antiphon is sung.

I saw water flowing from the right side of the temple,
alleluia. It brought God's life and his salvation, and
the people sang in joyful praise: alleluia, alleluia.

Or, during Lent:
I will pour clean water over you and wash away all
your defilement. A new heart will I give you, says the
Lord.

Another appropriate song may be sung.

13. After the sprinkling the bishop returns to the chair and, when the singing is finished, standing with hands joined, says:

May God, the Father of mercies,
dwell in this house of prayer.
May the grace of the Holy Spirit cleanse us,
for we are the temple of his presence.
℟. **Amen.**

HYMN

14. Then, except on Sundays or weekdays of Advent and Lent, the **Gloria** is sung.

OPENING PRAYER

15. When the hymn is finished, the following prayer is said except on the days listed in the Table of Liturgical Days, nos. 1-4, when the prayer of the day is used. The bishop, with hands joined, says:

Let us pray.

All pray in silence for a brief period. Then the bishop, with hands extended, says:

Lord,
bless this church,
which we have been privileged to build with your
   help.

May all who gather here in faith
to listen to your word
and celebrate your sacraments,
experience the presence of Christ,
who promised to be with those
gathered in his name,
for he lives and reigns with you and the Holy Spirit,
one God, for ever and ever.
℟. **Amen.**

LITURGY OF THE WORD

16. The readings are taken, in accordance with the rubrics (see above no.4), either from the texts in *The Lectionary* (nos. 704 and 706) for the rite of the dedication of a church or from the Mass of the day.

17. Neither lights nor incense are carried at the gospel.

18. After the gospel the bishop gives the homily, in which he explains the biblical readings and the meaning of the rite.

19. The profession of faith and the general intercessions are said in the usual way.

BLESSING OF THE ALTAR

20. Then the bishop goes to bless the altar. Meanwhile the following antiphon is sung.

May the children of the Church be like olive branches around the table of the Lord (alleluia).

Another appropriate song may be sung.

21. When the singing is finished, the bishop, standing without miter, speaks to the people in these or similar words:

Brothers and sisters, our community rejoices as it comes together to bless this altar. Let us ask God to look kindly on the Church's offering placed upon it and to receive his people as an everlasting gift.

All pray in silence for a brief period. Then the bishop, with hands extended, says:

**Blessed are you, Lord our God,
who accepted the sacrifice of Christ,
offered on the altar of the cross
for the salvation of the world.**

**Now with a Father's love,
you call upon your people to celebrate his memory
by coming together at his table.**

May this altar,
which we have built for your holy mysteries,
be the center of our praise and thanksgiving.

May it be the table
at which we break the bread which gives us life
and drink the cup which makes us one.

May it be the fountain
of the unfailing waters of salvation.

Here may we draw close to Christ,
the living stone,
and, in him, grow into a holy temple.

Here may our lives of holiness
become a pleasing sacrifice to your glory.
℟. Blessed be God for ever.

The bishop puts incense into some censers and incenses the
altar; receiving the miter, he returns to the chair, is incensed,
and then sits. Ministers, walking through the church, incense
the people and the main body of the church.

22. If the altar is to be dedicated, the profession of faith is
said, and the general intercessions are omitted, and what is
laid down in Chapter IV, nos. 43-56, is observed.

But if the altar is to be neither blessed nor consecrated (for
example, because an altar already blessed or dedicated has
been transferred to the new church), after the general intercessions the Mass proceeds as in no. 23 below.

LITURGY OF THE EUCHARIST

23. Ministers cover the altar with a cloth, and, if opportune,
decorate it with flowers. They arrange in a suitable manner
the candles needed for the celebration of Mass, and, if need
be, the cross.

24. When the altar is ready, some of the congregation bring
bread, wine, and water for the celebration of the Lord's sacrifice. The bishop receives the gifts at the chair. While the
gifts are being brought, one of the following antiphons may
be sung.

If you are bringing your gift to the altar, and there you remember that your neighbor has something against you, leave your gift in front of the altar; go at once and make peace with your neighbor, and then come back and offer your gift, alleluia.

Or:

Moses consecrated the altar to the Lord and offered sacrifices and burnt offerings; he made an evening sacrifice of sweet fragrance to the Lord God in the sight of the children of Israel.

Another appropriate song may be sung.

25. When all is ready, the bishop goes to the altar, removes the miter, and kisses the altar. The Mass proceeds in the usual way; however, neither the gifts nor the altar are incensed. But if the altar was not blessed or dedicated in this celebration, the incensation takes place in the usual way.

26. If a chapel of the blessed sacrament is to be inaugurated, when the communion of the congregation is finished, everything takes place as described in Chapter II, nos. 79-82.

BLESSING AND DISMISSAL

27. The bishop receives the miter and says:

The Lord be with you.
℟. And also with you.

Then the deacon, if appropriate, gives the invitation to the people in these or similar words:

Bow your heads and pray for God's blessing.

Then the bishop extends his hands over the people and blesses them, saying:

The Lord of the earth and heaven
has assembled you before him this day
to bless this house of prayer.
May he fill you with the blessings of heaven.
℟. Amen.

God the Father wills that all his children
scattered through the world

become one family in his Son.
May he make you his temple,
the dwelling place of his Holy Spirit.
℞. Amen.

May God free you from every bond of sin,
dwell within you and give you joy.
May you live with him for ever
in the company of all his saints.
℞. Amen.

The bishop takes the pastoral staff and continues:

May almighty God bless you,
the Father, and the Son, ✠ and the Holy Spirit.
℞. Amen.

28. Finally the deacon dismisses the people in the usual way.

CHAPTER VI

BLESSING OF AN ALTAR

INTRODUCTION

1. An altar is considered fixed if it is attached to the floor so that it cannot be moved. It is a movable altar if it can be transferred from place to place.[1]

A fixed altar is to be dedicated according to the rite described in Chapter IV. A movable altar too should be treated with religious respect because it is a table destined solely and permanently for the eucharistic banquet. Consequently it is desirable that before a movable altar is put to use, if it is not to be dedicated, it should at least be blessed with the following rite.[2]

2. A movable altar may be constructed of any solid material which is suitable to liturgical use, according to the traditions and culture of different regions.[3]

3. In erecting a movable altar, what is laid down in the Introduction to Chapter IV, nos. 6-10, after suitable adjustments have been made, is to be observed. However, it is not permissible to place the relics of saints in the base of a movable altar.

4. It is appropriate that a movable altar should be blessed by the bishop of the diocese or by the priest who is rector of the church.

5. A movable altar may be blessed on any day, apart from Good Friday and Holy Saturday. Insofar as possible a day should be chosen when as many of the people as possible can participate, especially Sunday, unless pastoral considerations suggest otherwise.

6. The Mass of the day is said in the rite of the blessing of a movable altar.

---

[1]*The Roman Missal*, General Instruction, no. 261.
[2]See *ibid.*, no. 265.
[3]See *ibid.*, no. 264.

7. The altar should be entirely uncovered until the beginning of the Liturgy of the Eucharist. Hence a cross (if need be), a cloth, candles, and everything else necessary for its furnishing should be prepared in a suitable place in the sanctuary.

RITE OF BLESSING

8. During Mass everything takes place in the usual way. When the general intercessions are finished the bishop goes to bless the altar. Meanwhile the following antiphon is sung.

May the children of the Church be like olive branches around the table of the Lord (alleluia).

Another appropriate song may be sung.

9. When the singing is finished, the bishop, standing without miter, speaks to the people in these or similar words:

Brothers and sisters, our community rejoices as it comes together to bless this altar. Let us ask God to look kindly on the Church's offering placed upon it and to receive his people as an everlasting gift.

All pray in silence for a brief period. Then the bishop, with hands extended, says:

**Blessed are you, Lord our God,
who accepted the sacrifice of Christ,
offered on the altar of the cross
for the salvation of the world.**

**Now with a Father's love,
you call your people to celebrate his memory
by coming together at his table.**

**May this altar,
which we have built for your holy mysteries,
be the center of our praise and thanksgiving.**

**May it be the table
at which we break the bread which gives us life
and drink the cup which makes us one.**

May it be the fountain
of the unfailing waters of salvation.

Here may we draw close to Christ,
the living stone,
and, in him, grow into a holy temple.

Here may our lives of holiness
become a pleasing sacrifice to your glory.
℟. Blessed be God for ever.

10. The bishop then sprinkles the altar with holy water and incenses it. Then he returns to the chair, receives the miter, is incensed, and then sits. A minister incenses the people.

11. Ministers cover the altar with a cloth, and, if opportune, decorate it with flowers; they arrange in a suitable manner the candles needed for the celebration of Mass, and, if need be, the cross.

12. When the altar is ready, some of the congregation bring bread, wine, and water for the celebration of the Lord's sacrifice. The bishop receives the gifts at the chair. While the gifts are being brought, the following antiphon is sung.

If you are bringing your gift to the altar, and there you remember that your neighbor has something against you, leave your gift in front of the altar; go at once and make peace with your neighbor, and then come back and offer your gift, alleluia.

Another appropriate song may be sung.

13. When all is ready, the bishop goes to the altar, removes the miter, and kisses the altar. The Mass proceeds in the usual way; however, neither the gifts nor the altar are incensed.

CHAPTER VII

BLESSING OF A CHALICE AND PATEN

INTRODUCTION

1. The chalice and paten in which wine and bread are offered, consecrated, and received,[1] since they are intended solely and permanently for the celebration of the eucharist, become "sacred vessels."

2. The intention, however, of devoting these vessels entirely to the celebration of the eucharist is made manifest before the community by a special blessing which is preferably imparted during Mass.

3. Any bishop or priest may bless a chalice and paten, provided these have been made according to the norms laid down in the General Instruction of *The Roman Missal*, nos. 290-295.

4. If it is a chalice or paten alone that is to be blessed, the text should be suitably adapted.

RITE OF BLESSING WITHIN MASS

5. In the liturgy of the word, apart from the days listed on the Table of Liturgical Days, nos. 1-9, one or two readings may be taken from those given below in nos. 6-8.

6. READINGS FROM SACRED SCRIPTURE

1. **1 Corinthians 10:14-22a (Gr. 10-22)**
Our blessing-cup is a communion with the blood of Christ.

2. **1 Corinthians 11:23-26**
This cup is the new covenant in my blood.

7. RESPONSORIAL PSALMS

1. Psalm 16:5 and 8, 9-10, 11
℟. (5a) **The Lord is my inheritance and my cup.**

---

[1] See *The Roman Missal*, General Instruction, no. 289.

2. Psalm 23:1-3a, 3b-4, 5, 6
℟. (5a, d) **You prepared a banquet before me; my cup overflows.**

8. GOSPELS

1. **Matthew 20:20-28**
You shall indeed drink my cup.

2. **Mark 14:12-16, 22-26**
This is my body. This is my blood.

9. After the reading of the word of God the homily is given in which the celebrant explains the biblical readings and the meaning of the blessing of a chalice and paten that are used in the celebration of the Lord's Supper.

10. When the general intercessions are finished, ministers or representatives of the community that are presenting the chalice and paten place them on the altar. The celebrant then approaches the altar. Meanwhile the following antiphon is sung.

I will take the cup of salvation and call on the name of the Lord.

Another appropriate song may be sung.

11. When the singing if finished, the celebrant says:

Let us pray.

All pray in silence for a brief period. The celebrant then continues:

Lord,
with joy we place on your altar
this cup and this paten,
vessels with which we will celebrate
the sacrifice of Christ's new covenant.

May they be sanctified,
for in them the body and blood of Christ
will be offered, consecrated, and received.

Lord,
when we celebrate Christ's faultless sacrifice on earth,

may we be renewed in strength
and filled with your Spirit,
until we join with your saints
at your table in heaven.

Glory and honor be yours for ever and ever.
℟. Blessed be God for ever.

12. Afterward the ministers place a corporal on the altar. Some of the congregation bring bread, wine, and water for the celebration of the Lord's sacrifice. The celebrant puts the gifts in the newly blessed paten and chalice and offers them in the usual way. Meanwhile the following antiphon may be sung with Psalm 116:10-19.

I will take the cup of salvation and offer a sacrifice of praise (alleluia).

Another appropriate song may be sung.

13. When he has said the prayer **Lord God, we ask you to receive us,** the celebrant may incense the gifts and the altar.

14. If the circumstances of the celebration permit, it is appropriate that the congregation should receive the blood of Christ from the newly blessed chalice.

RITE OF BLESSING OUTSIDE MASS

15. After the people have assembled, the celebrant, with alb or surplice and stole, goes to the chair. Meanwhile, an antiphon with Psalm 116:10-19 (see above, no. 12) may be sung or another appropriate song.

16. The celebrant greets the people saying:

The grace of our Lord Jesus Christ,
who offered for us his body and blood,
the love of God,
and the fellowship of the Holy Spirit
be with you all.
℟. And also with you.

Other suitable words taken preferably from sacred Scripture may be used.

17. Then the celebrant briefly addresses the people, preparing them to take part in the celebration and explaining to them the meaning of the rite.

18. Afterward one or more texts from sacred Scripture are read, especially from those proposed above, with a suitable intervening responsorial psalm (see above, nos. 6-8) or a period of silence.

19. After the reading of the word of God the homily is given, in which the celebrant explains the biblical readings and the meaning of the blessing of a chalice and paten that are used in the celebration of the Lord's Supper.

20. After the homily the ministers or representatives of the community that are presenting the chalice and paten place them on the altar. The celebrant then approaches the altar. Meanwhile the following antiphon may be sung.

I will take the cup of salvation and call on the name of the Lord.

Another appropriate song may be sung.

21. Then the celebrant says:

Let us pray.

All pray in silence for a brief period. The celebrant then continues:

Father,
look kindly upon your children,
who have placed on your altar
this cup and this paten.

May these vessels be sanctified ✠ by your blessing,
for with them we will celebrate
the sacrifice of Christ's new covenant.

And may we who celebrate these mysteries on earth
be renewed in strength

and filled with your Spirit
until we join with your saints
at your table in heaven.

Glory and honor be yours for ever and ever.
℟. Blessed be God for ever.

22. Afterward the general intercessions take place either in the usual way or as indicated below:

Let us pray to the Lord Jesus who continuously offers himself for the Church, as the bread of life and the cup of salvation. With confidence we make our prayer:
℟. Christ Jesus, bread of heaven, grant us eternal life.

Savior of all, in obedience to the Father's will, you drank the cup of suffering,
grant that we may share in the mystery of your death and thus win the promise of eternal life.

Priest of the most high, hidden yet present in the sacrament of the altar,
grant that we may discern by faith what is concealed from our eyes.

Good shepherd, you give yourself to your disciples as food and drink,
grant that, fed by this mystery, we may be transformed into your likeness.

Lamb of God, you commanded your Church to celebrate the paschal mystery under the signs of bread and wine,
grant that this memorial may be the summit and source of holiness for all who believe.

Son of God, you wondrously satisfy the hunger and thirst of all who eat and drink at your table,
grant that through the mystery of the eucharist we may learn to live your command of love.

Then the celebrant may introduce the Lord's Prayer in these or similar words:

Fastened to the cross, Christ was the way of salvation; in fulfilling the will of the Father he is acclaimed the master of prayer; let his prayer be the source of ours as we say:
All: **Our Father . . .**

The celebrant immediately continues:
**Lord,
by the death and resurrection of your Son
you have brought redemption to the entire world.**

**Continue in us the work of your grace,
so that, ever recalling the mystery of Christ,
we may finally rejoice at your table in heaven.**

**Grant this through Christ our Lord.
℟. Amen.**

23. Then the celebrant blesses the people in the usual way and dismisses them saying:

**Go in peace.
℟. Thanks be to God.**

CHAPTER VII

LITANY OF THE SAINTS

The cantors begin the litany; they add, at the proper place, names of other saints (the titular of the church, the patron saint of the place, and the saints whose relics are to be deposited, if this is to take place) and petitions suitable to the occasion.

Lord, have mercy   Lord, have mercy
Christ, have mercy   Christ, have mercy
Lord, have mercy   Lord, have mercy

Holy Mary, Mother of God   pray for us
Saint Michael   pray for us
Holy angels of God   pray for us
Saint John the Baptist   pray for us
Saint Joseph   pray for us
Saint Peter and Saint Paul   pray for us
Saint Andrew   pray for us
Saint John   pray for us
Saint Mary Magdalene   pray for us
Saint Stephen   pray for us
Saint Ignatius of Antioch   pray for us
Saint Lawrence   pray for us
Saint Perpetua and Saint Felicity   pray for us
Saint Agnes   pray for us
Saint Gregory   pray for us
Saint Augustine   pray for us
Saint Athanasius   pray for us
Saint Basil   pray for us
Saint Martin   pray for us
Saint Benedict   pray for us
Saint Francis and Saint Dominic   pray for us
Saint Francis Xavier   pray for us
Saint John Vianney   pray for us
Saint Catherine   pray for us
Saint Teresa   pray for us
All holy men and women   pray for us

Lord, be merciful   Lord, save your people
From all evil   Lord, save your people
From every sin   Lord, save your people
From everlasting death   Lord, save your people
By your coming as man   Lord, save your people
By your death and rising to new life   Lord, save your
    people
By your gift of the Holy Spirit   Lord, save your people

Be merciful to us sinners   Lord, hear our prayer
Guide and protect your holy Church
    Lord, hear our prayer
Keep the pope and all the clergy in faithful service
    to your Church   Lord, hear our prayer
Bring all peoples together in trust and peace
    Lord, hear our prayer
Strengthen us in your service
    Lord, hear our prayer
Make this church (altar) holy and consecrate it
    to your worship   Lord, hear our prayer
Jesus, Son of the living God   Lord, hear our prayer
Christ, hear us   Christ, hear us
Lord Jesus, hear our prayer   Lord Jesus, hear our
    prayer

APPENDIX I
RECEPTION OF THE BISHOP IN THE
CATHEDRAL CHURCH

Canonical Possession

Introductory Rites

Imposition of the Pallium

Greeting of the Bishop

Celebration of Mass

Participation of the Metropolitan

Reception of Coadjuter or Auxiliary Bishops

APPENDIX II
BLESSING OF PONTIFICAL INSIGNIA

APPENDIX III
BLESSING OF OILS AND
CONSECRATION OF THE CHRISM

Decree

Introduction (1-12)

The Oils (3-5)

The Minister (6-8)

Time of Blessing (9-10)

Place of Blessing in the Mass (11-12)

Blessing of Oils and Consecration of the Chrism (13-28)

Preparations (13)

Rite of Blessing (14-19)

Blessing of the Oil of the Sick (20)

Blessing of the Oil of the Catechumens (21-22)

Consecration of the Chrism (23-24)
    Consecratory Prayer (25)

APPENDIX I

RECEPTION OF THE BISHOP IN THE CATHEDRAL CHURCH

The ordination of a new bishop properly takes place in his cathedral church, in accord with the Roman Pontifical, and there is then no distinct rite for the reception or installation of the bishop. In some cases, however, the new bishop may have been ordained already as bishop of another church, or it may have been impossible for him to be ordained in his cathedral church. In these circumstances, the new bishop should be solemnly received in the cathedral church by the clergy and people of the local church when he first comes to the diocese.

This liturgical reception of the new bishop is sometimes called installation; its principal element is the eucharistic celebration at which the bishop presides for the first time with the college of priests and the deacons, and with people of the diocese taking full and active part.

CANONICAL POSSESSION

The new bishop may take canonical possession of the diocese before the liturgical reception. It is preferable, however, that this be done in the presence of the clergy and people, that is, by the presentation and reading of the apostolic letter at the beginning of Mass (below). The showing of the letter to the chapter of the cathedral church or to the board of consultors should be recorded by the chancellor.

INTRODUCTORY RITES

The bishop, vested for Mass, is received at the door of the cathedral church by the senior member of the presbyterium. This may be, for example, the senior member of the presbyteral council, the ranking dignitary of the chapter or board of consultors, the senior auxiliary bishop, or the rector of the church, according to local custom or circumstances.

The one who receives the bishop may offer him a crucifix to kiss and then give him the sprinkler with holy water. The bishop sprinkles himself and all who are present. The entrance procession through the church takes place as usual, while the entrance song is sung. (If the bishop has not vested for Mass, he may visit the chapel of the Blessed Sacrament with the priests, deacons, and other ministers and then go to the vesting chapel, sacristy, or other convenient place.)

When he has arrived at his chair or *cathedra*, the bishop greets the people and, wearing the miter, sits. One of the deacons reads the apostolic letter at the lectern. All sit and listen; at the end they say **Thanks be to God** or make some other appropriate acclamation or response.

IMPOSITION OF THE PALLIUM

In the case of the reception of the metropolitan (or other bishop who is to receive the pallium), it is appropriate that the imposition of the pallium take place on the occasion of the liturgical reception in the cathedral church. In this case the pallium is carried in the entrance procession by one of the deacons and placed upon the altar. The senior suffragan bishop or other bishop who is to impose the pallium takes a position in a suitable place in the sanctuary. After the reading of the apostolic letter the metropolitan goes to him, kneels, and makes the prescribed profession of faith and oath.

The bishop who is to impose the pallium then rises without the miter, takes the pallium from the deacon, and places it on the shoulders of the bishop. He says:

**To the glory of almighty God
and the praise of the Blessed Virgin Mary
and of the apostles Peter and Paul,
in the name of Pope N., Bishop of Rome,
and of the holy Roman Church,
for the honor of the Church of N.,
which has been placed in your care,
and as a symbol of your authority as metropolitan
archbishop:
we confer on you the pallium taken from the tomb of
Peter
to wear within the limits of your ecclesiastical province.**

May this pallium be a symbol of unity
and a sign of your communion with the Apostolic See,
a bond of love, and an incentive to courage.
On the day of the coming and manifestation of our
   great God and chief shepherd, Jesus Christ,
may you and the flock entrusted to you
be clothed with immortality and glory.
In the name of the Father, and of the Son, and of the
   Holy Spirit.
℟. Amen.

GREETING OF THE BISHOP

The penitential rite and **Kyrie** are omitted.

After the apostolic letter has been read (or after the imposition of the pallium), the bishop is greeted, according to local custom, by the one who received him at the door of the church and then by the chapter or board of consultors, representatives of the presbyteral and pastoral councils, and at least some of the priests, deacons, and lay people of the local church, and, depending on circumstances, by members of other churches and ecclesial communities, religious bodies, civil authorities, and others.

Then the **Gloria** is sung, or another appropriate song if the **Gloria** is not permitted.

CELEBRATION OF MASS

The bishop then invites the people to pray, and, after a period of silent prayer, sings or says the opening prayer of Mass.

The liturgy of the word and the liturgy of the eucharist are celebrated in the usual way. After the gospel, the bishop addresses the people of the local church for the first time.

PARTICIPATION OF THE METROPOLITAN

If the metropolitan brings the new bishop to the cathedral church, he presents the bishop to the one who is to receive him at the door of the church. The metropolitan presides over the introductory liturgical rite. After the entrance procession he goes to the bishop's chair, greets the people, and asks that the apostolic letter be read.

After the reading and the acclamation, the metropolitan invites the bishop to take his place at the chair, and the **Gloria** is sung, as described above.

The metropolitan goes to his own place within the sanctuary and joins the new bishop in the eucharistic celebration.

RECEPTION OF COADJUTOR OR AUXILIARY BISHOPS

The ordination of a coadjutor or auxiliary bishop properly takes place in the cathedral church of the bishop whom he will assist in the pastoral ministry. If, however, the coadjutor or auxiliary bishop has been ordained already, it is appropriate that he be introduced to the people of the local church by the bishop of the diocese, during the celebration of the eucharist, after the greeting of the people. The coadjutor or auxiliary bishop then joins the bishop of the diocese in the eucharistic celebration.

APPENDIX II

BLESSING OF THE PONTIFICAL INSIGNIA

The pastoral ring, staff, and miter may be blessed at a convenient time prior to the ordination of the bishop or abbot.

℣. Our help is in the name of the Lord.
℟. The Lord who made heaven and earth.

℣. The Lord be with you.
℟. And also with you.

Let us pray.

Almighty, eternal God,
bless these symbols (this symbol)
of the pastoral office and the pontifical dignity.
May the one who uses them (it)
receive the reward of his faithfulness
and enter into eternal life
with Christ, the High Priest and Good Shepherd
who lives and reigns with you for ever and ever.
℟. Amen.

The pontifical insignia are then sprinkled with holy water.

APPENDIX III

RITE OF THE BLESSING OF OILS
RITE OF CONSECRATING THE CHRISM

SACRED CONGREGATION FOR DIVINE WORSHIP

Prot. n. 3133/70

DECREE

Since the Holy Week rites of the Roman Missal have been revised, it seemed appropriate to make the necessary adaptations in the rites of the blessing of the oil of catechumens and the oil of the sick and of consecrating the chrism, for use in the chrism Mass.

Therefore the Sacred Congregation for Divine Worship has revised these rites and, with the approval of Pope Paul VI, publishes them to be used in place of those now given in the Roman Pontifical.

It is the responsibility of the conferences of bishops to prepare vernacular editions of these rites and to present them to this Congregation for confirmation.

Anything to the contrary notwithstanding.

From the Sacred Congregation for Divine Worship, December 3, 1970.

Benno Cardinal Gut
prefect

A. Bugnini
secretary

INTRODUCTION

1. The bishop is to be considered as the high priest of his flock. The life in Christ of his faithful is in some way derived and dependent upon the bishop.[1]

The chrism Mass is one of the principal expressions of the fullness of the bishop's priesthood and signifies the close unity of the priests with him. During the Mass, which he concelebrates with priests from various sections of the diocese, the bishop consecrates the chrism and blesses the other oils. The newly baptized are anointed and confirmed with the chrism consecrated by the bishop. Catechumens are prepared and disposed for baptism with the second oil. And the sick are anointed in their illness with the third oil.

2. The Christian liturgy has assimilated this Old Testament usage of anointing kings, priests, and prophets with consecratory oil because the name of Christ, whom they prefigured, means "the anointed of the Lord."

Chrism is a sign: by baptism Christians are plunged into the paschal mystery of Christ; they die with him, are buried with him, and rise with him;[2] they are sharers in his royal and prophetic priesthood. By confirmation Christians receive the spiritual anointing of the Spirit who is given to them.

By the oil of catechumens the effect of the baptismal exorcisms is extended. Before they go to the font of life to be reborn the candidates for baptism are strengthened to renounce sin and the devil.

By the use of the oil of the sick, to which Saint James is a witness,[3] the sick receive a remedy for the illness of mind and body, so that they may have strength to bear suffering and resist evil and obtain the forgiveness of sins.

[1]See II Vatican Council, Constitution on the Sacred Liturgy, *Sacrosanctum Concilium*, no. 42.
[2]*Ibid.*, no. 6.
[3]James 5:14.

I. THE OILS

3. The matter proper for the sacraments is olive oil or, according to circumstances, other plant oil.

4. Chrism is made of oil and perfumes or other sweet smelling matter.

5. The preparation of the chrism may take place privately before the rite of consecration or may be done by the bishop during the liturgical service.

II. THE MINISTER

6. The consecration of the chrism belongs to the bishop alone.

7. If the use of the oil of catechumens is retained by the conferences of bishops, it is blessed by the bishop with the other oils during the chrism Mass.

In the case of the baptism of adults, however, priests have the faculty to bless the oil of catechumens before the anointing in the designated stage of the catechumenate.

8. The oil used for anointing the sick must be blessed for this purpose by the bishop or by a priest who has this faculty, either from the law or by special concession of the Apostolic See.

The law itself permits the following to bless the oil of the sick:
a) those whom the law equates with diocesan bishops;
b) in case of true necessity, any priest.

III. TIME OF BLESSING

9. The blessing of the oil and the consecration of the chrism are ordinarily celebrated by the bishop at the chrism Mass celebrated on Holy Thursday morning.

10. If it is difficult for the clergy and people to assemble with the bishop on Holy Thursday morning, the blessing may be held on an earlier day, near Easter, with the celebration of the proper chrism Mass.

IV. PLACE OF THE BLESSING IN THE MASS

11. According to the tradition of the Latin liturgy, the blessing of the oil of the sick takes place before the end of the eucharistic prayer; the blessing of the oil of catechumens and the consecration of the chrism, after communion.

12. For pastoral reasons, however, the entire rite of blessing may be celebrated after the liturgy of the word, according to the order described below.

BLESSING OF OILS AND CONSECRATION OF THE CHRISM

PREPARATIONS

13. For the blessing of oils the following preparations are made in addition to what is needed for Mass:

In the sacristy or other appropriate place:
—vessels of oils;
—balsam or perfume for the preparation of the chrism if the bishop wishes to mix the chrism during the liturgical service;
—bread, wine, and water for Mass, which are carried with the oils before the preparation of the gifts.

In the sanctuary:
—table for the vessels of oil, placed so that the people may see the entire rite easily and take part in it;
—chair for the bishop, if the blessing takes place in front of the altar.

RITE OF BLESSING

14. The chrism Mass is always concelebrated. It is desirable that there be some priests from the various sections of the diocese among the priests who concelebrate with the bishop and are his witnesses and the co-workers in the ministry of the holy chrism.

15. The preparation of the bishop, the concelebrants, and other ministers, their entrance into the church, and everything from the beginning of Mass until the end of the liturgy of the word take place as indicated in the rite of concelebration. The deacons who take part in the blessing of oils walk ahead of the concelebrating priests to the altar.

16. After the renewal of commitment to priestly service the deacons and ministers appointed to carry the oils or, in their absence, some priests and ministers together with the faithful who will carry the bread, wine, and water, go in procession to the sacristy or other place where the oils and other offerings have been prepared. Returning to the altar, they follow this order: first the minister carrying the vessel of balsam, if the bishop wishes to prepare the chrism, then the minister with

the vessel for the oil of the catechumens, if it is to be blessed, the minister with the vessel for the oil of the sick, lastly a deacon or priest carrying the oil for the chrism. The ministers who carry the bread, wine, and water for the celebration of the eucharist follow them.

17. During the procession through the church, the choir leads the singing of the hymn "O Redeemer" or some other appropriate song, in place of the offertory song.

18. When the procession comes to the altar or the chair, the bishop receives the gifts. The deacon who carries the vessel of oil for the chrism shows it to the bishop, saying in a loud voice: **The oil for the holy chrism**. The bishop takes the vessel and gives it to one of the assisting deacons to place on the table. The same is done by those who carry the vessels for the oil of the sick and the oil of the catechumens. The first says: **The oil of the sick;** the second says: **The oil of catechumens.** The bishop takes the vessels in the same way, and the ministers place them on the table.

19. Then the Mass continues, as in the rite of concelebration, until the end of the eucharistic prayer, unless the entire rite takes place immediately (see no. 12). In this case everything is done as described below (no. 26).

BLESSING OF THE OIL OF THE SICK

20. Before the bishop says **Through Christ our Lord/you give us all these gifts** in Eucharistic Prayer I, or the doxology **Through him** in the other eucharistic prayers, the one who carried the vessel for oil of the sick brings it to the altar and holds it in front of the bishop while he blesses the oil. The bishop says or sings this prayer:

Lord God, loving Father,
you bring healing to the sick
through your Son Jesus Christ.
Hear us as we pray to you in faith,
and send the Holy Spirit, man's Helper and Friend,
to serve the needs of men.
May your blessing ✠
come upon all who are anointed with this oil,

that they may be freed from pain and illness
and made well again in body, mind, and soul.
Father, may this oil be blessed for our use
in the name of our Lord Jesus Christ
(who lives and reigns with you for ever and ever.
℟. **Amen.)**

The conclusion **Who lives and reigns with you** is said only
when this blessing takes place outside the eucharistic prayer.

When Eucharistic Prayer I is used, the beginning of the
prayer **Through Christ our Lord/you give us all these gifts** is
changed to: **Through whom you give us all these gifts.**

After the blessing, the vessel with the oil of the sick is returned to its place, and the Mass continues until the communion rite is completed.

BLESSING OF THE OIL OF CATECHUMENS

21. After the prayer after communion, the ministers place the
oils to be blessed on a table suitably located in the center of
the sanctuary. The concelebrating priests stand around the
bishop on either side, in a semicircle, and the other ministers
stand behind him. The bishop then blesses the oil of
catechumens, if it is to be blessed, and consecrates the
chrism.

22. When everything is ready, the bishop faces the people
and, with his hands extended, sings or says the following
prayer:

Lord God, protector of all who believe in you,
bless ✠ this oil
and give wisdom and strength
to all who are anointed with it
in preparation for their baptism.
Bring them to a deeper understanding of the gospel,
help them to accept the challenge of Christian living,
and lead them to the joy of new birth
in the family of your Church.
We ask this through Christ our Lord.
℟. **Amen.**

CONSECRATION OF THE CHRISM

23. Then the bishop pours the balsam or perfume in the oil and mixes the chrism in silence, unless this was done beforehand.

24. After this he sings or says the invitation:

**Let us pray
that God our almighty Father
will bless this oil
so that all who are anointed with it
may be inwardly transformed
and come to share in eternal salvation.**

CONSECRATORY PRAYER

25. Then the bishop may breathe over the opening of the vessel of chrism. With his hands extended, he sings or says one of the following consecratory prayers.

**God our maker,
source of all growth in holiness,
accept the joyful thanks and praise
we offer in the name of your Church.**

**In the beginning, at your command,
the earth produced fruit-bearing trees.
From the fruit of the olive tree
you have provided us with oil for holy chrism.
The prophet David sang of the life and joy
that the oil would bring us in the sacraments of your
    love.**

**After the avenging flood,
the dove returning to Noah with an olive branch
announced your gift of peace.
This was a sign of a greater gift to come.
Now the waters of baptism wash away the sins of
    men,
and by anointing with olive oil
you make us radiant with your joy.**

**At your command,
Aaron was washed with water,**

and your servant Moses, his brother,
anointed him priest.
This too foreshadowed greater things to come.
After your Son, Jesus Christ our Lord,
asked John for baptism in the waters of Jordan,
you sent the Spirit upon him
in the form of a dove
and by the witness of your own voice
you declared him to be your only, well-beloved Son.
In this you clearly fulfilled the prophecy of David,
that Christ would be anointed with the oil of gladness
beyond his fellow men.

All the celebrants extend their right hands toward the chrism,
without saying anything, until the end of the prayer.

And so, Father, we ask you to bless ✠ this oil you
    have created.
Fill it with the power of your Holy Spirit
through Christ your Son.
It is from him that chrism takes its name
and with chrism you have anointed
for yourself priests and kings,
prophets and martyrs.

Make this chrism a sign of life and salvation
for those who are to be born again in the waters of
    baptism.
Wash away the evil they have inherited from sinful
    Adam,
and when they are anointed with this holy oil
make them temples of your glory,
radiant with the goodness of life
that has its source in you.

Through this sign of chrism
grant them royal, priestly and prophetic honor,
and clothe them with incorruption.
Let this be indeed the chrism of salvation
for those who will be born again of water and the
    Holy Spirit.
May they come to share eternal life

in the glory of your kingdom.
We ask this through Christ our Lord.
℟. Amen.

Or:

Father, we thank you for the gifts
you have given us in your love:
we thank you for life itself and for the sacraments
that strengthen it and give it fuller meaning.

In the Old Covenant you gave your people
a glimpse of the power of this holy oil
and when the fullness of time had come
you brought that mystery to perfection
in the life of our Lord Jesus Christ, your Son.

By his suffering, dying, and rising to life
he saved the human race.
He sent your Spirit to fill the Church
with every gift needed to complete your saving work.

From that time forward,
through the sign of holy chrism,
you dispense your life and love to men.
By anointing them with the Spirit,
you strengthen all who have been reborn in baptism.
Through that anointing
you transform them into the likeness of Christ your
    Son
and give them a share
in his royal, priestly, and prophetic work.

All the concelebrants extend their right hands toward the
chrism without saying anything, until the end of the prayer.

And so, Father, by the power of your love,
make this mixture of oil and perfume
a sign and source ✠ of your blessing.
Pour out the gifts of your Holy Spirit
on our brothers and sisters who will be anointed
    with it.
Let the splendor of holiness shine on the world
from every place and thing
signed with this oil.

**Above all, Father, we pray
that through this sign of your anointing
you will grant increase to your Church
until it reaches the eternal glory
where you, Father, will be the all in all,
together with Christ your Son,
in the unity of the Holy Spirit,
for ever and ever.**
℟. **Amen.**

26. When the entire rite of blessing of oils is to be celebrated after the liturgy of the word, at the end of the renewal of commitment to priestly service the bishop goes with the concelebrants to the table where the blessing of the oil of the sick and of the oil of the chrism are to take place, and everything is done as described above (nos. 20-25).

27. After the final blessing of the Mass, the bishop puts incense in the censer, and the procession to the sacristy is arranged.

The blessed oils are carried by the ministers immediately after the cross, and the choir and people sing some verses of the hymn "O Redeemer" or some other appropriate song.

28. In the sacristy the bishop may instruct the priests about the reverent use and safe custody of the holy oils.